TOKYO
MIDTOWN
HIBIYA

New
Technique
of Town
Planning

東 京
ミッドタウン
日 比 谷

新 た な
街 づくりの
手 法

新建築社

002 目次

004 ［ステートメント］
「街づくり」を通して
社会の課題解決に挑戦
菰田正信［三井不動産 代表取締役社長］

008 周辺からの眺め
018 日比谷ステップ広場
028 商業エリア
036 TOHOシネマズ 日比谷
040 オフィス
046 Base Q
047 オフィスサポート
048 パークビューガーデン
057 基本図面＋設計データ

062 ［対談］
「日比谷らしさ」を共有した新たな街づくり
小野澤康夫［三井不動産］×大松敦［日建設計］

PHASE 1

ビジョンメイキング——
日比谷の新たな街づくり

068 PHASE 1

070 街の歴史と性格を理解する

072 日本の西洋化の先駆けとなった日比谷

080 日比谷公園の価値を再認識

084 文化・演劇、エンターテイメントの中心地
東宝の新たな街づくり
山下誠［東宝 取締役 不動産経営担当］
太田圭昭［東宝 不動産経営部次長］
日生劇場と日比谷
松本勝嗣［日生劇場 劇場部部長］

088 千代田区第1号地区計画（1985年）

090 日比谷パティオ（2008年12月〜2011年6月）

092 土地区画整理事業、地区計画、
都市再生特別地区

094 「Park Side」から「In the Park」へ

PHASE 2

街づくりのビジョンを
デザイン・計画として具現化する

096 PHASE 2

098 「Dancing Tower」で実現する
日比谷らしさ
場所とディテールの重要性
——品質と洗練
マイケル・ホプキンス［ホプキンス・アーキテクツ］
柔らかさのデザイン
サイモン・フレーザー［ホプキンス・アーキテクツ］

106 全関係者が一堂に会する
重要な会議体「ワークセッション」

108 デザインと並行して進む
都市計画の協議

109 景観と事業性を両立させる
曲面のタワー形状

112 景観を決定付ける外装ディテール

116 人が集い賑わう広場

121 初心を確認するための
グランドデザイン会議

CONTENTS

004 ［STATEMENT］
Addressing Social Challenges with
Town Planning
Masanobu Komoda [Mitsui Fudosan, President and
Chief Executive Officer]

008 View from the surroundings
018 Hibiya Step Square
028 Commercial zone
036 TOHO Cinemas Hibiya
040 Office
046 Base Q
047 Office support
048 Park View Garden
057 Basic drawing and data

062 ［DIALOGUE］
New Town Planning by Sharing
"Hibiya-ness"
Yasuo Onozawa [Mitsui Fudosan] ×
Atsushi Omatsu [Nikken Sekkei]

PHASE 1

Vision making
— new town planning in Hibiya

068 PHASE 1

070 Understanding history and
characteristics of the town

072 Hibiya, the forerunner of
Westernization in Japan

080 Reevaluation of Hibiya Park

084 Center for culture and theatrical
entertainment
New town planning by TOHO
Makoto Yamashita [TOHO]
Yoshiaki Ota [TOHO]
Nissay Theatre and Hibiya
Yoshitsugu Matsumoto [Nissay Theatre]

088 The first Chiyoda district plan (1985)

090 Hibiya Patio (Dec. 2008 - Jun. 2011)

092 Land readjustment project,
district planning, special urban
renaissance districts

094 From "Park Side" to "In the Park"

PHASE 2

Embodiment of urban
development as design/plan

096 PHASE 2

098 Hibiya-style realization of
"Dancing Tower"
The importance of place and detail
– quality and sophistication
Michael Hopkins [Hopkins Architects]
Design of softness
Simon Fraser [Hopkins Architects]

106 "Work sessions" were important
meetings of concerned individuals in
one place

108 Discussion of urban plan in parallel
with design

109 Curved tower shape that offers both
scenic view and commercial potential

112 Exterior details with decided scenery

116 Bustling plaza where people gather

121 Grand design conference to confirm
the original intention

PHASE 3
**実現に向けた
デザインの深化と検証**

122

124 新たなデザイナーの参画

125 記憶を継承しながらも
先進性のある商業インテリア

130 オフィスワーカーが舞うステージ

134 公園のような柔らかなランドスケープ

136 街を上品に照らし出すライティング

138 アクティビティのきっかけを生むアート
歴史を表す3つの石が生み出す
人との対話
和泉正敏[彫刻家]
伝統産業の和紙と最先端技術の
融合がつくり出す豊かな空間
堀木エリ子[和紙デザイナー]

142 着工に向けて1番列車を走らせる
──実施設計1

148 デザインを実現する設計図面への
落とし込み

150 総合検討を深めるための2番列車を
走らせる──実施設計2

154 モックアップで確認・検討し、
合意形成を進める

PHASE 4
**技術と人に支えられ
実現した街づくり**

158

160 36カ月にわたる工事のスタート

166 いよいよ建物が立ち上がる

170 建物の機能を止めない備え(BCP)

172 地下鉄との接続

174 Dancing Towerを印象付ける
外装取り付け

178 街への存在感が立ち現れる

180 たくさんの職人に支えられる工事現場
たくさんの人の関わりで実現した
難易度の高い工事
桐生雅文[鹿島建設 東京ミッドタウン日比谷現場所長]

003

186 街びらき

196 [論考]
新しい文化を取り込む日比谷エリアの
特性と可能性
岸井隆幸[日本大学理工学部 特任教授]

198 建築データ・クレジット

PHASE 3
**Detailing and verification of design
oriented for implementation**

122

124 Participation of new designers

125 Commercial interiors that are advanced,
at the same time inheriting memories

130 Stage where office workers dancing

134 Soft landscape like that of a park

136 Lighting, which elegantly illuminates
the city

138 Art that will create a chance for activity
3 stones revealing History,
in dialogue with the people visiting
Masatoshi Izumi [Stone sculptor]
A Rich Space Created by the Fusion of
Traditional Japanese Industry of Washi
and the State-of-the-Art Technology
Eriko Horiki [Washi designer]

142 Run train No.1 oriented towards
starting the construction
– The execution design 1

148 Capture the drawing for design creation

150 Run train No.2 for comprehensive
study – The execution design 2

154 Promote confirmation, consideration
and consensus building by mock-up

PHASE 4
**Town Development Realized by the
Power of Technology and People**

158

160 Construction which takes 36 months
started

166 The building finally erected

170 Preventative Measures against
Disruption of the Building (BCP)

172 Connecting a tunnel to the subway

174 Finishing Exterior to Make the
Dancing Tower Unique

178 The existence of the building is
emerging

180 The construction site where many
craftsmen contributed to this project
A Difficult Construction Work
Realized with the Involvement of
Many People
Masafumi Kiryu [Kajima Corporation]

186 Opening of the Town

196 [ESSAY]
Characteristics and Possibilities of
Hibiya Area, Embracing New
Cultures
Takayuki Kishii [Professor of Nihon University]

198 Data / Credit

CONTENTS

1周年を迎えた手応え

「東京ミッドタウン日比谷」が2018（平成30）年3月29日に開業して約1年が経ちましたが、当初われわれが期待していた通り、人の流れが大きく変わりました。日比谷は、商業エンターテインメントゾーンの有楽町、銀座、ビジネスゾーンの丸の内、大手町、さらには政治、官庁の中心である霞が関など日本の要衝の中心にあります。また、帝国ホテルや宝塚劇場のように目的性の高い魅力的な施設もあります。一方、いわゆる不特定多数の人が来られる集客施設はありませんでした。ここに人が集まる核となる施設ができればたくさんのお客様に訪れていただける街となると考えていました。開業後、実際に大きく人の流れが変わりました。来街者数は年間1,200万人を目標としていましたが、実際には半年で目標を達成しました。どんなプロジェクトでも開業景気はあるので当初は人の流れができますが、1年経っても来街者数が変わらないプロジェクトは珍しい。われわれの考えていた通り、核となる施設ができると、街全体が魅力的になり一時的ではなく構造的に人の流れが変わることを立証できたと思います。来られた方に感想をおうかがいすると、この場所の歴史や特徴を活かした街づくりをしたことをご評価いただいているのかなと思いました。日比谷公園や皇居外苑など都心には珍しい豊かな水と緑があること、そして東宝や宝塚が古くから映画館や劇場をつくられた日本のエンターテインメントの発祥の地であること、さらに鹿鳴館や帝国ホテルのような海外の方をお招きしてきた日本の近代化の歴史があること。それらの特徴を活かしたことで、われわれが目指した街づくりの成果が現れたと思っています。

日比谷の歴史と文化を引き継ぐ

われわれ三井不動産としても、日比谷は特別な場所なのです。明治時代に「有楽町三井集会所」がありました。ここでは国内外からのお客様をお招きしたり、三井グループの最重要事項を審議・決定していました。周囲には鹿鳴館や帝国ホテルなど近代化の象徴となる建物があり、日比谷公園も日本で最初の近代的な洋風の公園ですから、常に新しいものが発信されてきた地と言えます。昭和時代にはさまざまな劇場が建ち並びエンターテイメントの拠点となりました。「東京ミッドタウン日比谷」の敷地には、デザイン性の高い「三信ビルディング」（1930［昭和5］年）や東洋一のビルと謳われた「日比谷三井ビルディング」（1960［昭和35］年）が建てられ、日本の建築の近代化を牽引しました。「日比谷三井ビルディング」を建設した鹿島建設も、「日比谷三井ビルディング」で初めて本格的な近代建築の建設に取り組まれ、そこで培われた技術や経験が、日本初の超高層ビルである「霞が関ビルディング」（1968［昭和43］年）に結び付きました。

「東京ミッドタウン日比谷」のデザインには、この場所の歴史や街の風景などが引き継がれています。低層部の石張りの外壁には「三信ビルディング」や「日比谷三井ビルディング」の記憶が再現されています。デザインはイギリスのホプキンス・アーキテクツにお

Feedback after a Year

It's been about a year since the Tokyo Midtown Hibiya opened its door on March 29, 2018. As we had expected, the flow of people has significantly shifted. Hibiya is located in a strategic area of Japan with Yurakucho and Ginza as notable commercial and entertainment areas, Marunouchi and Otemachi as business areas, and the center of government, Kasumigaseki. We can't miss highly-attractive facilities such as the Imperial Hotel Tokyo and the Tokyo Takarazuka Theater. For a while, however, there have been no venues that can attract general people. We considered that the establishment of a core complex where people can visit would change this area into the place that can attract many customers. The opening of the Tokyo Midtown Hibiya brought about a significant change in the flow of people. Our target number of people visiting this area first was 12 million on a yearly basis, which was actually achieved within sixth months. Usually in every project, the opening boom can maintain the flow of people to a certain degree. But here, the number of people coming to this area remained almost the same throughout the year. This project demonstrated that core facilities can make the area attractive and generate a big shift in the flow of people not temporarily, but structurally. Customers visiting Hibiya that answered our interview seem to appreciate our town planning that took advantage of the history and the characteristics of this area. Hibiya, rather unusual for central Tokyo, is a place with wealth of water as well as greenery based on Hibiya Park and the outer garden of the Imperial Palace. Hibiya has served as the Mecca of Japanese entertainment with movie and performing theaters built by TOHO and Takarazuka. Hibiya also symbolizes modern Japanese history by inviting and entertaining overseas guests at the Rokumeikan and the Imperial Hotel. We believe that leveraging these characteristics bore fruit as the achievements of our town planning.

Inheriting the History and Culture of Hibiya

Hibiya is a special place for Mitsui Fudosan. In the Meiji Era, the Yurakucho Mitsui Shukaijo (assembly house) was located. Here, we used to invite our domestic and international guests and held meetings to examine and decide the most important matters for the Mitsui Group. With other notable buildings that symbolize the westernization of Japan, such as the Rokumeikan Hall and the Imperial Hotel including Hibiya Park as the first modernistic western park in Japan, Hibiya has served as the source of new things. In the Showa Era, Hibiya was reborn as the entertainment hub where various theaters were built. Hibiya has also taken the initiative in the construction modernization of Japan with the Sanshin Building (1930) with its sophisticated design and the Hibiya Mitsui Building (1960) called the best Oriental building that once existed on the site of the Tokyo Midtown Hibiya. The construction of the Hibiya Mitsui Building was the starting point for the builder, Kajima Corporation, to work on full-scale modern architecture. The technical skills and experience that were cultivated through this construction project later led to such success as the construction of Japan's first-ever skyscraper, the Kasumigaseki Building (1968).

願いしましたが、非常に柔らかなものになったと思っています。丸の内から大手町にかけては直線的なデザインのビルがほとんどですが、独特の緩やかな曲線美のデザインが、このプロジェクトをより一層際立たせていると思います。超都心に広場を生み出したことも特徴的で、東宝の「日比谷シャンテ」など周辺施設とも連携して地域一体となって街づくりを進めたことにより、有楽町全体が大きく変わりました。千代田区のご判断により日比谷仲通りを歩行者専用道路にしていただきましたが、日比谷シャンテも日比谷仲通りから直接入ることができるカフェを設置するなど街全体を魅力的にするためにリノベーションを実施いただきました。また、日比谷仲通りから繋がる日比谷ステップ広場、アトリウムに至るまでを連担したひとつの大きな広場としたことで、人びとが集いやすく、さまざまなイベントを行うことで新たなコミュニティが生まれる場所ができ上がったと思っています。そうした特徴がたくさんあるのが東京ミッドタウン日比谷の面白さで、人びとが新しい感動や潤いを感じられる場所があり、来ていただくだけで楽しくなる、それが街の魅力になっているのでしょう。

個 性 を 活 か し て 東 京 の 魅 力 を 高 め る

日比谷だけでなく東京には核となるクラスターがいくつもあります。これだけいろいろな核を持っている都市は世界でも珍しい。たとえば、ロンドンでは主にシティとウェスト・エンドの2極に分かれ、ニューヨークのマンハッタンでは、アップタウン、ミッドタウン、ダウンタウンといったエリアに分かれている程度です。東京を世界的な都市として魅力あるものにするために必要なことは、まず、東京の中にあるエリアの個性を活かすことです。それぞれのクラスターが固有の街として独自の魅力を発信していくことによって、東京は世界的に魅力的な都市になっていくと思います。2点目は、いわゆる先進国、成熟化した国が必ず直面するであろう社会的な課題、エネルギー問題や環境問題、あるいは少子化・高齢化、産業の新陳代謝などの諸課題の解決に、街づくりを通して取り組んでいくことです。日比谷においても、水と緑を活かして環境と共生したり、エネルギー負荷のない街づくりをしたり、新しい才能を育てる拠点づくりをしたり、現代の課題を街づくりで解決しようとしています。また、3点目は、デジタル技術が発達してきているので、オフィスビルでも商業施設でも、あるいは住宅でも、街全体でデジタル技術を取り込んでいくことです。それによって、働く、買い物する、暮らす、泊まるといった人びとの活動がストレスなく快適にできるようになります。その際に価値を持ってくるものは、デジタル技術で代替できない現実の空間、生身の空間とも言うべきリアルな場の体験です。リアルな場の価値とは、水や緑など手で触れて匂いで感じる自然環境の豊かさや潤いであり、ネット配信される映像や音楽では得られない、劇場での臨場感や体験であり、インターネットでは伝わらない生身の人間同士のふれあいや出会い、何かを一緒にやる連帯感です。リアルな場の価値はデジタル技術が発達すればするほど貴重になります。ロンドンやニューヨークなど他の街と比べても「やっぱり東京っていいよ

The design of the Tokyo Midtown Hibiya tactfully incorporates the history of this area including cityscapes. The stone-clad outer walls on the lower floors reproduce the memories of the Sanshin Building and the Hibiya Mitsui Building. To design these facilities, we asked a prominent British architectural firm, Hopkins Architects. Many construction and buildings within the areas from Marunouchi through Oteamachi are designed entirely with straight lines. Unlike those buildings, the beautifully unique design of the Tokyo Midtown Hibiya based on gentle curves accentuates this project. Another characteristic point is a spacious square that appears in the center of Tokyo. Our community-based town planning in collaboration with the surrounding facilities including TOHO's Hibiya Chanter significantly has changed the entire Yurakucho area. While the Hibiya-Nakadori Street was pedestrianized in accordance with the decision made by the Chiyoda Ward Office, the area based on this street was nicely renovated with various attractions, such as a café that directly leads visitors to Hibiya Chanter from the Hibiya-Nakadori Street. Combining the Hibiya Step Square open space connecting the Hibiya-Nakadori Street with another space named Atrium provides an attractive place for people to hold a wide variety of events so that new communities can be generated. These various features characterize the Tokyo Midtown Hibiya as a place where people can be inspired and enrich their lives, which results in promoting the attractiveness of this area.

Make Use of Originality to Enhance Tokyo's Attractiveness

In addition to Hibiya, Tokyo has several core clusters, which is rare in most cities in the world. For example, London is mainly divided into only the City and the West End, and Manhattan, New York, is zoned with areas of Uptown, Midtown, and Downtown. In order to make Tokyo attractive on a global basis, we need to make use of the originality of each Tokyo area. Providing the attractions of each cluster as a unique city will surely lead to us making Tokyo globally attractive. Another approach based on town planning is to address various social challenges that advanced countries will face, such as energy or environmental issues, declining birthrates and aging population along with industrial metabolism. Hibiya is also trying to solve various modern-day challenges with town planning by achieving a nature-friendly environment taking advantage of water and greenery, producing an environment with minimal energy load, and creating new hubs for human-resource development. The third approach is to introduce advanced digital technology, in the entire city, into offices and commercial facilities, or even into homes. Digital technology can make people's activities comfortable, as to how they work, shop, and lodge. When this takes place, what can be valuable is experience of real matters that cannot be substituted with digital technology. The real matters referred here include wealth and richness of the natural environment that we can feel by touching and smelling such as water , the leaves of trees, the real experience at a theater that cannot be obtained through online video and music streaming, real contact and encounters with people that cannot be experienced in a virtual world, and a sense of solidarity that we can have when

ね」と、国内はもちろん、海外から来られた方にも感じていただくために、ここにしかできないことに力点を置いて取り組んでいきたいと思います。

「街づくり」から世界、未来へ発信する

われわれの考える「街づくり」は、建物が竣工した時がゴールではなく、むしろスタートだと位置付けています。完成した後、時間が経過すればするほど街の魅力が増していく経年優化の街づくりを目指します。また、「東京ミッドタウン日比谷」は、日比谷から内幸町、日比谷公園にかけての街づくりのゲートウェイとなるプロジェクトです。このプロジェクトを通して得られた経験や学んだことを、今後の広域な街づくりに活かしていきたいと考えています。「東京ミッドタウン日比谷」にも広場をつくりたくさんの緑を取り込みましたが、日比谷公園との連携はさらに深めていけると思います。商業施設のスペースももっと広くとる考え方もありますが、街はこのプロジェクトだけで構成されているわけではありません。街全体が連携し多様であれば、ここにすべてが揃っている必要はありません。今後は、エネルギーの面でも、地域ごとに自立分散型でエネルギーを供給できる体制も必要になると思います。レジリエンス(強靭性)と言いますか、災害に非常に強い、また平時にもエネルギー効率の高い街にしていく必要があります。それも今後の街づくりの中にどのように備えていくのか、今後われわれが取り組まなくてはいけない課題だと思います。三井不動産が2020年の東京オリンピックのゴールドパートナーになった大きな目的は、場を提供することでオリンピックムーブメントを加速し、日本を盛り上げることです。「東京ミッドタウン日比谷」でもこれまでオリンピック関係のイベントをしましたが、オリンピック開催期間中もパブリックビューイングをしたり、海外から来られた方々をこの場所にお迎えして日本のよさを体感していただいたり、リアルな場の提供によって東京の魅力を世界へ発信し、国際競争力の強化に貢献しようと思います。2025年に開催が決まった大阪・関西万博においても、「Society5.0」という超スマート社会を実現するための街のあり方を展覧する観点からしっかりと発信し、未来に繋げていきたいと考えています。
われわれの本業は「街づくり」であり、社会的使命として今後も「街づくり」を通じて社会の課題解決に挑戦し、未来を見据えて新たな価値を創造し続けていきたいと思います。

[2019年1月28日、東京ミッドタウン日比谷にて|文責:新建築社編集部]

trying to achieve something. Value of real experience becomes more precious as digital technology advances further. Focusing on what only this place can achieve, we put forth great effort to make Tokyo more attractive so that local and international visitors can feel that Tokyo is a nice place even when compared to other world cities such as London or New York.

Town Planning to Provide Attractiveness to the World and the Future

Through our town planning, we consider the completion of the construction not to be the end, but rather the beginning. Our town planning aims to create a place that can strengthen its attractiveness as time passes after completion. The Tokyo Midtown Hibiya is a gateway project for creating an area from Hibiya and Uchisaiwaicho to Hibiya Park. We want to take advantage of what we learned and experienced through this project in our broader town projects in the future. While the Tokyo Midtown Hibiya incorporated greenness through a spacious square, we will deepen our collaboration with Hibiya Park more than before. There is an idea to secure a broader space for commercial facilities; however, the entire city is not sorely composed by this project. There is no need to have everything within the area if the city is entirely coordinated and diversified. In terms of energy, each community needs to establish an autonomous decentralized system for its energy supply. This requires making the community energy-efficient during peaceful times and promoting disaster-prevention, or resilience, so to speak. How should these goals be incorporated into the future town planning? This is also a future challenge that we must work on.
Our major purpose of serving as a Tokyo 2020 Olympics Gold Partner is to liven up Japan by shifting the Olympic momentum into high gear through the location that we provide. Several Olympic-related events have been held at the Tokyo Midtown Hibiya. During the Tokyo 2020 Olympics, we are also planning various events including a public viewing event of the Olympic Games and an event to entertain international visitors to experience the attractiveness of Japan. By providing a location that offers real experiences, we will try to spread Tokyo's originality to the world and to contribute to strengthening Japan's global competitiveness.
As for the Expo 2025 Osaka, Kansai, our focus is on putting out our message to achieve a smart society based on the concept "Society 5.0" from the perspective of how a community should exist as it moves toward the future.
Our primary business is town planning. We will continue to address social challenges through town planning as our societal mission, in order to create new values while looking toward the future.
[At Tokyo Midtown Hibiya on January 28, 2019 – edited by Shinkenchiku-sha]

猫田正信|こもだ・まさのぶ
1954年東京都生まれ/1978年東京大学法学部卒業、三井不動産入社/1999年同社業務企画室長/2003年同社経営企画部長/2005年同社執行役員/2008年同社常務執行役員/2009年同社常務取締役常務執行役員/2010年同社専務取締役専務執行役員/2011年〜同社代表取締役社長社長執行役員

Masanobu Komoda
1954 Born in Tokyo, Japan / 1978 Graduated from the Bachelor of Laws, Tokyo University, Joined Mitsui Fudosan / 1999 General Manager, Office Building Fund Planning Department, Office Building Division / 2003 General Manager, Corporate Planning Department / 2005 Managing Officer / 2008 Executive Managing Officer / 2009 Executive Managing Director, Executive Managing Officer / 2010 Senior Executive Managing Director, Senior Executive Managing Officer / 2011– President and Chief Executive Officer

飯田橋方向から、皇居・日比谷公園越しに見る。
View from Iidabashi direction, across the Imperial Palace and the Hibiya Park.

南西側俯瞰。左に日比谷公園、皇居。奥に丸の内、大手町。
Overlooking view of the south west side. The Hibiya Park and the Imperial Palace are on the left. Marunouchi and Otemachi are at the far back.

北桔橋門の皇居のお堀越しに見る。
View across the moat on the north side of the Imperial Palace.

北東側から見る。JR線の高架が横切るのが見える。
View from the northeast side. The overpasses of the JR lines in the front.

日比谷公園から見る。
View from the Hibiya Park.

日比谷通りから見る。低層部は以前この敷地に建っていた三信ビルディングのファサードの印象を花崗岩と金属で表現している。
View from the Hibiya-dori street. Adopting the facade of the Sanshin Building which was located on this site before, the lower levels of the building employs granite-clad and metallic exterior.

晴海通り側から日比谷仲通りを見る。高層部のカーテンウォールは、
「Dancing Tower」をコンセプトにドレープをイメージさせる
曲線的な形状が採用されている。

View of the Hibiya-Nakadori street from the Harumi-dori street.
The curtain wall for the higher levels of the building is fabricated
in a sweeping shape like gracefully draped cloth,
based on the concept of "Dancing Tower."

日比谷ステップ広場を見る。パブリックスペースとして開放され、イベントなどが開催される。
View of the Hibiya Step Square.
The Hibiya Step Square is open to people as a public space. Events take place here.

日比谷ステップ広場夕景。緩やかな階段状の空間で、円形広場を囲む観客席のように使用することができる。
Evening view of the Hibiya Step Square. The gentle stairs in the space can be used as audience seats surrounding the round area.

日比谷ステップ広場を見下ろす。
イベント時には、円形広場は内部のアトリウムと
一体的に使用することも可能。
Looking down the Hibiya Step Square.
When holding an event,
the round area and the Atrium inside of the building
can be used integrally.

024

日比谷ステップ広場の階段部分から
日比谷シャンテ方向を見る。
Looking toward Hibiya Chanter
from the stairs of the Hibiya Step Square.

歩行者専用道路として整備された
日比谷シャンテとの間の道路を見る。
View of the street between Tokyo Midtown Hibiya
and Hibiya Chanter.
The street is improved as a pedestrian-only road.

4階から日比谷ステップ広場越しに日比谷通りを見る。
View of the Hibiya-dori street from the fourth floor,
across the Hibiya Step Square.

タワー部見上げ
Looking up the tower

円形の日比谷ステップ広場からエントランスを見る。
View of the entrance from the round Hibiya Step Square.

3階から商業エリアのアトリウムを見下ろす。伝統的な劇場空間をイメージした緩やかな曲線が用いられた内装。

Looking down the Atrium in the commercial zone from the third floor.
The interior adopts gentle curves, inspired by traditional theatrical spaces.

商業エリアのアトリウム夕景。
Evening view of the Atrium in the commercial zone.

TOKYO MIDTOWN HIBIYA

3階商業エリアから日比谷ステップ広場を見る。
View of the Hibiya Step Square from the commercial zone on the third floor.

2階飲食エリア。日比谷公園側にテラスを設け、店舗と接続してテラス席としても利用できる。
The food and drink zone on the second floor.
The balcony is built on the side facing the Hibiya Park.
This area can be used as a place for terrace tables when connected with restaurants.

地下1階日比谷アーケードを見通す。三信ビルディングの意匠を踏襲したアーチ天井。東京メトロ日比谷線と千代田線がこの日比谷アーケードを通して接続する。

Looking through the Hibiya Arcade in the first basement. Adopting the design of the Sanshin Building, the ceiling is arched. Tokyo Metro Hibiya Line and Chiyoda Line are connected by the Hibiya Arcade.

地下1階日比谷アーケードを見る。右奥は東京メトロ千代田線日比谷駅のコンコース。
View of the Hibiya Arcade in the first basement.
The concourse of the Hibiya Station on the Tokyo Metro Chiyoda Line is seen in the right back.

地下1階の東京メトロ日比谷線日比谷駅コンコースへと接続する通路。
A passage in the first basement, which connects to the concourse of the Hibiya Station on the Tokyo Metro Hibiya Line.

地下1階のフードホールフロア。
The food hall floor in the first basement.

地下1階フードホールフロアから日比谷アーケードへ接続する動線。
地下鉄との接続のためレベル差がある。
The flow line from the food hall floor in the first basement to the Hibiya Arcade.
Since it connects to the subway, there is a level difference.

4階TOHOシネマズ 日比谷。11スクリーン、約2,200席を有する。隣接する東京宝塚ビル内の2スクリーンを加えると、都内最大級のシネマコンプレックスとなる。
TOHO Cinemas Hibiya on the fourth floor. It houses 11 screens and about 2,200 seats in total.
When the two screens in the adjacent Tokyo Takarazuka Building are included, it is one of the largest cinema complex in Tokyo.

038

4階TOHOシネマズ 日比谷から6階を見上げる。吹き抜けを上るエスカレータ。
Looking up the sixth floor from TOHO Cinemas Hibiya on the fourth floor.
The escalator across the atrium.

スクリーン1内部。456席（3席の車椅子席を含む）。
Inside of the Screen 1. Houses 456 seats (including three wheelchair seats).

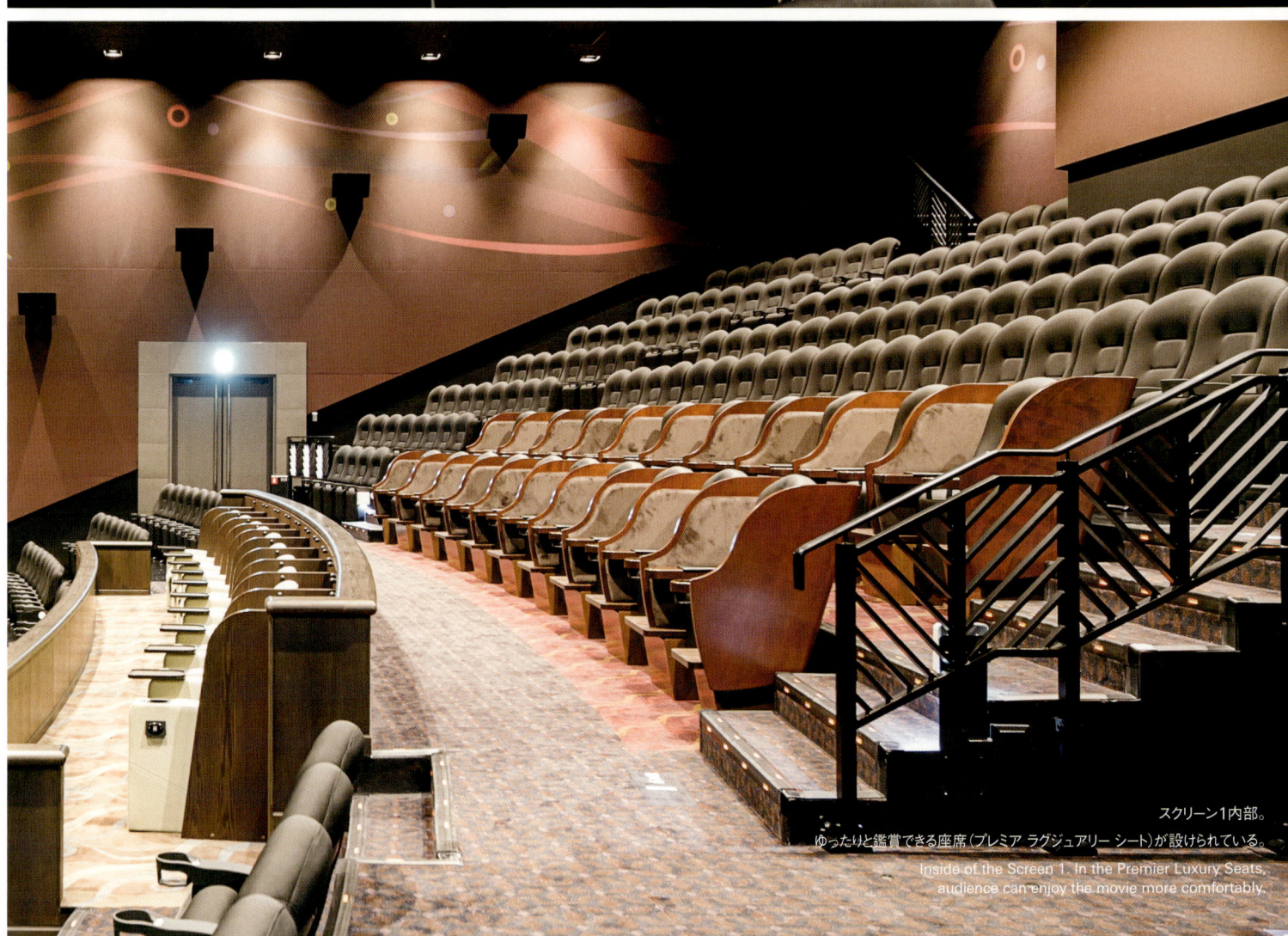

スクリーン1内部。
ゆったりと鑑賞できる座席（プレミア ラグジュアリー シート）が設けられている。
Inside of the Screen 1. In the Premier Luxury Seats,
audience can enjoy the movie more comfortably.

2層吹き抜けの9階スカイロビー。日比谷公園や皇居を望むことができる。天井にはシャンデリアアートが設置されている。
The double-story sky lobby on the ninth floor. People can enjoy the view of the Hibiya Park and the Imperial Palace.
The ceiling is decorated with the chandelier art.

9階スカイロビーから日比谷公園を見る。
View of the Hibiya Park from the sky lobby on the ninth floor.

9階スカイロビーから、10階に接続するエスカレータを見る。右手のゲートから各バンクのエレベータホールに繋がる。
The escalators connecting to the tenth floor looked from the sky lobby on the ninth floor.
The gate on the right connects to the elevator hall. People can go to each office floor from there.

9階シャトルエレベータホールから、スカイロビーを見る。
約60人乗りのエレベータ8基。エレベータの各かご室には、
堀木エリ子氏によるすべて異なるデザインの和紙アートが施されている。
Looking the sky lobby from the shuttle elevator hall on the ninth floor.
Eight elevators are available, and each one can accommodate about 60 people.
Each elevator cabin is decorated with different Washi art by Eriko Horiki.

基準階オフィスフロア。1フロアの専有部は約3,000m²、天井高さ2,900mm。
Typical office floor. The private area of one floor is about 3,000m², and the height from the floor to the ceiling is 2,900mm.

基準階オフィスフロアから北側を見る。
Looking toward the north side from the typical office floor.

6階の新産業創出を支援するビジネス連携拠点として開設された「BASE Q」。BASE Qラウンジを見る。

"BASE Q" on the sixth floor, which is opened as a business collaboration hub for supporting creation of new industries. Looking the BASE Q lounge.

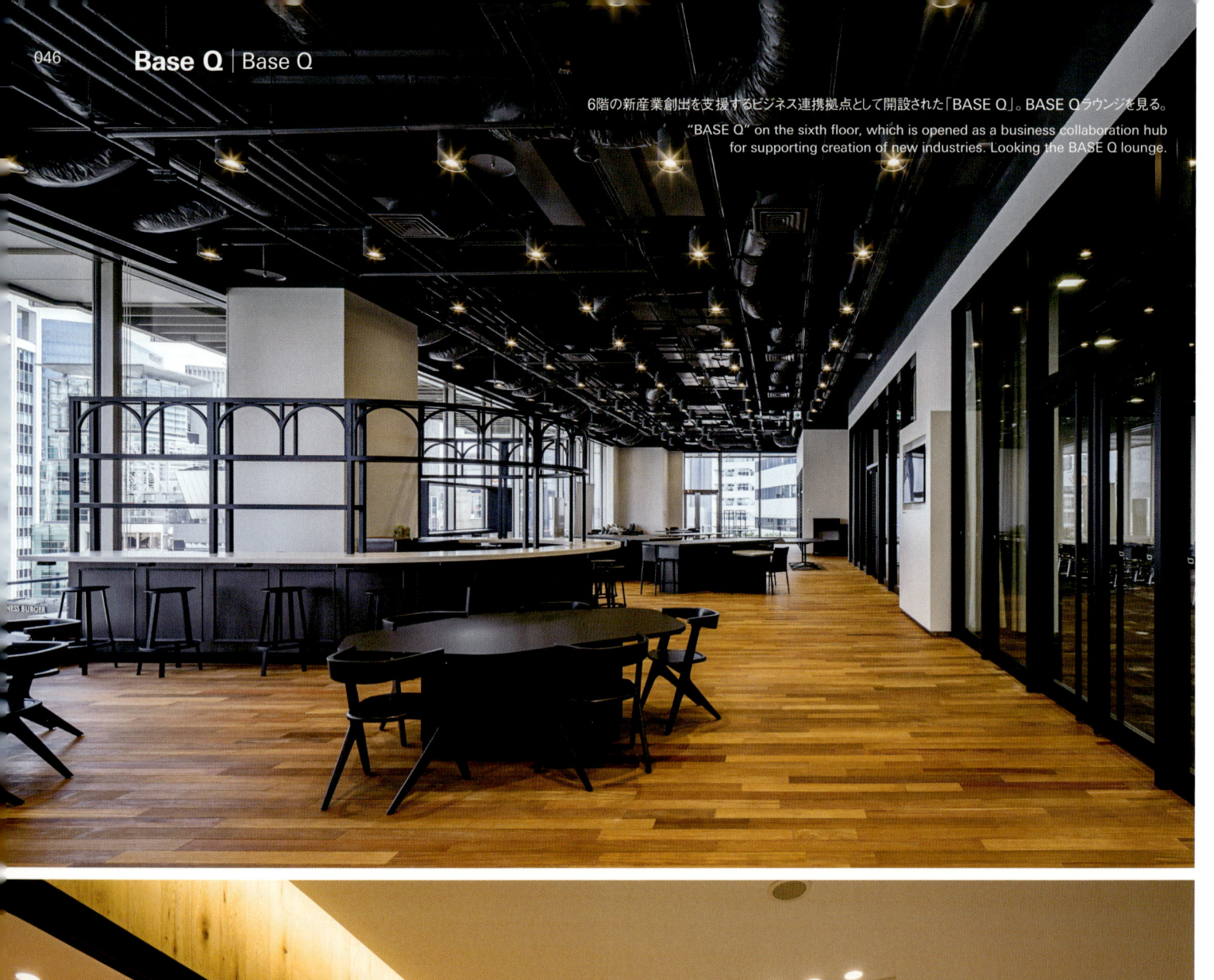

6階 BASE Q。キッチンスペースからホールを見る。
The BASE Q on the sixth floor. Looking the hall from the kitchen space.

9階日比谷三井カンファレンスの貸会議室ROOM6。
The rental conference room ROOM 6 of Hibiya Mitsui Conference on the ninth floor. About 60 seats are available.

9階日比谷三井カンファレンスの貸会議室ROOM6。
The rental conference room ROOM 6 of Hibiya Mitsui Conference on the ninth floor.

8階パークウェルネス。
The Park Wellness on the eighth floor.

8階日比谷三井カンファレンスのROOM1+2。
ROOM 1+2 of Hibiya Mitsui Conference on the eighth floor.

8階パークウェルネスのパウダールーム。
The powder room of Park Wellness on the eighth floor.

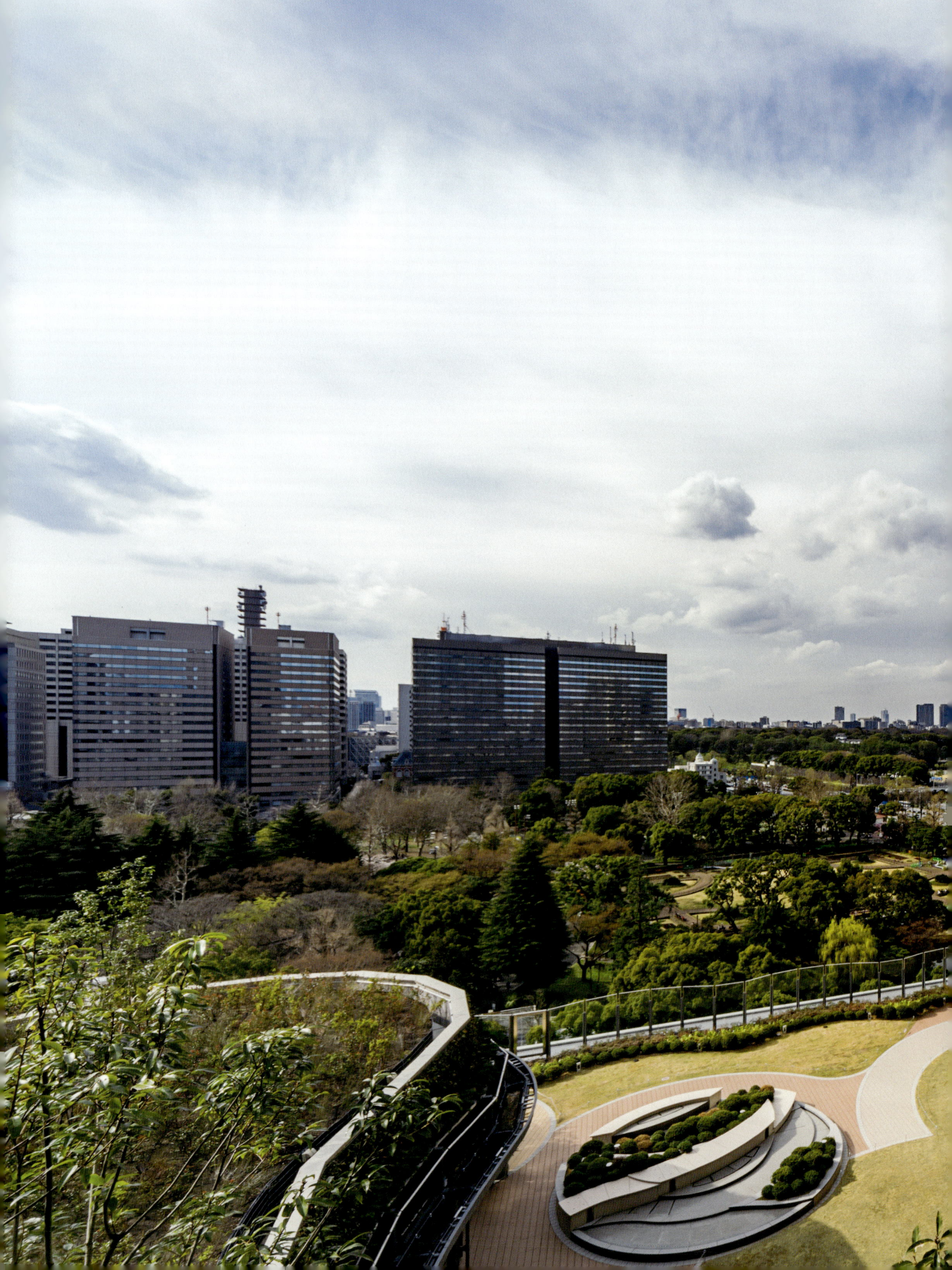

6階パークビューガーデン越しに日比谷公園方向を見る。
Looking toward the Hibiya Park across the Park View Garden on the sixth floor.

7階エグゼクティブラウンジ。
Executive lounge on the seventh floor.

7階バンケットルーム。
Banquet hall on the seventh floor.

7階エグゼクティブラウンジから日比谷公園方向を見る。左は高層タワー部を支える柱。
Looking toward the Hibiya Park from the executive lounge on the seventh floor.
The pillar on the left supports the high-rise tower part.

6階パークビューガーデン。9階スカイガーデンへ段状に緑が繋がる
Park View Garden on the sixth floor. The green extends to the Sky Garden on the ninth floor in a terraced form.

6階パークビューガーデンから日比谷公園方向を見る。
Looking toward the Hibiya Park from the Park View Garden on the sixth floor.

6階Qカフェのテラス席とパークビューガーデン。
The terrace tables of the Q Cafe and the Park View Garden on the sixth floor.

北側から見る。低層部の日比谷公園側の屋上部はパークビューガーデンとして開放されており、日比谷公園方向の眺望が確保されている。
View from the north side. The roof terrace of the lower level part on the Hibiya Park side is open as the Park View Garden, and the view toward the Hibiya Park is secured.

056

飯田橋方向から見る夕景。タワー部のラップ部分とクラウン部分が光る特徴的な照明計画。

Evening view from the Iidabashi direction.
A distinguishing illumination plan in which the wrap part and the crown part of the tower light up.

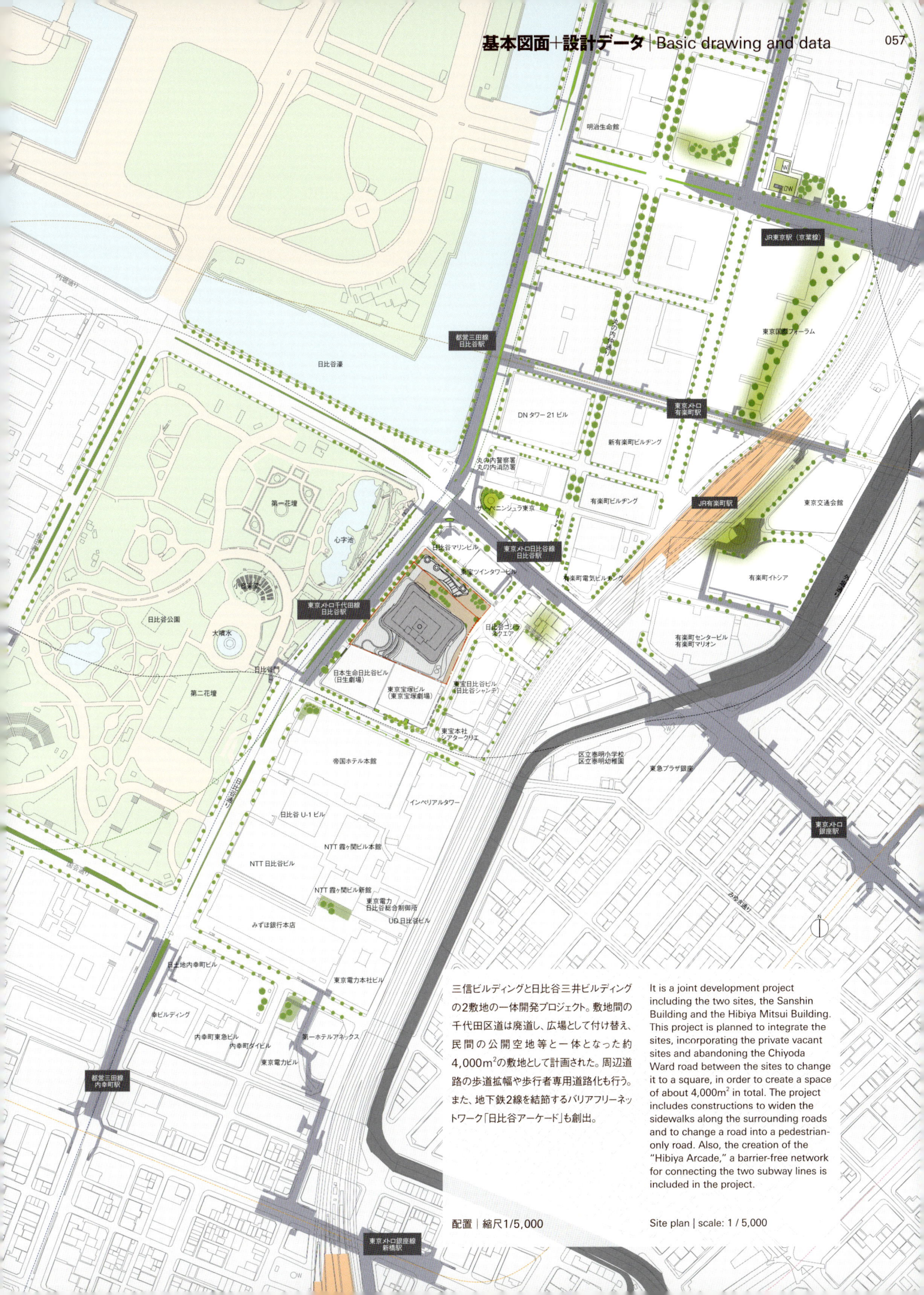

明治生命館

JR東京駅（京葉線）

東京国際フォーラム

都営三田線
日比谷駅

日比谷濠

DN タワー 21 ビル

丸の内警察署
丸の内消防署

新有楽町ビルヂング

東京メトロ
有楽町駅

有楽町ビルヂング

JR有楽町駅

東京交通会館

ザ・ペニンシュラ東京

東京メトロ日比谷線
日比谷駅

有楽町電気ビルヂング

有楽町イトシア

日比谷マリンビル

有楽町センタービル
有楽町マリオン

東京メトロ千代田線
日比谷駅

東京ツインタワービル

日比谷ゴジラ
スクエア

第一花壇

心字池

日比谷公園

大噴水

日本生命日比谷ビル
（日生劇場）

東京宝塚ビル
（東京宝塚劇場）

東宝日比谷ビル
（日比谷シャンテ）

第二花壇

日比谷門

東宝本社
アーク・クリエ

区立泰明小学校
区立泰明幼稚園

東急プラザ銀座

帝国ホテル本館

東京メトロ
銀座駅

インペリアルタワー

日比谷 U-1 ビル

NTT 霞ヶ関ビル本館

NTT 日比谷ビル

NTT 霞ヶ関ビル新館

東京電力
日比谷総合制御所

U9 日比谷ビル

みずほ銀行本店

東京電力本社ビル

日土地内幸町ビル

幸ビルディング

都営三田線
内幸町駅

内幸町東急ビル

内幸町ダイビル

第一ホテルアネックス

東京電力ビル

東京メトロ銀座線
新橋駅

三信ビルディングと日比谷三井ビルディングの2敷地の一体開発プロジェクト。敷地間の千代田区道は廃道し、広場として付け替え、民間の公開空地等と一体となった約4,000㎡の敷地として計画された。周辺道路の歩道拡幅や歩行者専用道路化も行う。また、地下鉄2線を結節するバリアフリーネットワーク「日比谷アーケード」も創出。

It is a joint development project including the two sites, the Sanshin Building and the Hibiya Mitsui Building. This project is planned to integrate the sites, incorporating the private vacant sites and abandoning the Chiyoda Ward road between the sites to change it to a square, in order to create a space of about 4,000m² in total. The project includes constructions to widen the sidewalks along the surrounding roads and to change a road into a pedestrian-only road. Also, the creation of the "Hibiya Arcade," a barrier-free network for connecting the two subway lines is included in the project.

配置｜縮尺1/5,000

Site plan | scale: 1 / 5,000

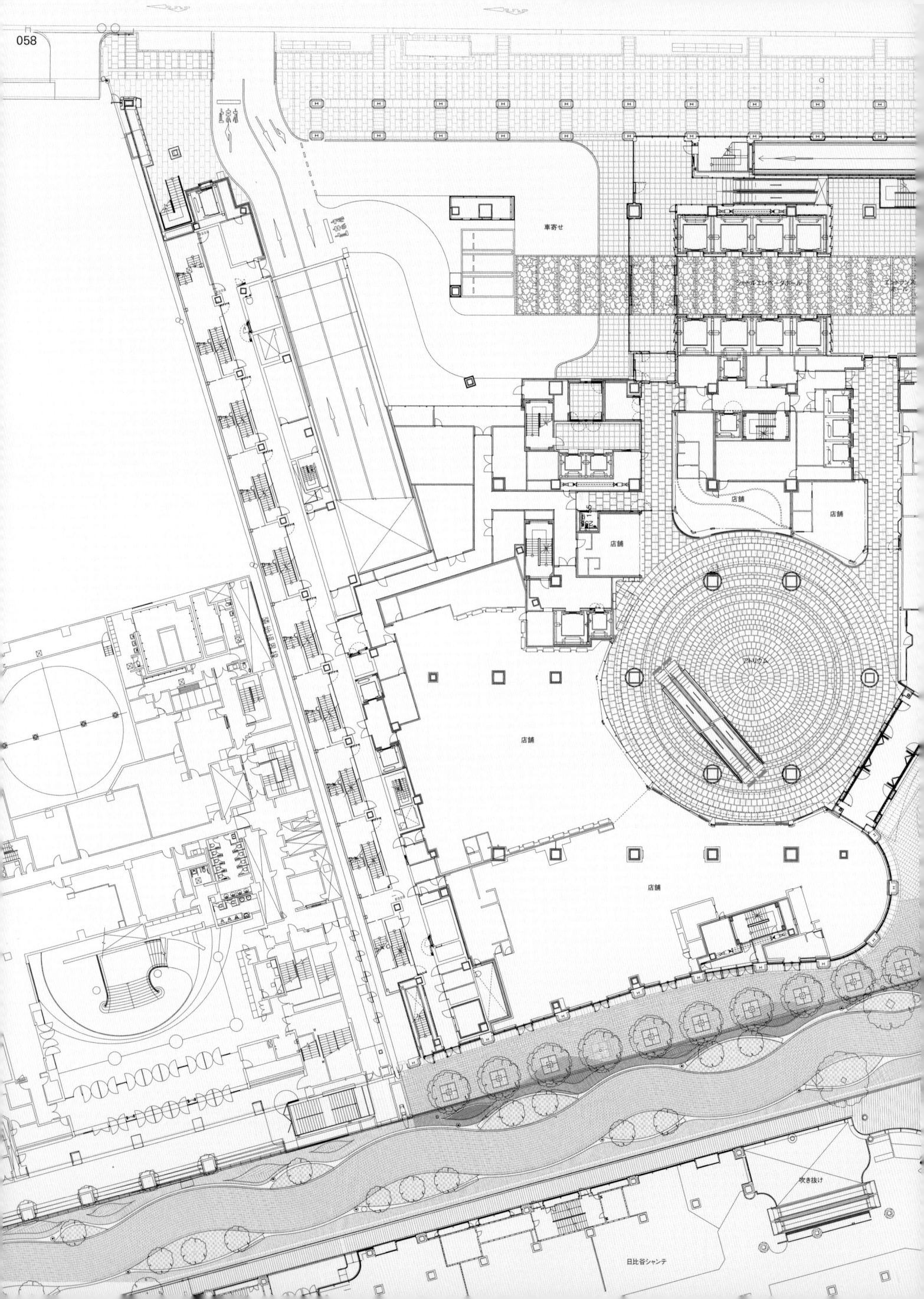

車寄せ

シャルルモンタダホール

エオラワンホール

店舗

店舗

店舗

アトリウム

店舗

店舗

店舗

吹き抜け

日比谷シャンテ

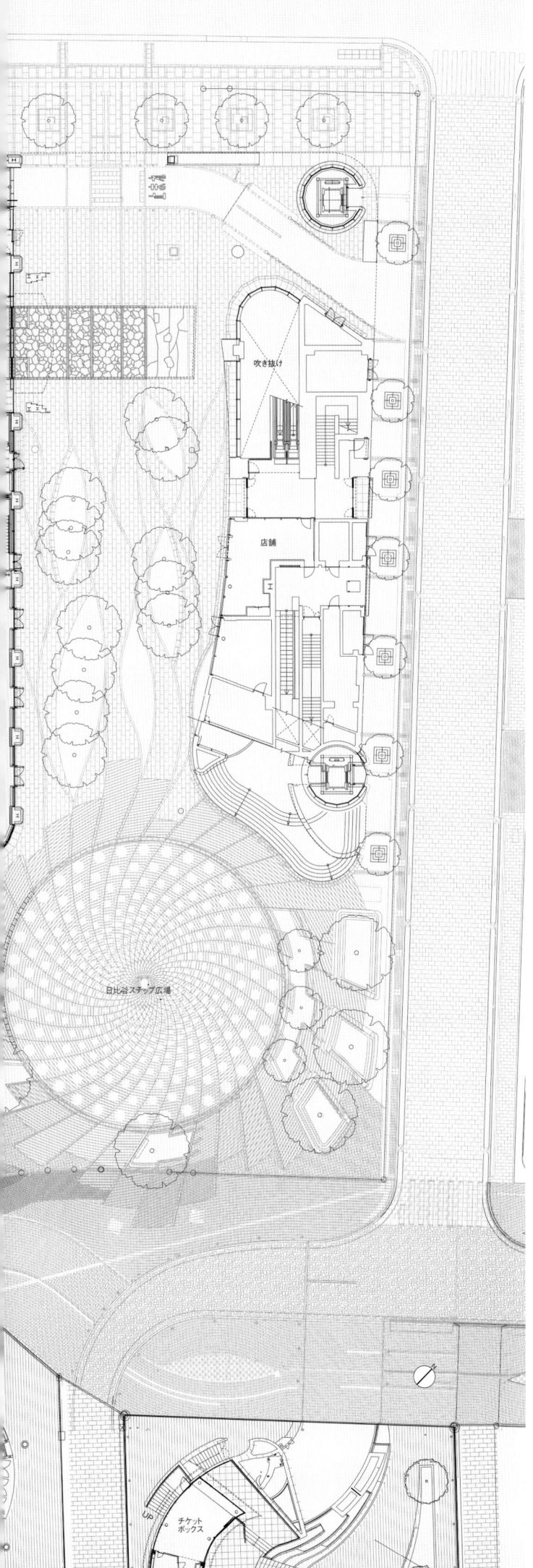

事業主
三井不動産
設計
マスターデザインアーキテクト
ホプキンス・アーキテクツ
　ガーデンデザイナー
　マーカスバーネットスタジオ
　照明デザイナー
　DHAライティング
都市計画・基本設計・デザイン監修
日建設計
実施設計・監理
KAJIMA DESIGN
　外構実施設計協力
　ランドスケープデザイン
　外構・外観照明実施設計協力
　フォーライツ
商業環境デザイン
乃村工藝社
オフィス共用部環境デザイン
イリア
サインデザイン
井原理安デザイン事務所
施工
鹿島建設

敷地面積
10,702.32m²（日比谷三井タワー）＋
1,990.01m²（日比谷ステップ広場関連施設）
建築面積
8,652.41m²（日比谷三井タワー）＋
930.69m²（日比谷ステップ広場関連施設）
延床面積
189,244.95m²（日比谷三井タワー）＋
3,602.43m²（日比谷ステップ広場関連施設）
階数（日比谷三井タワー）
地下4階／地上35階／塔屋1階
階数（日比谷ステップ広場関連施設）
地下2階／地上2階
構造（日比谷三井タワー）
鉄骨造／鉄筋コンクリート造／
鉄骨鉄筋コンクリート造
構造（日比谷ステップ広場関連施設）
鉄筋コンクリート造
工期
2015年1月−2018年2月

Developer
Mitsui Fudosan
Master design architect
Hopkins Architects
　Garden designer
　Marcus Burnet Studio
　Master lighting designer
　DHA lighting
Urban planning, schematic design, design supervisor
Nikken Sekkei
Local architect, Supervisor
KAJIMA DESIGN
　Local landscape architect
　Landscape Design
　Local lighting designer
　FORLIGHTS
Commercial designer
NOMURA
Office interior designer
Ilya Corporation
Sign designer
Rian Ihara Design Office
Constructor
Kajima Corporation

Site area
10,702.32m² (Hibiya Mitsui Tower) +
1,990.01m² (Hibiya Step Square-related facilities)
Building area
8,652.41m² (Hibiya Mitsui Tower) +
930.69m² (Hibiya Step Square-related facilities)
Total floor area
189,244.95m² (Hibiya Mitsui Tower) +
3,602.43m² (Hibiya Step Square-related facilities)
Number of stories (Hibiya Mitsui Tower)
-4, +35, rooftop structure +1
Number of stories (Hibiya Step Square-related facilities)
-2, +2
Structure (Hibiya Mitsui Tower)
Steel frame, reinforced concrete, steel reinforced concrete
Structure (Hibiya Step Square-related facilities)
Reinforced concrete
Construction period
January, 2015 - February, 2018

1階平面兼配置｜縮尺1/5,000

1st floor plan and site plan ｜ scale: 1 / 5,000

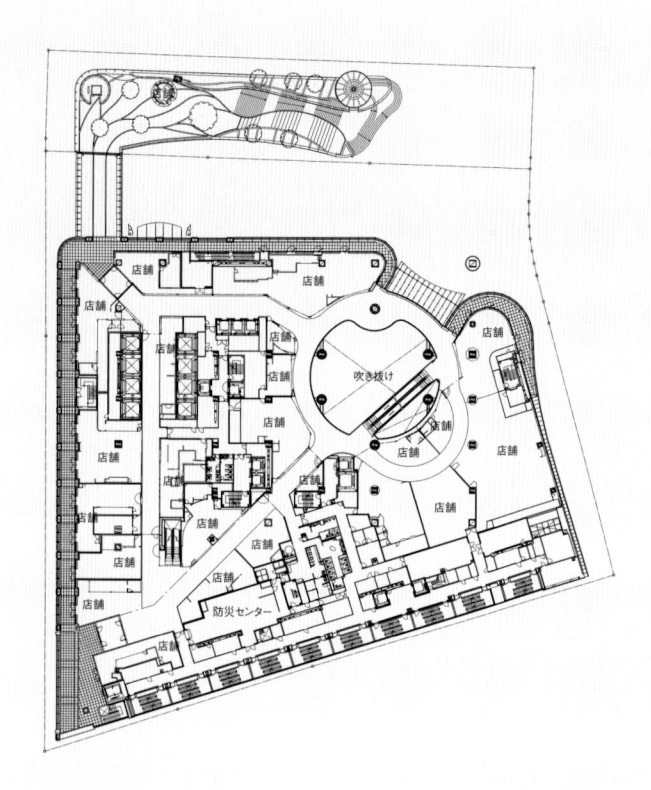

2階平面
2nd floor plan

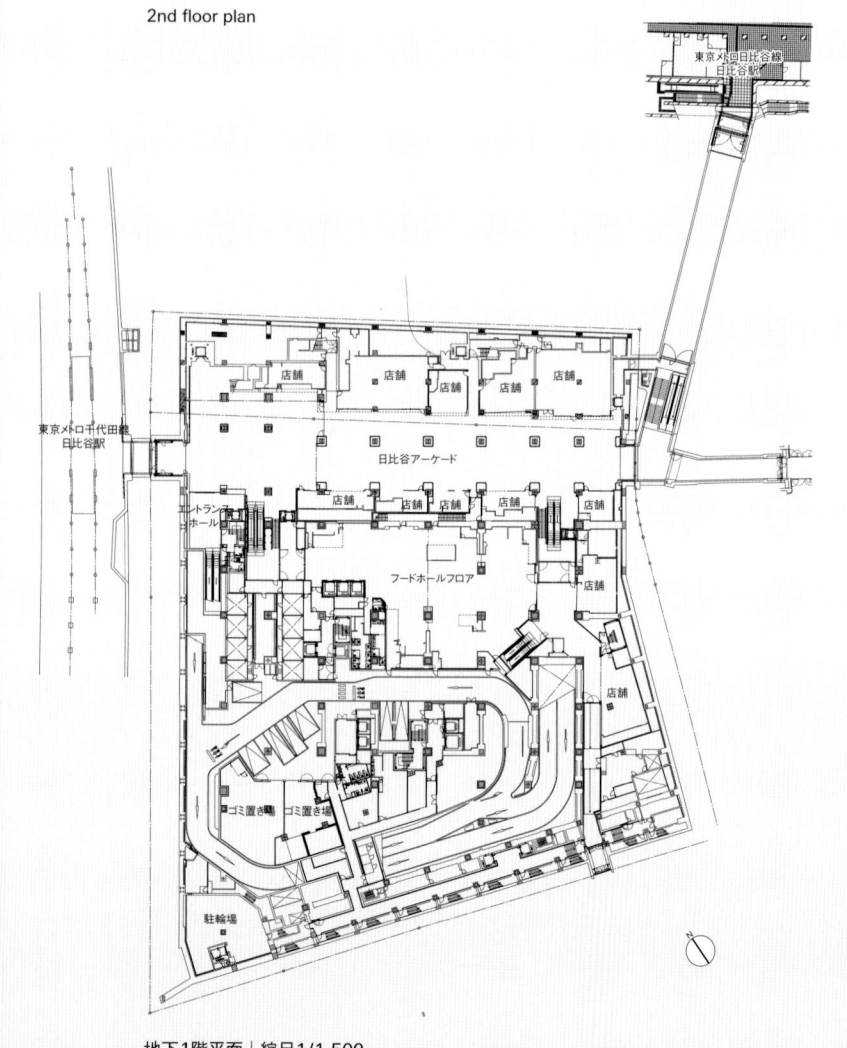

地下1階平面｜縮尺1/1,500
Basement 1st floor plan | scale: 1/ 1,500

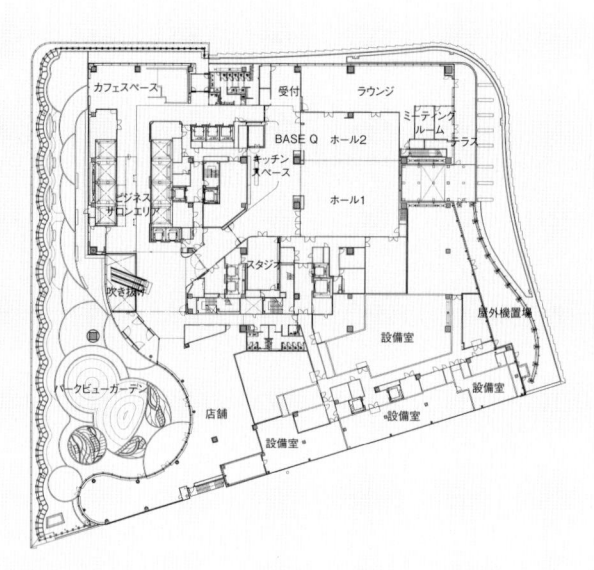

6階平面
6th floor plan

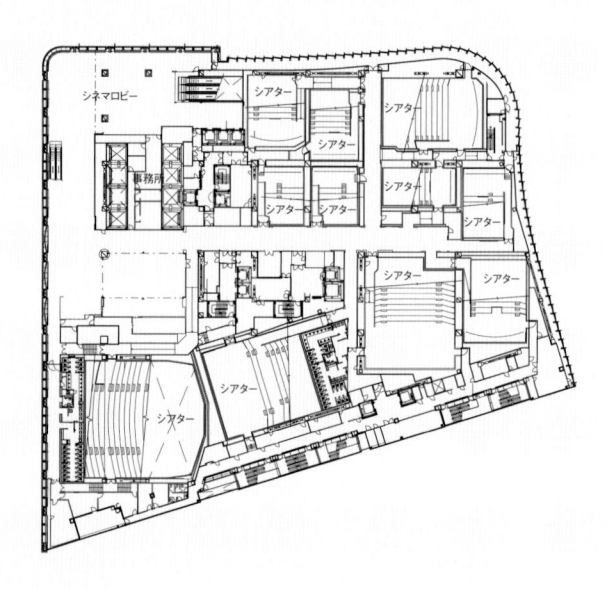

4階平面
4th floor plan

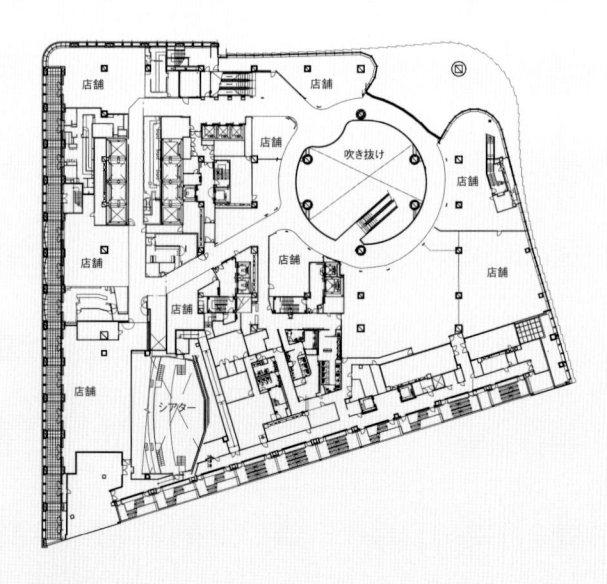

3階平面
3rd floor plan

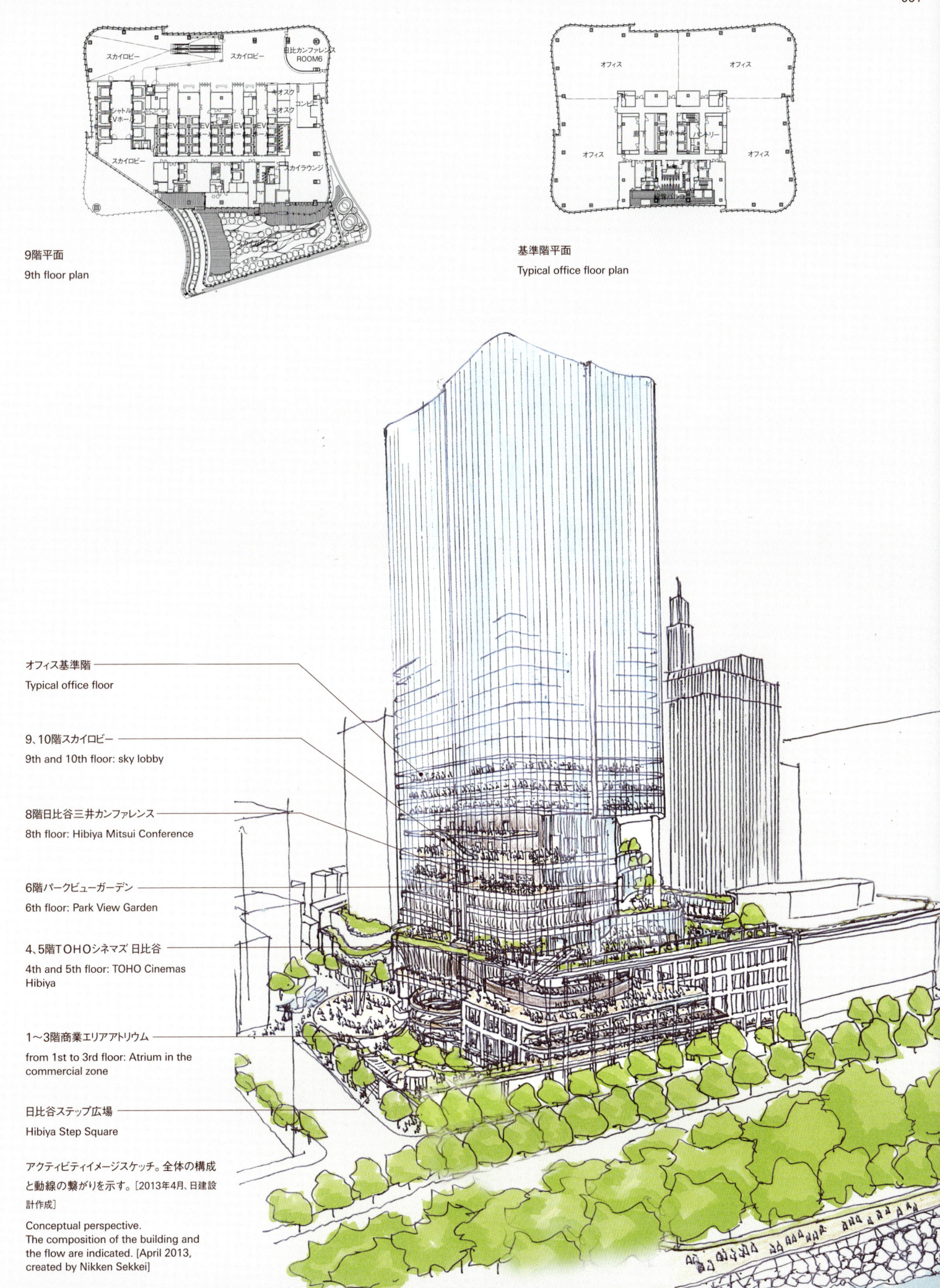

9階平面
9th floor plan

基準階平面
Typical office floor plan

オフィス基準階
Typical office floor

9、10階スカイロビー
9th and 10th floor: sky lobby

8階日比谷三井カンファレンス
8th floor: Hibiya Mitsui Conference

6階パークビューガーデン
6th floor: Park View Garden

4、5階TOHOシネマズ 日比谷
4th and 5th floor: TOHO Cinemas Hibiya

1〜3階商業エリアアトリウム
from 1st to 3rd floor: Atrium in the commercial zone

日比谷ステップ広場
Hibiya Step Square

アクティビティイメージスケッチ。全体の構成と動線の繋がりを示す。[2013年4月、日建設計作成]

Conceptual perspective. The composition of the building and the flow are indicated. [April 2013, created by Nikken Sekkei]

New Town Planning by Sharing "Hibiya-ness"

Yasuo Onozawa [Mitsui Fudosan] ×
Atsushi Omatsu [Nikken Sekkei]

夢を描き、前人未到の山を目指す

●——2008年に「東京ミッドタウン日比谷」のプロジェクトが始動しました。その当初から大切にしてきた考え方を教えてください。

小野澤康夫[以下、小野澤]——2008(平成20)年当時、三信ビルディング(1930[昭和5]年竣工、設計：横河工務店[松井貴太郎])が既に解体され、日比谷三井ビルディングでもテナントの立ち退きが始まっていました。このふたつの敷地でいったいどのような街づくりをなすべきか。そこで日建設計とタッグを組み、2008年の初夏にコンセプトづくりの合宿を行いました。振り返るとそれがこのプロジェクトの原点になりました。

街づくりのコンセプトを考える時、プロジェクトの立ち位置をどのくらい広い地図の中にイメージできるかがとても大切です。このエリアに、世界中からどんな人たちが訪れ、働き、ビジネスや文化的な交流がどんな風に繰り広げられるのか。近隣との関係においてもプロジェクトエリアの意識は重要で、自分たちのエリアを超えて、近接する人たちにもあまねく開かれて繋がっていることが重要だと考えていました。こういったイメージは開発が進んだ後から慌てて付け加えてデザインしようとしても手遅れになってしまいます。合宿の中でわれわれはこの日比谷でイメージできるさまざまな夢を描きました。実現の可能性とかビジネスのことは取りあえず脇に置いて、その夢をちゃんと突き詰めてみたいと思ったのです。われわれはこのプロジェクトを100年に一度の街づくりのチャンスだと捉えていました。そこで登るべき山はどんな山なのか、そしてその頂上からどんな景色が見たいのか、日々議論を重ねていきました。

大松敦[以下、大松]——街づくりの検討にあたっては、歴史的にも景観的にも価値のある三信ビルディングを解体する、という厳しい判断が前提となりました。もちろん単純に容積を積んで新しい建物に建て替え、ということではなく、その前提にふさわしい街を提案することが必要なことは明白でした。

三信ビルディングがあった頃の日比谷は、私も子どもの頃に訪れた時の印象が少し記憶にあるのですが、とても華やかだったことが思い出されます。新しい映画のロードショーが次々と公開され、映画や演劇を通して西洋文化に触れられるような場所でした。そんな日比谷の街の活気は、本プロジェクトがスタートした2008(平成20)年頃には霞んでしまっており、近接する銀座や丸の内がどんどん発展していくのに比べて、取り残されている感じがありました。かつての日比谷の華やかさをどのように取り戻すのか、さらにこれからの東京の核となる街としてどうつくっていけるのか。この敷地だけでなく、日比谷公園や内幸町、大丸有などの隣接するエリア、線路を越えた銀座など、もっと視野を広げて全体で賑わいをつくり出すためにはどうすればよいか。そういったことをチームで散々議論しました。

小野澤——チームの議論の中で常に考え方の指針となっていたことは、自分たちの街づくりが社会的使命に照らして世に問うにふさわしい群を抜く水準にあるかということでした。それを日々自分たちに問いかけ続けていました。

Having a Dream and Climbing an Unexplored Mountain

●——In 2008, the project of "Tokyo Midtown Hibiya" launched. Could you explain the concept you have considered important from the beginning?

Yasuo Onozawa—— In 2008, Sanshin Building (built in 1929, designed by Kitaro Matsui in Yokogawa Building Contractor's Office) was already demolished and eviction of tenants from Hibiya Mitsui Building already started. I wondered what kind of town I should make on the two sites. Therefore, we partnered up with Nikken Sekkei and had a training camp for creating a concept early in summer in 2008. When I looked back, it became the origin of this project. When considering a concept of town planning, it is very important to have an idea for the position of the project with the largest map possible to think about the questions such as "what kinds of people visit and work in this area?" and "how do business and cultural exchanges take place?" The awareness of the project area is also important even in a relationship with the neighborhood, and we considered it was important that an area was widely open and connected to its neighborhood outside of the area. Adding such an idea to a design after starting a development is too late. During the training camp, we imagined various dreams in this Hibiya. We wanted to put their feasibility and business matters aside and to pursue the dreams. We considered the project as a once-100-years chance of town planning. We discussed what kind of a mountain we should climb and what kind of scenery we want to see from the summit every day.

Atsushi Omatsu—— In the town planning, demolishing Sanshin Building, which was the historically and visually valuable, was a prerequisite but a difficult decision. Of course, it was clear that we needed to propose a town appropriate to the prerequisite instead of simple replacement with a new building with a larger capacity.

I vaguely remember that Hibiya with Hibiya Sanshin Building where I visited in my childhood was very brilliant. It was a place where new movies were released one right after the other and people were able to come into contact with western culture through movies and theatrical plays. In 2008, when the project was launched, Hibiya was less vibrant and seemed to be left behind while neighboring towns such as Ginza and Marunouchi were developing. As a team, we discussed subjects such as "how do we retrieve the past glory of Hibiya?" "how do we create Hibiya as a future core town of Tokyo?" "what should we do to give liveliness not only to the site but also to other areas including adjacent areas such as Hibiya Park, Uchisaiwaicho, and Daimaruyu and Ginza beyond a railway as a whole?"

Onozawa—— Our guideline of thinking during discussions in the team was always that our town planning should be at an outstanding level in the context of social missions. We kept asking ourselves this question every day.

Altruistic Attitude Supported by the Government and Related Land Owners

Onozawa—— If we had replaced the building on each of the two sites, we could have made a certain contribution at

行政や関係地権者から支持された
利他的な姿勢

小野澤——ふたつの敷地それぞれで建て替えを行えば収益面でも早期に一定の貢献はできるはずですが、100年に一度というチャンスを前にしてわれわれが目指すべき水準は未踏の頂であるべきだと考えた末に、チームで練りあげた街づくりのコンセプトは、「ふたつの敷地の間を通る区道を付け替えて敷地を一体化し、賑わいの核となる広場を中心に作り、日比谷への豊かな人の流れをつくろう」というものでした。このふたつの敷地は、元を辿るとひとつの敷地でした。関東大震災後の復興区画整理の際に、敷地の一部を都電の引き込み線用地として提供し2敷地となったのです。都電が廃止されてはや半世紀、引き込み線としての使命は終えてはいましたが、通過交通量もそれなりの区道を廃止して他用途として付け替えるには、プロジェクトが有する公共的な価値を行政に理解してもらい賛同していただくことが必要でした。

大松——2011年3月11日の東日本大震災発生直後には、日比谷公園や三信ビルディングが解体された跡地を暫定利用した日比谷パティオに、近隣のビルの方が次々と一時避難して余震に備えていました。本プロジェクトではちょうど基本構想ができた後で、いよいよ区画整理に向かっている時期でしたが、日比谷公園や日比谷パティオのような一般に広く提供され人びとが集まることのできる広場が都市の中に必要だという実感が、地域のみなさんの中に生まれたと思います。その後、区道を廃止して付け替えるという区画整理事業が千代田区議会で全会一致で可決されたのです。われわれが日比谷で実現しようとしている大きなビジョンを、みなさんに共有していただいたのだと感じました。

●——今回、行政だけでなく、さまざまな地元の関係者との議論・検討や多くの協力があったと思います。具体的にどのようなことが議論され、東京ミッドタウン日比谷での街づくりが共有されたのでしょうか。

小野澤——これまで日比谷の地を愛し、人びとの営みを支えてこられた有楽町町会のお店の皆さんや、近隣の東宝、日本生命といった地元関係者の方々にとって、セイムボートだと思ってもらえるプロジェクトかどうかということを第一に考えていました。日比谷まちづくり検討会を幾度も開催し、皆さんが日比谷という街に抱いていらっしゃる思いをしっかりと理解し、われわれがここでやろうとしていることと皆さんの思いとがマッチするのかどうかをじっくりと見極めながら、街づくりのコンセプトをつくり上げていきました。自分たち事業者のためだけに進めるプロジェクトではなく、日比谷の街を、そこで暮らしを営む人たち、訪れてくれる人びとにとってもっとよいものにしようという、利他的といってもよいかと思える開発の基本理念が、行政の方々も含めて皆さんに支持いただけたのだと思います。

大松——ちょうどプロジェクトがスタートする直前の2007(平成19)年、六本木の「東京ミッドタウン」が竣工しました。私はそちらにも参画していましたが、日比谷と同じように、地元のみなさんとじっくりと協

an early date in terms of profits. However, in the face of the once-100-years chance, we considered that we should aim at an unexplored height. As a result, the concept of town planning developed by the team was "removing the public road between the two sites to unify them, creating a square as a core of liveliness, and creating a flow of many people to Hibiya." Those two sites were originally one section. In a land readjustment for reconstruction after the Great Kanto Earthquake, a part of the section was given for a sidetrack of the Metropolitan streetcar. A half a century after discontinuation of the streetcar, the sidetrack had finished its role. However, to remove a public road with a certain amount of traffic to use it for other purposes, it was necessary to achieve the government's understanding and approval of the public value of the project.

Omatsu—— Just after the Great East Japan Earthquake on March 11, 2011, office workers of nearby buildings evacuated to Hibiya Park and Hibiya Patio, which was the site where Sanshin Building once had stood, one after another because of the possibility of aftershock. At the time, we just created the basic concept of the project and were about to start the land readjustment, and I think people in the area came to consider that a square open to the public where people could gather such as Hibiya Park and Hibiya Patio was necessary in a city. After that, the Chiyoda Ward council unanimously approved the plan of land readjustment including removal of the public road. We felt that everyone shared the large vision we were going to realize in Hibiya.

●——I think you made discussions and examinations with not only the government but also related local people and got a great deal of cooperation from them. What kinds of subjects did you discuss in detail to share the town planning of Tokyo Midtown Hibiya?

Onozawa—— What came to our mind at first was whether related local people, including shop owners consisting of the Yurakucho town assembly and members of TOHO and Nippon Life, considered the project as a common interest or not. We held Hibiya town planning meetings many times, understood their feeling for the town of Hibiya, checked without haste if our concept could match with what they were feeling, and developed the concept of town planning. I think that the government and everyone supported our basic stance on the development because it pursues the project to make the town of Hibiya better, not only for business operators but also for residents and visitors, which we can call it as an altruistic attitude.

Omatsu—— In 2007, just before the launch of the project, "Tokyo Midtown" in Roppongi was completed. I participated its project, too, and was impressed that they had discussions carefully with local people as we did in Hibiya. Because the completion of Tokyo Midtown Roppingi and the proper reconstruction of Hinokicho Park increased the liveliness of the town and rapidly activated the place, we consider that they understood that the large urban development based on a proper vision was not only for business operators but also for the society and the town. Without such mutual trust, the project in Hibiya could not have been achieved. Such an altruistic attitude is necessary because a town is not created by the characteristics of one

議を行われていたことが印象に残っています。東京ミッドタウン六本木ができて、檜町公園もしっかりと再整備され、賑わいが向上することでどんどん街が活性化されていくことで、正しいビジョンに基づいた大規模な都市開発が事業者のためだけでなく、社会のため、街のためであるということを理解していただけたと思います。そうした相互信頼がなくては日比谷のプロジェクトは実現できませんでした。街はひとりの個性でつくられるものではなく、ダイバーシティによって構成されているため、そんな利他的な姿勢が必要なのだと思います。そのダイバーシティにこそが街の魅力に繋がっていることにも改めて気付かされました。

小野澤——街づくりにかけるわれわれの利他的な姿勢は、周囲の方々にも連鎖していきました。たとえば、東宝は東京宝塚劇場との間の歩行者専用道路、この歩専化にも相当難儀しましたが、に面した日比谷シャンテの低層部を歩道に開かれた形にリニューアルし、合歓の広場も東京ミッドタウン日比谷の広場と一体的になるように建物が減築され、日比谷ゴジラスクエアとして生まれ変わりました。エリアマネジメントに新たな自立的取り組みを導入できたのも千代田区の英断があったからこそです。また、隣接する日生劇場でも、日比谷三井ビルディングを解体した際に顕わになってしまう北側の壁に、日比谷の街の景観を損なわないよう石でお化粧をしたいというお話をいただきました。このプロジェクトを契機に、皆さんの日比谷という街に対する愛着のようなものが湧き出してきた感じがありました。

ビジョンを共有した
シームレスな設計プロセス

●——大型物件では、設計プロセスにもさまざまな立場の人たちが参加しますが、どのようにして街づくりのコンセプトを共有して具現化していったのでしょうか。

小野澤——練りあげたコンセプトを具現化するために、当代一流のタレントに集まっていただいたのはもちろんです。しかし、彼らがベストを尽くしてくれるかどうかは、われわれが彼らのハートに火を付けられるかどうかにかかっているんです。そのためには、街づくりのイメージとその魅力をきちんと理解していただく一方で、目指す山が峻嶮であれば当然そこに伴うであろう困難を必ず克服していくんだというこちら側の決意が彼らに伝わらなければいけません。

大松——先にお話したプロジェクトのコンセプトを決める合宿で議論していたビジョン。それが、プロジェクトのどの段階においてもシームレスに生き続けていたと思います。プロジェクトが進行すると新しく様々な専門家がチームに参加してきますが、そういった多様な専門家チームの中で、そのビジョンはさまざまな人のさまざまな意見を受け入れながら継承されていきました。もちろん、どんどん変わっていく部分もあるのですが、根底に流れているビジョンは変わらなかった。それが素晴らしい成果に繋がったと思います。

小野澤——マスターデザインをお願いしたホプキンス・アーキテクツには、われわれの抱いている夢やそれまで練り上げてきた構想

person but by a diversity. I reaffirmed that the diversity led to the attractiveness of the town.

Onozawa—— Our altruistic attitude to the town planning had impacts on people around us. For example, as for the pedestrian road in between Tokyo Takarazuka Theater, which was also very tough to make it pedestrianized, we renewed the low-level floor of Hibiya Chanter facing the pedestrian road to make it open and demolished the building to unify Nemu Square and the square of Tokyo Midtown Hibiya so that they were reborn as Hibiya Godzilla Square. Thanks to an excellent decision made by the Chiyoda Ward, we were able to introduce a new independent approach for area management. In addition, Nissay Theatre, the next-door neighbor, expressed their intention to cover the north wall, which would be exposed after disassembling Hibiya Mitsui Building, with stones not to impair scenery in Hibiya. I felt that their attachment to Hibiya or the like was triggered by the project.

Seamless Design Process
with a Shared Vision

●——In a large project, people in different positions participate its design process. How did you share and realize the concept of town planning?

Onozawa—— To realize the concept which was carefully developed, of course we invited the most talented people of the day. However, it fully depended on how we should ignite their soul to do their best. For fulfilling the purpose, we needed to make them properly understand the idea of the town planning and its attractiveness, and convey our determination to overcome inevitably accompanying difficulties like a steep road of the mountain we aimed at.

Omatsu—— There was a vision we discussed in the training camp in which we set the concept of the project as mentioned earlier. I think that it seamlessly stayed alive in every stage of the project. As the project proceeded, new experts joined the team from the various backgrounds. In the team with various experts, the vision was taken over while accepting different opinions from various people. Some parts were largely changed, of course, but the underlying vision was not changed, which led to a wonderful result.

Onozawa—— Hopkins Architects, which we requested to make the master design, fully understood and shared our dreams and the concept we had developed through detailed and repeated communication. The concept we considered to express Hibiya-ness in the future is "In the Park," and I feel the expression "everything is carried out at a town in the park" took a role as a common language which easily understood when participants shared the vision.

Omatsu—— For example, the three-story open ceiling of the commercial area, a large waiting room in the cinema complex on the fourth floor, and a scenery toward Hibiya Park may be excessive from the point of view of real estate business. There may have been some other ways which can increase areas to be rented to tenants as well as profits. However, because of the vision we had shared in the team for a long time, we were able to examine a space design to create "Hibiya-ness" without hesitation.

The vision played a large role when examining the floor level

を、細やかなコミュニケーションを重ねるなかでよく理解し共有してもらえたと思います。われわれの考えるこれからの日比谷らしさを表したコンセプトが「In the Park」ですが、「公園の中にある街で全てが営まれる」という表現は、参画するメンバーがビジョンを共有する上でとても分かりやすい共通言語としての役割を果たしていたと感じます。

大松——たとえば、商業部分の大きな3層吹き抜けや、4階のシネマコンプレックスの待合ロビーの大空間や日比谷公園側への眺望などはおそらく、不動産ビジネス的に考えると過剰だったかもしれません。もっとテナントへの貸床面積が広くなり収益が上がるようなやり方もいくらでもあったと思います。しかし、チームでずっと共有してきているビジョンがあったので、「日比谷らしさ」をつくり出すため、チーム内でも迷いなく空間デザインの検討を進めることができました。

地下の日比谷アーケードの床レベルの検討においてもビジョンは大きな役割を果たしました。接続する東京メトロ千代田線のコンコースと同じレベルに設定したことで、街におけるこの空間の価値は比類なきものになりました。実はビルの地下1階と地下鉄のコンコース階にはレベル差があり、地下のアーケードはビルの地下1階とはスキップフロアで接続しています。普通、効率を考えると、階段やエスカレータなどの動線を設けないといけなくなるので、ビル側と同じレベルにしたいと考えるところなのですが、日比谷への人の流れをつくり出すこと優先して考え、地下鉄を利用してこの街を訪れる人にとって連続してアクセスできるようなレベル設定としています。その結果、地下のアーケード空間も高い天井が取れました。ビジネス的な判断ではなく、共有していたビジョンがあったからこそ、実現した空間だと思います。

企業を越えた人の繋がりで実現する新しい街づくり

●——東京ミッドタウン日比谷が完成し、このプロセスによって得たものは何ですか。またそれは、今後どのように活きてくると思われますか。

小野澤——このプロジェクトでは、構想段階から竣工に至るまで、関係地権者や行政、有識者、デザイナー、アーティスト、設計者、施工者を始めとして、さまざまな方々と日比谷らしさについて議論しながらチームとして協働させていただきました。それぞれの立場の違いはありますが、日比谷をもっと魅力溢れる街にしたいという同じ夢を追いかけるひとつの大きなチームがつくれたと思います。これまでにない高みを目指そうというチームの目標は、メンバー個々の自律性を高め、同時に相互の信頼を揺るぎないものにしました。目標自体が突破力を内包するということも改めて自覚できました。この経験によって得られたことは、プロジェクトの完成にとどまらない目に見えない素晴らしい財産です。

大松——一般的な市街地再開発事業では、あるエリアの権利区分を共有化して、共同で一気に新しい街をつくっていきます。本

of the underground arcade. Setting the floor at the same level as that of the concourse of the Tokyo Metro Chiyoda Line, it made the space in the town incomparably valuable. In fact, there is a difference in level between the basement level 1 of the building and the concourse floor of the subway. The underground Hibiya Arcade is connected to the basement level 1 with skip floors. Normally, the floor is set at the same level as that of the building for efficiency, because a difference in level requires setting of traffic lines including stairs and escalators. But we prioritized making the flow of people to Hibiya and set the level so that people who visit the town using a subway have straight access. As a result, the arcade in the basement has a high ceiling. I think that the space was realized by the shared vision, not because of a business decision.

New Town Planning Achieved by Communication between People across Companies

●——Tokyo Midtown Hibiya was completed. What did you get through the process? And how do you think it will be used in the future?

Onozawa—— In this project from the stage of planning to the completion, we worked with many people including related land owners, the government, experts, designers, artists, architects, and constructors as a team while discussing what Hibiya-ness should be. Though each had a different role, I think we were able to form one large team following the same dream of making Hibiya more attractive. Our goal of reaching to an unexplored height increased self-discipline of each member and solidified mutual trust. I also realized that the goal itself included a breakthrough. What I got from this experience is not only the completion of the project but also an invisible and wonderful asset.

Omatsu—— Generally, in an urban redevelopment project, the ownership of a certain area is commoditized to create a new town at once. This project did not employ the method, and we created a city with a sense of unity as a whole by figuring out its network, scenery, management, and operation while securing the ownerships of existing neighboring buildings. I think this process will have large impacts on the future town planning. I think that the value of this town planning will be clarified while many people in different positions will give us opinions.

Onozawa—— In March this year, "Tokyo Midtown Hibiya" made its grand opening, and fortunately, it has attracted many people and is always crowded. We can say this is one of our goal, but I look forward to seeing how our dream of "In the Park" will grow in the future. And I expect that new possibilities developed in the Hibiya project will be actively used in urban development in the future.

[On December 3, 2018, in Tokyo Midtown Hibiya. Edited by the editorial department of Shinkenchiku]

プロジェクトではそういった方式をとらず、それぞれの隣接する既存建物の権利関係を担保しながら、ネットワークや景観調整、管理運営上の工夫を図ることで全体としては一体感のある街をつくっていきました。このプロセスはこれからの街づくりに大きな影響をもたらすと思います。これからもいろいろな立場の方から意見をいただくことになると思いますが、その中で今回の街づくりの価値がはっきり見えてくるのではないでしょうか。

小野澤——今年3月に「東京ミッドタウン日比谷」はグランドオープンを迎え、ありがたいことにたくさんの方々に注目していただきいつも賑わっています。ここがひとつのゴールという言い方もできると思うのですが、われわれの抱いた「In the Park」という夢が未来に向かってどのように成長していくのかを、これからも楽しみに見続けていくつもりです。そして、この日比谷プロジェクトによって拓かれた都市開発の新たな可能性が、今後の街づくりにも活かされていくのではないかと期待しています。

[2018年12月3日、東京ミッドタウン日比谷にて | 文責：新建築社編集部]

小野澤康夫 | おのざわ・やすお
1959年長野県生まれ/1981年一橋大学商学部卒業、三井不動産入社/2004年同社ビルディング本部業務推進室長/2008年同社ビルディング本部千代田開発部長/2009年同社執行役員/2011年同社常務執行役員/2016年同社取締役常務執行役員/2017年〜同社取締役専務執行役員

—

大松敦 | おおまつ・あつし
1960年東京都生まれ/1983年東京大学工学部建築学科卒業、日建設計入社/1998年同社企画開発室長/2003年同社プロジェクトマネジメント室長/2011年同社執行役員/2015年同社常務執行役員/2016年〜同社取締役常務執行役員

Yasuo Onozawa
1959 Born in Nagano, Japan / 1981 Graduated from the Bachelor of commerce and management, Hitotsubashi University, Joined Mitsui Fudosan / 2004 General Manager, Strategy Planning and Administration Department Office Building Division / 2008 General Manager, Chiyoda Project Department, Office Building Division / 2009 Managing Officer / 2011 Executive Managing Officer / 2016 Managing Director, Executive Managing Officer / 2017– Managing Director, Senior Executive Managing Officer

—

Atsushi Omatsu
1960 Born in Tokyo, Japan / 1983 Graduated from Department of Architecture and Building Engineering, University of Tokyo, Joined Nikken Sekkei / 1998 General Manager of Project Development Section / 2003 General Manager of Project Management Section / 2011 Executive Officer / 2015 Senior Executive Officer / 2016– Senior Executive Officer & Member of the Board

以降の頁では「東京ミッドタウン日比谷」の街づくりのプロセスを4つのフェーズに分けて紹介する。それぞれの記名テキストは、ワークセッションのコアメンバーによる座談会（2018年8月1日、8月9日の2回実施）や、関係者の執筆原稿によって構成している。記名テキストの凡例は以下の通り。

[凡例]	
MF	三井不動産
HA	ホプキンス・アーキテクツ
NS	日建設計
KD	KAJIMA DESIGN
LD	ランドスケープデザイン
FL	フォーライツ
MB	マーカスバーネットスタジオ
DHA	DHAライティング
NK	乃村工藝社
IL	イリア
IZ	和泉正敏氏
HO	堀木エリ子氏
TS	TOSHIO SHIMIZU ART OFFICE
IH	井原理安デザイン事務所
KC	鹿島建設

[座談会参加者]	
MF	藤井拓也[三井不動産 日比谷街づくり推進部 グループ長]
	中村仁[三井不動産アーキテクチュアルエンジニアリング CM本部 プロジェクト推進部長]
HA	星野裕明[日本代表 プロジェクトディレクター]
NS	小嶋隆[設計部門 設計部長]
	高田絵美[都市部門 主管]
	谷内啓太郎[設計部門]
KD	深井繁人[建築設計統括グループ グループリーダー]
	久保田聡[建築設計統括グループ チーフアーキテクト]
LD	岩崎哲治[設計部 部長]
NK	數坂幸生[クリエイティブ本部 グループリーダー]
	西本陽[第二事業本部 部長]

The following pages introduce the town planning process of "Tokyo Midtown Hibiya" separated into 4 phases. Each article with author names consist of discussions of core members in work sessions in meetings (held twice in August 1 and August 9, 2018) and notes writings by related people. The explanatory notes of articles with author names are as follows.

[Explanatory notes]	
MF	Mitsui Fudosan
HA	Hopkins Architects
NS	Nikken Sekkei
KD	KAJIMA DESIGN
LD	Landscape Design
FL	FORLIGHTS
MB	Marcus Barnett Studio
DHA	DHA Lighting
NK	NOMURA
IL	Ilya Corporation
IZ	Masatoshi Izumi
HO	Eriko Horiki
TS	Toshio Shimizu Art Office
IH	Rian Ihara Design Office
KC	Kajima Corporation

[Participant in a discussion meeting]	
MF	Takuya Fujii [Executive Manager, Hibiya Urban Planning and Development Department of Mitsui Fudosan]
	Hitoshi Nakamura [General Manager, Construction Management Division of Mitsui Fudosan Architectural Engineering]
HA	Hoshino Hiroaki [Project Director, Representative in Japan]
NS	Takashi Kojima [General Manager, Design Section]
	Emi Takata [Urban Development Planning Section]
	Keitaro Taniuchi [Design Section]
KD	Shigeto Fukai [Group Leader, Architectural Design Department]
	Akira Kubota [Chief Architect, Architectural Design Department]
LD	Tetsuji Iwasaki [General Manager]
NK	Sachio Suzaka [Group Leader, Creative Department]
	Yo Nishimoto [Director, Buisiness Unit 2]

座談会の様子。
（2018年8月1日、東京ミッドタウン日比谷にて）

A discussion meeting. (On August 1, 2018, in Tokyo Midtown Hibiya)

PHASE 1

ビジョンメイキング
—日比谷の新たな街づくりへ

Vision making — new town planning in Hibiya

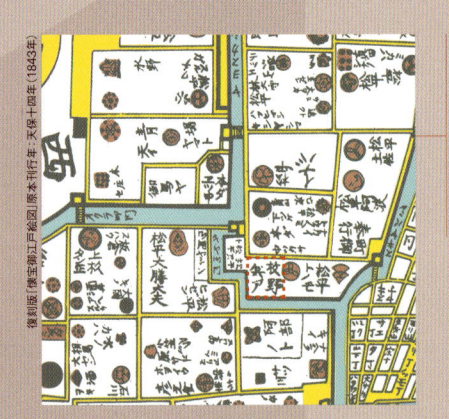

1848年頃の敷地周辺。
常陸国（現在の茨城県）に存在した笠間藩の屋敷があったと言われている。

The site and its surroundings around 1848. It is said that there was a residence of Kasama Domain, which was in Hitachi Province (Ibaraki Prefecture at the present day).

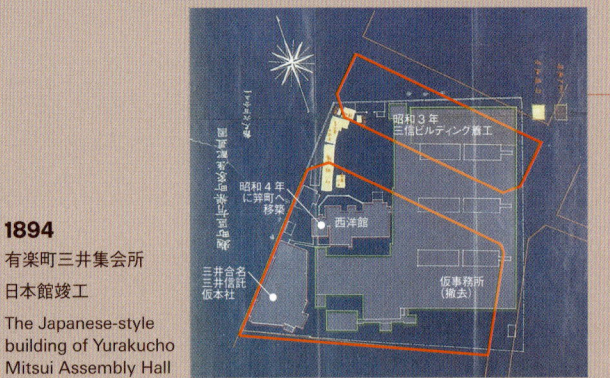

1894
有楽町三井集会所
日本館竣工

The Japanese-style building of Yurakucho Mitsui Assembly Hall was completed

1898
有楽町三井集会所
西洋館竣工

The Western-style building of Yurakucho Mitsui Assembly Hall was completed

1924
帝国復興計画

Imperial capital restoration plan

**東京ミッドタウン
日比谷の敷地での
出来事**

**Events on
Tokyo Midtown
Hibiya site**

1875
明治時代に入り、しばらく居住して居た大隈重信が土地を伊勢神宮司庁に譲り転出

When the Meiji period came, Shigenobu Okuma, who lived on the site for a period, gave it to the Ise Shrine and moved

1880
皇太神宮遥拝殿
（後の日比谷大神宮）落成

Kotai Jingu Worship Hall (which was renamed to Hibiya Grand Shrine later) was completed

1887
三井銀行が神宮司庁から当該敷地を取得

Mitsui Bank obtained the site from the Ise Shrine

周辺地域・その他の出来事 | Surrounding area / Other events

1868
明治維新

The Meiji Restoration started

1871
現在の日比谷公園周辺が軍用地に

The site of the current Hibiya Park became a military park

1883
鹿鳴館竣工

Rokumeikan was completed

1890
帝国ホテル
（初代）竣工

The original Imperial Hotel was completed

1899−1903
日比谷濠の埋め立て

Hibiya Moat was reclaimed

1903
日比谷公園
開園

Hibiya Park was opened

1906
日比谷図書館
完成

Hibiya Library was completed

1908
有楽座完成

Yurakuza was completed

1923
帝国ホテル
ライト館竣工

設計：
フランク・ロイド・ライト

Imperial Hotel (Wright hotel) was completed. designed by Frank Lloyd Wright

1560
徳川家康入府「天下普請」により
日比谷入江の埋立開始

Ieyasu Tokugawa came to Tokyo, and under "the government order", the reclamation of Hibiya Inlet was started

「天下普請」では、江戸城防衛などを理由に港を東へ移転し、日比谷入江の埋め立てが行われた。埋立地は親藩や譜代大名の屋敷となった。

Under "the government order", for reasons including the defense of Edo Castle, a port was moved to the east and Hibiya Inlet was reclaimed. Residents of collateral and hereditary daimyos were built on the reclaimed land.

1907年頃の敷地周辺地図。
明治期、日比谷は欧化政策の中心であり、大名屋敷跡に鹿鳴館や帝国ホテルが建てられた。

The site and its surroundings around 1907. In the Meiji period, Hibiya was the center of Europeanization, and Rokumeikan and Imperial Hotel were built on sites where residences of daimyos (feudal lords) had stood.

「東京ミッドタウン日比谷」の街づくりのプロセスを4つのフェーズに分けて紹介する。
PHASE1では、敷地である日比谷という街がどのような歴史やポテンシャルを持つ場所であるかを議論し、
そこから「日比谷らしさ」を導き出し、新しい街づくりのビジョンを策定して共有するまでのプロセスを紹介する。

The planning process of the town of "Tokyo Midtown Hibiya" is introduced by categorizing into four phases.
In PHASE 1, we introduce the process from the discussion of history and potentials of the town of Hibiya (the planning site),
deriving "Hibiya-ness" from the discussion, drafting a new vision of town planning, up until sharing.

1923年の関東大震災を受け、東京市の帝都復興計画（構想：後藤新平）を策定。これにより、それまで一体だった敷地を、三信ビルディングが建つことになる北側と、日比谷三井ビルディングが建つ南側に分けることが計画された。

After the Great Kanto Earthquake in 1923, an Imperial capital restoration plan was created in Tokyo City (by Shinpei Goto). It included separation of the site into the north part, where Sanshin Building stood, and the south part, where Hibiya Mitsui Building stood.

1929
有楽町三井集会所閉鎖
Yurakucho Mitsui Assembly Hall was closed

1930
三信ビルディング竣工
設計：横河工務所（松井貴太郎）
Sanshin Building was completed.
designed by Kitaro Matsui in Yokogawa Building Contractor's Office

1941
三井不動産設立
Mitsui Fudosan was founded

1947
三信ビルディングGHQにより接収
Sanshin Building was requisitioned by GHQ

1950
接収解除
Sanshin Building was returned

1960
日比谷三井ビルディング竣工
Hibiya Mitsui Building was completed

2005
プロジェクトの検討スタート
The examination of the project was started

2008
三信ビルディング解体
跡地で日比谷パティオ開始
Sanshin Building was demolished and Hibiya Patio was opened on the site

1929
日比谷公会堂開館
Hibiya Public Hall was opened

1934
**日比谷映画劇場開業
東京宝塚劇場完成**
Hibiya Movie Theater was opened, and Tokyo Takarazuka Theater was completed

1935
**小林一三が
日本劇場を買収・
有楽座再建**
Ichizo Kobayashi purchased Nihon Theater and rebuilt Yurakuza

1945
第二次世界大戦終戦
World War II ended

1957
東宝本社ビル竣工
（みゆき座、千代田劇場、芸術座開業）
TOHO Headquarters Building was completed (Miyukiza, Chiyoda Theater, and Geijutsuza were opened)

1959
日比谷公園に大噴水が完成
A large fountain was built in Hibiya Park

1961
日生劇場竣工
Nissay Theatre was completed

1970
3代目帝国ホテル竣工
The third Imperial Hotel was completed

1987
日比谷シャンテ竣工
Hibiya Chanter was completed

2007
三信ビルディング閉館　解体開始
Sanshin Building was closed and the demolishing of the building was started

2007
ザ・ペニンシュラ東京開業
有楽町イトシア開業
東宝本社建て替えにより
シアタークリエ開業
The Peninsula Tokyo was opened and Yurakucho Itocia was opened / Theatre Creation was opened because of reconstruction of TOHO Headquarters Building

1934年の東京宝塚劇場オープンを端緒に、日比谷公会堂や日生劇場、映画館の数々が立ち並んだ日比谷は昭和エンターテインメントの聖地だった。

Since the opening of Tokyo Takarazuka Theater in 1934, with Hibiya Public Hall, Nissay Theatre, and many movie theaters, Hibiya had been a sanctuary for entertainment in the Showa period.

PHASE 1

街の歴史と性格を理解する

Understanding history and characteristics of the town

■「これからの日比谷らしさ」を描いた街づくり

NS 2005(平成17)年から三井不動産と日建設計で、日比谷の将来像についての検討をスタートしました。日比谷の街を理解するため、歴史や特性、課題を分析すると共に、50年後100年後を見据えるため、両社共にプロジェクト関係者以外のさまざまな部門にも声をかけ、計画・設計フェーズだけではなく、エリアマネジメントのような運営フェーズまで視野を広げ、複数回大規模なワークショップを行い、多様な視点からアイデアを吸い上げる工夫を行いました。

地元の方々との対話や、ワークショップや日比谷公園に関する学識の方々との対話も行い、この場所で開発を行う責任や意義、期待、課題、ハードル等も確認しながら、夢だけでも現実だけでもない複眼的な将来像の検討を積み重ねました。2008(平成20)年には、合宿スタイルでの集中ワークショップや海外視察等でイメージを共有しながら、これまでの議論を集約した街づくりコンセプト、具体的なガイドライン、CG、模型、VR等のアウトプットとしてとりまとめ、プロジェクトの目指すべき将来像を構築しました。クライアントとコンサルタントが共に将来像を構築し、さらにそこに至る難しさも共有することができたからこそ、両社が足並みを揃え、協力しながら、それぞれの役割を果たしていくという関係性が構築されたと考えています。

設計フェーズに入った後も、グランドデザイン会議というコンセプト検討を行う会議体を立ち上げ、ハード・ソフト両面での検討を継続しました。ヒューマンファクターの手法を用い、街の観察や、働く人やよく来る人へのインタビューから多くの「気づき」を得ています。また、テキストマイニングの手法も活用し、ネット上での日比谷の情報を分析し、他エリアと比較した街のポジショニングを検討しました。将来予測を基にした50年、100年後の日比谷を思い描くシナリオプランニングや、ペルソナを設定したある日のシーンやストーリーづくりも行うなど、チーム全員で日比谷の目指すべき方向性を、多角的、継続的に模索し続けたことも、このプロジェクトのビジョンメイキングの大きな特徴です。

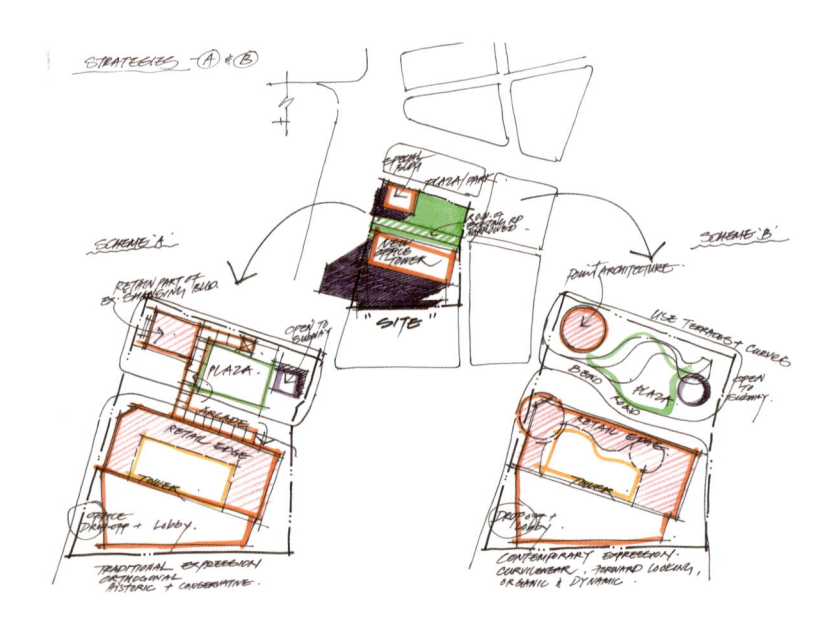

3点:三井不動産と日建設計でスタートした日比谷の街の将来像についての検討。
[2006年3月、日建設計作成]
上:A案とB案の2パターンのゾーニング。A案は2敷地をアーケードで接続。一方B案は2敷地を一体的に開発。
下2点:B案の断面スケッチ。

3 items: Examination of the Hibiya town in the future started by Mitsui Fudosan and Nikken Sekkei. [March 2006, created by Nikken Sekkei]
Top: 2 patterns of zoning: Plan A and Plan B. The 2 sites are connected with an arcade in Plan A while the 2 sites are developed as a whole in Plan B.
2 items at the bottom: Cross-sectional sketches of Plan B.

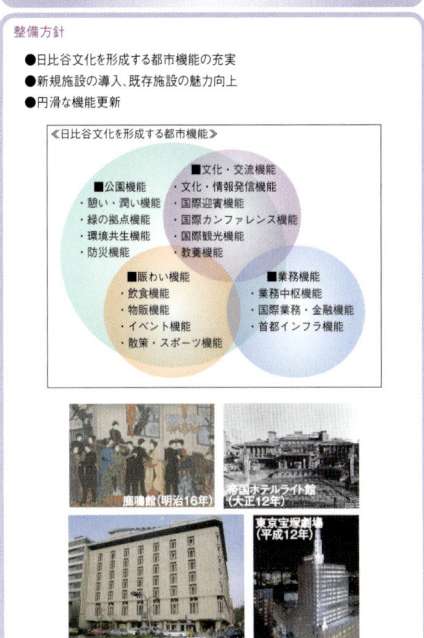

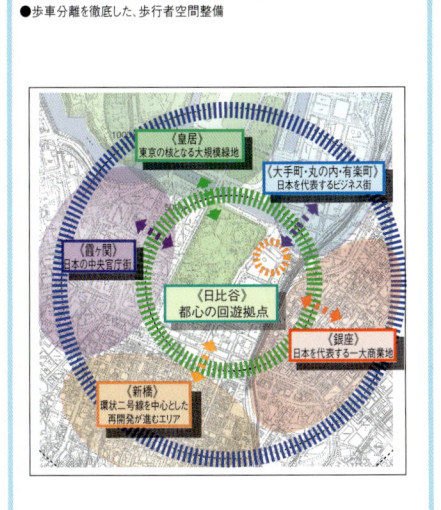

コンセプトⅠ
公園をまちへ、まちを公園へ
〜街区と日比谷公園が相互に価値を高めあうまちづくり〜

整備方針
- 公園の緑や園路が街区に繋がる、潤いと憩いに満ちた空間整備
- 公園の象徴性を活かした景観形成
- 文化・交流施設や店舗・レストラン等の最適配置

コンセプトⅡ
歴史をつむぐ、文化をはぐくむ
〜歴史的な機能集積を活かした個性あふれるまちづくり〜

整備方針
- 日比谷文化を形成する都市機能の充実
- 新規施設の導入、既存施設の魅力向上
- 円滑な機能更新

コンセプトⅢ
日比谷に集う、日比谷から広がる
〜都心の回遊拠点となる歩いて楽しいまちづくり〜

整備方針
- 大丸有・新橋・銀座・霞ヶ関など周辺エリアとの歩行者アクセス改善
- 南北の賑わい軸・個性的なシンボル空間の整備
- 歩車分離を徹底した、歩行者空間整備

上：2008年に合宿スタイルで行った集中ワークショップや海外視察などの議論をとりまとめたコンセプト。[2008年10月、日建設計作成]
右2点：グランドデザイン会議で行った、日比谷の街の観察から得た気づき。[2012年6月、インフィールドデザイン作成]

Top: Concepts as the results of discussions in a concentrated workshop as a training camp in 2008 and an oversea inspection. [October 2008, created by Nikken Sekkei]
2 items on the right: Discoveries found by observation of the town of Hibiya in the grand design meeting.
[June 2012, created by infield design]

買い物で両手を満たすのではなく、心を満たしに来る場所

余韻を楽しむことができる街

■ Town planning by drawing "future of Hibiya-ness"

NS Mitsui Fudosan and Nikken Sekkei have started reviewing the future image of Hibiya since 2005. In order to understand the town of Hibiya, we analyzed the history, characteristics, and issues. At the same time, in addition to the planning/designing phase, both companies expanded their horizons for an operation phase, which included area management. They conducted several large-scale workshops and gathered ideas from various viewpoints by inviting other departments besides project related personnel to look 50 to 100 years into the future.

We also interacted with local residents, held workshops, and consulted with experts in knowledge of Hibiya Park, and continuously examined a multifaceted future vision, neither a dream nor reality, while recognizing the responsibility, meanings, expectations, tasks, and hurdles for developing a new town here. In 2008, while sharing our visions through intense workshops and an inspection tour abroad by having a training camp, we summarized the concept of town planning, detailed guideline, CG, model, VR, etc. based on all of our discussions, and built an ideal future image of the project.

The client and the consultant can align, cooperate, and fulfill own roles by trusting each other. We believe such a relationship was established because they have built a future vision and shared difficulties reaching the goal. Even after moving forward to the design phase, we launched a meeting committee structure, which was designated as a ground design meeting for examining the concept and continued examining both hardware and software. We observed the city and interviewed working people and frequent visitors based on the human factor method and gained "awareness." Also, we analyzed information of Hibiya on the Internet, examined positioning of the town in comparison to other areas based on the text mining method. One of the major features of vision making of this project is that we continued searching for the direction of goals for Hibiya multidirectionally with the entire team by drawing a scene and story of persona, and creating scenarios of Hibiya in 50 to 100 years based on future predictions.

日本の西洋化の先駆けとなった日比谷

Hibiya, the forerunner of Westernization in Japan

▌鹿鳴館　1883年竣工 | Rokumeikan - completed in 1883

上：海外からの賓客や外交官を接待するために建てられた社交場「鹿鳴館」。建設地に決まったのは、内山下町の旧薩摩藩装束屋敷跡（現在の「日比谷U-1ビル」）。華やかな文明開化の時代はこの場所から始まった。

左下：鹿鳴館テラス。
右下：鹿鳴館内観。

Top: "Rokumeikan", a meeting place built for entertaining guests and diplomats from overseas. The construction site was land of Uchiyama-Shitacho where a house of Satsuma Domain for changing clothes stood (where "Hibiya U-1 Building" stands at the present). The age of brilliant cultural enlightenment started from the place.
Bottom left: Terrace of Rokumeikan.
Bottom right: Interior of Rokumeikan.

1884年の日比谷一帯の地図（参謀本部陸軍部測量局による測量図）。中央の日比谷練兵場（後の日比谷公園）の南東方向に面した内山下町一丁目に鹿鳴館が建っている。現在地図左上枠外に位置する国会議事堂は当時まだなく、1936年に竣工している。

A map of the Hibiya district in 1884 (a survey map prepared by the Ordnance Survey Office of the Department of the Army General Staff). Rokumeikan stood in Uchiyama-Shitacho 1 chome facing the southeast of Hibiya Drill Ground (that was changed to Hibiya Park later), which is in the center of the map. The National Diet Building, which is outside of the top left corner of the map, did not exist at that time and was completed in 1936.

鹿鳴館は1883（明治16）年に明治政府により、現在の日比谷U-1ビルの位置に、国賓や外国の外交官を接待する外交施設として建てられた。ジョサイア・コンドルの設計によるイタリア・ルネッサンス様式に英国様式を加えた煉瓦づくりの2階建ての建築であった。

当時は明治に入り、日本の近代国家としての発展を諸外国に示す必要があった。鹿鳴館は欧州文化が積極的に取り入れられた上流階級の社交場として、毎晩のようにパーティが開催されていたという。鹿鳴館を中心にした諸外国との交渉は「鹿鳴館外交」とも言われた。

しかし中心人物であった当時の外務卿・井上馨が失脚すると、短い繁栄の時は終わり、1894（明治27）年には宮内庁に払い下げられて華族会館となった。その後、民間へとわたり、太平洋戦争中の1940（昭和15）年に解体された。

於鹿鳴館貴婦人慈善会之図（揚洲周延筆）。上流階級の人びとが洋装の正装で集い、華やかな欧風の社交場として栄えた。

Ladies' Charity Party at the Rokumeikan (painted by Yoshu Chikanobu). It was a brilliant European-style meeting place where upper-class people in Western dress gathered.

In 1883, the Rokumeikan was built by the Meiji government as a diplomatic facility to host state guests and foreign diplomats at the current location of the Hibiya U-1 Building. It was a large two-story brick building in the English style adding to the Italian renaissance style designed by Josiah Conder.
At that time, the Meiji era had just begun, and the government wanted to show the development of Japan as a modern nation to foreign countries. The Rokumeikan became famous for its nightly parties as a social meeting place for the upper class and introduced European culture. A negotiation with foreign countries centering on the Rokumeikan was also called "Rokumeikan Gaiko (diplomacy)."
However, when Foreign Minister Kaoru Inoue, who was a central figure at that time, was discredited and resigned, the glorious era ended short. In 1894, the building was sold by the Imperial Household Agency and became the Kazoku Kaikan (Peers Club). Later on, the building went over to the private sector and was demolished in 1940 during the Pacific War.

■帝国ホテル　初代・1890年竣工、2代目・1923年竣工、3代目・本館：1970年竣工、3代目・タワー：1983年竣工
The first Imperial Hotel - completed in 1890, the second - completed in 1923, the third - the main building: completed in 1970, the third - the tower: completed in 1983

帝国ホテルは初代から3代目の現在に至る約130年間にわたって日比谷の地に建ち、時代に応答しつつも歴史や伝統を守ってそのブランドを保ち続けている。

初代・帝国ホテルは1890(明治23)年、鹿鳴館の隣接地に日本初の本格洋風ホテルとして建てられた。鹿鳴館同様、近代国家を目指す日本の迎賓館として、宿泊施設の整備を目的に井上馨や渋沢栄一ら政財界人の働きかけによって誕生し

た。初代・帝国ホテルは内務省技師・渡辺譲設計によるネオ・ルネッサンス式の木骨煉瓦造の3層構造で、現在は埋め立てられた外濠に面していた。

2代目はフランク・ロイド・ライト設計による通称ライト館である。4年間の工事を経て1923(大正12)年に竣工し、オープニングの日に関東大震災に見舞われたがほぼ無傷で、戦後までその姿を保った。大谷石、スクラッチ・タイル、テラコッタを使い細部

にまで幾何学的な装飾を設けた建築は高い評価を得て、海外からの賓客も数多く訪れた。

1968(昭和43)年にライト館が解体された後(一部は明治村に移築)、1970(昭和45)年に地下3階・地上17階の本館が、1983(昭和58)年にはその東側に地下4階・地上31階のインペリアルタワーが建ち、現在に至っている。

左上：初代・帝国ホテル外観。木骨煉瓦造のネオ・ルネッサンス式洋風建築。／右上：初代・帝国ホテル談話室。当時、室料は最下等で50銭、2食付きで2円50銭だった。／左下：日比谷公園上空から見る2代目・ライト館俯瞰。／右下：北東側から見る現在の帝国ホテル。手前にインペリアルタワー、奥に本館。

Top left: Exterior of the original Imperial Hotel. A Neo-Renaissance Western-style timber-framed brick building. / Top right: Lounge of the original Imperial Hotel. The least expensive room rate at that time was 0.5 yen and the rate including breakfast and dinner was 2.5 yen. / Bottom left: View of the second Wright hotel from the sky over Hibiya Park. / Bottom right: The present Imperial Hotel seen from the northeast side. The tower is on the near side and the main building is on the far side.

The Imperial Hotel has been standing in Hibiya for about 130 years since the first generation up to the present which is the third generation and adapting to each era while retaining the brand of history and tradition. The first generation of the Imperial Hotel was built next to the Rokumeikan as the first authentic Western style hotel in 1890. Like Rokumeikan, the hotel was backed by political leaders, such as Kaoru Inoue and Eiichi Shibusawa, and built as a state guesthouse for improving accommodation facilities. The first

generation of the Imperial Hotel was a three-story wood frame and brick structure in the neo-Renaissance style designed by an engineer from the Home Ministry, Yuzuru Watanabe, and facing the outer moat, which is now reclaimed.

The second generation was known as the Wright hotel designed by Frank Lloyd Wright. The building was completed in 1923 after four years of construction. Although the building was hit by the Great Kanto earthquake, it was unaffected and remained intact until the

post-war. Many guests from overseas also visited the building, which received a reputation for the detailed geometric decorations using Oya stone, scratch tiles, and terracotta.

After the Wright hotel was demolished in 1968 (some sections were rebuilt at the Meiji-mura), the main building of three under- and 17 above-ground floors was built in 1970 and the Imperial Tower of four under- and 31 above-ground floors was built on the east side in 1983, which remain to this day.

上：ライト館、池越しに見る全景。
下：宴会場。幾何学的な装飾が家具や照明など細部にまで現れる。

Top: Overall view of Wright hotel beyond a pond.
Bottom: Banquet hall. Detailed geometrical decorations can be seen on the furniture and lighting apparatus.

PHASE 1

■ 三信ビルディング　1930年竣工 | Sanshin Building - completed in 1930

三信ビルディングは1930(昭和5)年に竣工した、当時最先端の構造技術が導入された鉄骨鉄筋コンクリート造の本格的オフィスビルである。横河工務所・松井貴太郎設計、大林組施工(基礎は清水建設)による地下2階・地上8階の建物で、1階が店舗、2〜8階が事務室。2層吹き抜けのアーチ型の天井を持つアーケードやアール・デコ様式のディテールなどデザイン性の高いオフィスだった。竣工当時、丸の内一帯では貸しオフィスの需要が落ち着いて空室が目立つ時期で、三信ビルディングは7割埋まれば上出来と言われる貸しオフィスの中で、7〜8割が埋まるという人気ぶりだったという。

1947〜50(昭和22〜25)年のGHQによる接収期間を経て、その後大規模な改修増築工事を行った。1960(昭和35)年には日比谷三井ビルディングとの連絡通路がつくられ、1970(昭和45)年には地下鉄千代田線日比谷駅に接続する連絡通路がつくられた。日比谷を象徴する建物として親しまれたが、耐震・防災上の観点から2007(平成19)年に解体された。

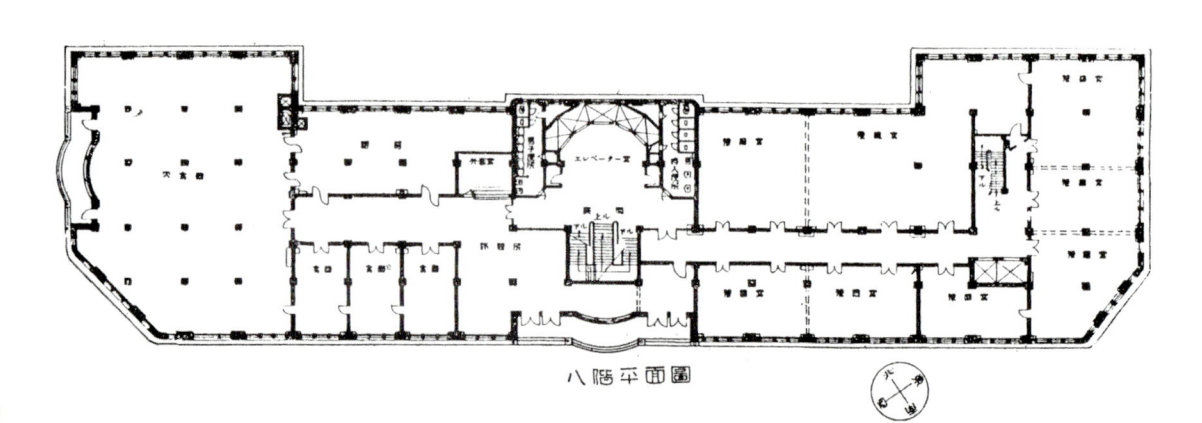

八階平面圖

8階平面

The Sanshin Building was completed in 1930. It was a full-scale office building with a steel framed reinforced concrete structure which was the cutting-edge structural technology at the time. The building was designed by Kitarou Matsui of Yokogawa Building Contractor's Office and constructed by Obayashi (the foundation was by Shimizu Corporation). It had two under- and eight above-ground floors, and there were retailers on the first floor and offices on the second to eighth floors. It was an office building with a sophisticated design such as an arch shaped 2-story atrium ceiling and detailed art deco style. Despite the vacancy around the Marunouchi area at the time of building completion, where the occupancy of 70% was considered successful, the Sanshin Building was popular and had 70 to 80% occupancy.

After a period of requisition by the GHQ (General Headquarters) from 1947 to 1950, the building underwent large scale repair and expansion. A connection passage was built between the Hibiya Mitsui Building in 1960, and another one connecting to Hibiya station in Chiyoda line in 1970. Although the building was popular as a symbol of Hibiya, it was demolished due to safety measures for earthquake and disaster.

左上：8階オフィスの廊下。／右上：基準階オフィス。／左下：1、2階吹き抜けのアーケード。／右中：アーケード照明脇の彫像。／右下：1階エレベータホール。

Top left: View from a corridor in the office space on the 8th floor / Top right: An office on the standard floor. / Left bottom: Arcade with a 2-story ceiling / Center right: Statue at the side of a lamp of the arcade. / Bottom right: Elevator hall on the 1st floor.

左頁：三信ビルディング南西側外観。関東大震災での経験を踏まえ、鉄骨鉄筋コンクリート造で建設された。当時の最先端の構造技術が用いられたオフィスビルは、貸しオフィスとして人気が高かった。

Left page: Exterior of the southwest side of Sanshin Building. It was a steel-reinforced concrete building based on the experience of the Great Kanto Earthquake. The office building built by leading-edge construction technology at that time was popular as an office space for rent.

▍日比谷三井ビルディング 1960年竣工 | Hibiya Mitsui Building - completed in 1960

日比谷三井ビルディングは、横河工務所と松田平田設計事務所の設計・監理、鹿島建設の施工によって1960(昭和35)年に竣工した。

地下5階・地上9階の鉄骨鉄筋コンクリート造で、建設にあたっては鉄筋・鉄骨各7,000t、コンクリート7万㎥の大量の資材を用いており、基礎工事を地下5階まで行うなど数々の技術的難題を解決してできた東洋最大級のオフィスビルだった。日比谷公園など周囲との調和を考慮し、外装にはアルミなどの金属材料を活用して水平ラインを強調するデザインを取り入れるなど、画期的な案を採用したデザインで高く評価された。

また日比谷三井ビルディング側に三信ビルディング用の冷凍機を設置して地下連絡通路を通じてパイピングすることで、地下が狭かった三信ビルディングへの供給を可能にした。また地下には東京電力千代田変電所と駐車場が入れられた。

日比谷公園側約60%の部分に三井銀行本店が入ったりと三井グループの一拠点を築いたが、再開発事業に伴い2011(平成23)年に解体された。

The Hibiya Mitsui Building was designed and supervised by Yokogawa Building Contractor's Office, and MHS Planners, Architects & Engineers, and constructed by Kajima Corporation, and completed in 1960.

The building had a steel frame reinforced concrete structure with five under- and nine above-ground floors. For construction, a massive amount of materials, 7,000 tons each of reinforcing rod and steel, and 70,000m³ of concrete were used. Several technical challenges were overcome, such as building five underground floors, which became the largest building in the Orient. The building had an external design that emphasized horizontal lines using aluminum in order to be in harmony with the surroundings including Hibiya Park. It was known for its groundbreaking design.

Also, by installing a centrifugal chiller unit for the Sanshin Building on the side of the Hibiya Mitsui Building and piping through the underground connection, it made it possible to supply cooler air to the Sanshin Building where underground space was limited. In addition, the basement floors were used for the Chiyoda substation of the Tokyo Electric Power Company and parking spaces. Although the building became one of the Mitsui Group's base by occupying 60% including the head office of Mitsui Bank on the side of Hibiya Park, it was demolished in 2011 due to a redevelopment project.

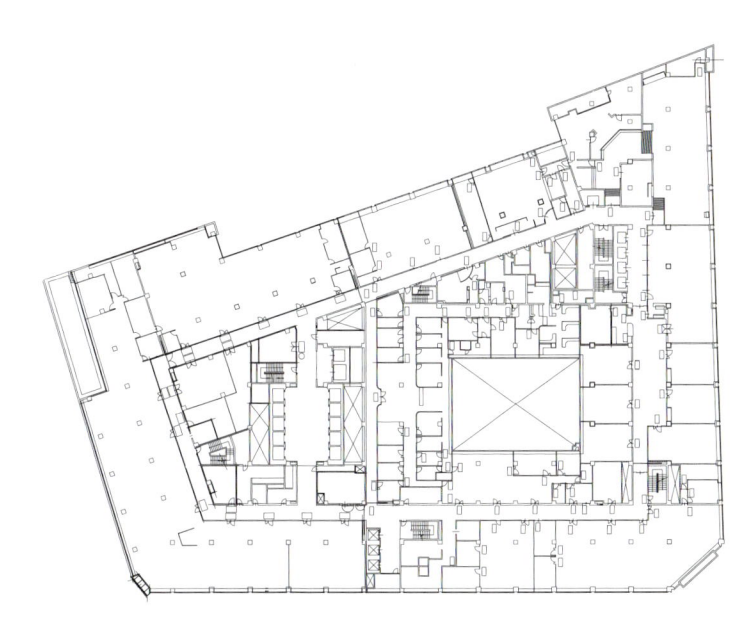

基準階平面　縮尺1/800
Typical floor plan (scale:1/800)

左頁上：戦後復興以降のビルブームの中で、日比谷三井ビルディングでは高さ31m制限の中で最大級の大きさのオフィスビルが実現された。外装には周囲との調和のためアルミなどの金属材料が用いられているのも特徴的。／左下：正面玄関。／右下：エントランスホール。
本頁右上：工事中の風景。
日比谷三井ビルディングで使用されていた石は保存され、東京ミッドタウン日比谷の地下1階オフィスエントランスで再利用されている。

Top on the left page: During a building boom in restoration after the war, Hibiya Mitsui Building was built as the tallest office building within a height limitation of 31 meters. As a characteristic, metallic materials including aluminum are used for the exterior to harmonize with the surroundings. / Bottom left: Main entrance. / Bottom right: Entrance hall. Top right of this page: View under construction.

PHASE 1

緑豊かな環境

日比谷公園の価値を再認識

Green environment

Reevaluation of Hibiya Park

日比谷公園から見る建設中の東京ミッドタウ
ン日比谷。

Tokyo Midtown Hibiya under
construction seen from Hibiya Park.

▌緑と水の豊かな都市の中の公園

1903（明治36）年の誕生から115年以上を経て、日比谷のシンボルとなっている日比谷公園。緑と水を

もたらす都会のオアシスとして、たくさんの木々が育つ日比谷公園は街を彩り、人びとの憩いの場として多くの人に親しまれてきた。周辺に位置する建物群も、公園の豊かな緑の恩恵を受けている。

約16万m²の敷地には、花壇や池や芝生のほか、公会堂、大音楽堂、テニスコート、陳列場、飲食店などの機能を有し、豊かな都市の公園となっている。

▌A park with rich green space and waterscapes in a city

Hibiya Park has been the symbol of Hibiya for over 115 years since its formation in 1903. As

an oasis nourishing the city with green space and waterscapes, Hibiya Park has been coloring the town with many trees and is a popular place for everyone to relax. Buildings surrounding the park also benefit from its rich greenery.

On the site of about 160,000m², in addition to flower beds, ponds, and grassy areas, there are facilities such as a public hall, a large open-air concert hall, tennis courts, a small museum, and restaurants. It has become a rich city park.

上：日比谷公園側からの俯瞰。[2018年11月]
左下：日比谷濠越しに見る。[2016年6月]
右下、下2点：日比谷公園から見る日比谷三
井ビルディング。[2016年5月〜2018年4月]

Top: Overhead view from the Hibiya Park side / Bottom left: View from Hibiya Moat. Bottom right, 2 pictures at the bottom: Hibiya Mitsui Building viewed from Hibiya Park.

■日本初の近代的洋風公園
Japan's first modern Western-style park

江戸末期まで松平肥前守の旧大名屋敷が建っていた場所は、明治に入って陸軍の練兵場(日比谷練兵場)となっていた。しかし周辺の市街地化に伴って、日比谷公園が日本初の近代的洋風公園として整備され、開園したのが1903(明治36)年のことである。計画から誕生までは15年の歳月を要した。現在も引き継がれる、都市の中の緑と水の豊かな公園という性格は、設計にあたった植物学博士の本多静六の尽力があった。近代的洋風公園など誰も知らなかった日本で、留学先のドイツの公園を手本に設計案が練られた。S字型の大園路、花壇や池、洋風喫茶店や音楽堂なども、開園当時から現在まで引き継がれる日比谷公園の魅力のひとつである。

The former site of the former Daimyo residence of Matsudaira in the Hizen Province, which was standing until the end of the Edo era, had become a parade ground for the Japanese army (Hibiya Parade Ground) after the Meiji era. However, along with the urbanization of the park surroundings, Hibiya Park was developed as the first Western style park in Japan and opened in 1903. It took 15 years to complete from planning to birth.
The characteristic of the park: rich green space and waterscapes in the city, has been sustained thanks to the efforts of a botanist professor, Dr. Seiroku Honda who designed the park. He referenced a park plan in Germany where he stayed as a student and designed the park when no one in Japan knew how a Western style park should look like. The large S-shaped garden path, flower beds and ponds, Western style cafe, and an open-air concert hall have been maintained since the opening of the park, and they are part of Hibiya Park's charm.

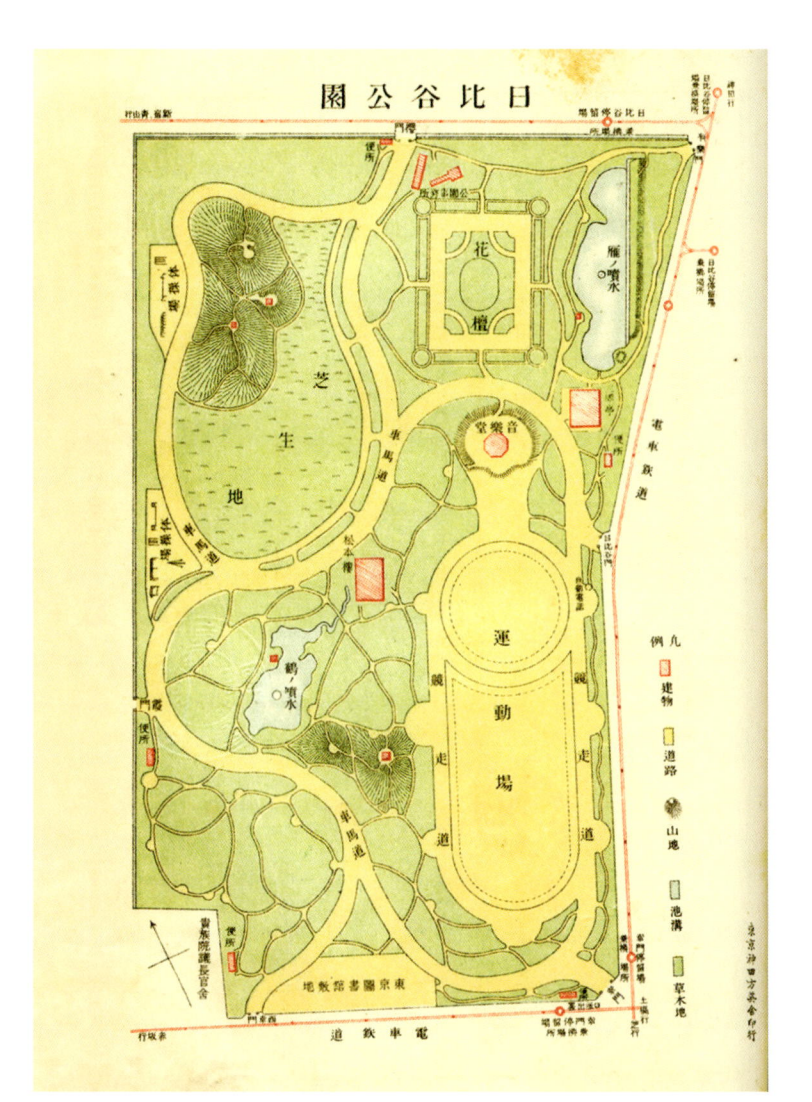

左下:日比谷練兵場の絵画(1874年)。
右上:日比谷公園、開園初期の配置図。当時は大きな運動場が設けられていた。
右中:日比谷公園の野外音楽室。八角形の鉄骨銅板屋根を持つステージに多くの人が集った。
中下:雲形池(鶴の噴水の池)を望む。
右下:公園開園と同時にオープンした、明治37年頃の洋風喫茶店(現在の松本楼)。

Bottom left: Picture of Hibiya Drill Ground (in 1874).
Top right: Layout of Hibiya Park in the early days after the opening. There was a large playground at that time.
Center right: Open-Air Concert Hall in Hibiya Park. Many people gathered at the stage with an octagon steel-framed copper roof.
Bottom center: View of Cloud Form Pond (a pond with a crane-shaped water spray).
Bottom right: Western style cafe opened at the time of the opening of the part around 1904 (the restaurant Matsumotoro at the present)

PHASE 1

文化・演劇、エンターテインメントの中心地

Center for culture and theatrical entertainment

▌日本のブロードウェイとして栄えた昭和から新たな時代へ

有楽町一丁目一帯は、映画館や劇場が建ち並ぶ文化の発信地としての顔を持つ。その第一号となった、1934（昭和9）年に開館した東京宝塚劇場（東宝の前身）に始まる。宝塚の創立者である小林一三は丸の内を中心に、劇場と映画館の娯楽施設が密集した地域形成を計画していた。これを皮切りに、同年日比谷映画劇場が、翌年には東京宝塚劇場直営の有楽座がオープンした。

戦後になると、演劇専用劇場や映画館が続々とオープンする。有楽町と新橋の間、帝国ホテル向かいの東宝の本社付近には映画街が形成され、1960年代には日比谷映画劇場・有楽座・千代田劇場・みゆき座・日比谷スカラ座の5館の映画館があり、いずれも東宝のチェーンマスター劇場（メイン館）だった。また隣接して演劇の劇場である宝塚劇場・芸術座、少し離れた皇居側に日生劇場、第一生命館の向かいには帝国劇場が位置し、映画・演劇のメッカとなった。

その後閉館や建て替えなどを経て形を変えながらも、現在に至るまでエンターテインメントの中心地として発展を遂げている。

▌From Showa, when it flourished as a Japanese Broadway, to a new era

There were movie and performance theaters in the area of Yurakucho 1-Chome, and the area was known to be a cultural hub. The initiator was the Tokyo Takarazuka Theater (former TOHO), opened in 1934. Ichizo Kobayashi, the founder of Takarazuka, was planning to form a district with entertainment facilities for performance and movie theaters centering around Marunouchi. Starting with this, the Hibiya Movie Theater was opened in the same year, and the Yurakuza, direct operation of the Tokyo Takarazuka Theater, in the following year.

After the war, performance exclusive theaters as well as movie theaters were opened successively. A movie town was formed near the headquarters of TOHO, across from the Tokyo Imperial Hotel, between Yurakucho and Shinbashi. In the 1960's, there were five theaters: Hibiya Movie Theater, Yurakuza, Chiyoda Theater, Miyukiza, and Hibiya Scalaza, which were all TOHO's chain master theaters. There were Takarazuka Theater and Geijutsuza for performances next to each other, Nissay Theater on the far side of the Imperial Palace, Imperial Theater across from the Daiichi Seimei Kan. The area became a Mecca for movies and performances.

Although it has changed its look over the years due to closing and rebuilding, it has developed as a center of entertainment to this day.

左頁：1962年頃の日比谷映画館街。帝国ホテル前から北側を見る。約200mの間に映画館や劇場が建ち並んだ。正面に三信ビルディング。
本頁右上：日比谷エリアの空撮。［1963年撮影］

Left page: The Hibiya Cinema Town around 1962. View of the north side from the front side of Imperial Hotel. Cinema houses and theaters stood within a distance of 200 meters or around. There was Sanshin Building in the front side.
Top right of this page: View of the Hibiya area from the sky.

1：日本劇場（1933年開館・1981年閉館）。有楽町マリオンへと建て替え。
2：日比谷映画劇場（1934年開館・1984年閉館）。
3：東京宝塚劇場（1934年開館・1997年建て替え）。
4：有楽座（1935年開館・1984年閉館）。日比谷シャンテへと建て替え。

5：東宝演芸場（1938年開館・1980年閉館）、スカラ座（1940年開館）。
6：千代田劇場。のち日比谷映画に改称。（1957年開館・2005年閉館）。
7：東京宝塚劇場（2001年開館）。
8：シアタークリエ（2007年開館・芸術座跡地）。

1: Nihon Theater (opened in 1933 and closed in 1981), rebuilt as Yurakucho Mullion later.
2: Hibiya Movie Theater (opened in 1934 and closed in 1984).
3: Tokyo Takarazuka Theater (opened in 1934 and rebuilt in 1997).
4: Yurakuza (opened in 1935 and closed in 1984), rebuilt as Hibiya Chanter later.

5: TOHO Entertainment Hall (opened in 1938 and closed in 1980) and Scala-za (opened in 1940).
6: Chiyoda Theater (opened in 1957 and closed in 2005), renamed to Hibiya Movie Theater later
7: Tokyo Takarazuka Theater (opened in 2001).
8: Theatre Creation (opened in 2007 on the site where Geijutsuza once stood).

東宝の新たな街づくり

山下誠［東宝　取締役 不動産経営担当・左］
太田圭昭［東宝　不動産経営部次長・右］

New town planning by TOHO

Makoto Yamashita [TOHO·left]
Yoshiaki Ota [TOHO·right]

日比谷はわれわれ東宝のスタートの地です。創業者の小林一三（1873〜1957年）が当時帝国劇場や日本劇場があった日比谷に着目し、「有楽町アミューズメント・センター構想」を描き、東京宝塚劇場や日比谷映画劇場（いずれも1934年開場）などをつくり、映画や演劇という文化をこの日比谷という街で面的に展開しました。それから施設の老朽化や映画興行の変化などにより、日比谷映画劇場と有楽座の跡地に商業をメインとした日比谷シャンテを1987年に建設しました。それに合わせて、映画・演劇と商業の相乗効果で賑わう歩きたくなる街となるよう、千代田区第1号の地区計画として歩車分離や駐車場出入口の集約化が実現しました。これは、「東京ミッドタウン日比谷」の地区計画でも引き継いでいただき、広い範囲がさらに歩きやすい街となりました。

弊社は「東京ミッドタウン日比谷」の計画段階から、街の構成員として意見を出し合う会議体に定期的に参加して、改めて日比谷公園のよさを再認識し、いかに連携してこのエリアを盛り上げていくかということを議論しました。それが「日比谷ステップ広場」として実現され、この管理についてもエリアマネジメント組織をつくり、行うということが計画されました。

「東京ミッドタウン日比谷」が開業したことにより、薄れつつあったかつての「日本のブロードウェイ」というイメージが、改めて印象付けられたのではないかと思っています。また、今回のオープンに合わせ、弊社も新ゴジラ像を中心とした「日比谷ゴジラスクエア」の再生や「日比谷シャンテ」のリニューアルを行い、一体となって街の賑わい創出の一助を担うことを考えました。今後も、日比谷の特徴の映画・演劇を楽しむワクワクとした雰囲気を最大限活かせるような街づくりを、さまざまな手段で目指していきます。

Hibiya is the beginning place for TOHO. Ichizo Kobayashi (1873 - 1957), the founder, set his eyes on Hibiya where Imperial Theatre and Nihon Gekijo were already there, and built Tokyo Takarazuka Theater and Hibiya Movie Theater (both of them were opened in 1934) at that time, created "Yurakucho Amusement Center Plan", and fully developed cultural works including movies and theatrical plays in the town of Hibiya. After that, because of getting old of these facilities and changes in the movie industry, our company constructed Hibiya Chanter, which was focused on commercial purposes, in 1987 at the site where Hibiya Movie Theater and Yurakuza once used to be. Along with construction, as the first district plan in the Chiyoda Ward, pedestrian-vehicle separation and centralization of entrances of parking lots were implemented to make the town bustling with the combined effect of movies and theatrical plays and shopping where people want to walk. The district plan of "Tokyo Midtown Hibiya" took over the plan, which made the wide area easier to walk.

Our company has periodically participated meetings as a member of the town from the stage of planning "Tokyo Midtown Hibiya", recognized good points of Hibiya Park, and discussed how to cooperate with each other to boost the area. This plan was implemented as "Hibiya Step Square" to plan to form the area management organization for maintaining the area.

We consider that the opening of "Tokyo Midtown Hibiya" bolstered the image of "Broadway in Japan", which had been fading away. Along with the opening, we reconstructed "Hibiya Godzilla Square" centering on a new Godzilla statue, renewed "Hibiya Chanter", and considered contributing to liveliness to the town. We will continue to develop the town to maximize the exciting atmosphere which characterizes Hibiya and enable people to enjoy movies and theatrical plays in various ways.

左：「日比谷ゴジラスクエア」の既存建物を減築し、ローチケ 日比谷チケットボックスを誘致。高さを抑えて「日比谷ステップ広場」との連続性をつくり出した。右：歩行者専用道路より「日比谷シャンテ」のファサードを見る。2018年の改修で、一部店舗は歩行者専用道路に面した出入口が設けられた。

Left: An existing building in "Hibiya Godzilla Square" was downsized and a ticket box was invited. Continuity with "Hibiya Step Square" was created by limiting its height. Right: The facade of Hibiya Chanter seen from a pedestrian road. By the renovation in 2018, some stores have entrances facing the pedestrian road.

1963年竣工、村野藤吾設計の日生劇場（日本生命日比谷ビル）。総花崗岩張りの外装。1,334席を有する劇場内部の天井にはアコヤ貝が貼られている。

Nissay Theatre designed by Togo Murano and completed in 1963. The exterior is fully covered with granite. The ceiling of the theatre with 1,334 seats is covered with pearl oyster shells.

日生劇場と日比谷

松本勝嗣［日生劇場　劇場部部長］

日比谷という街は不思議な魅力がある。大人の街として華やかに気分を高めてくれるかと思えば、昭和の雰囲気を残すガード下で酔いに興ずることもできる。大きく育った日比谷公園の緑は一服の清涼剤となる。そして、日比谷の街をかたちづくってきた多くの先人たちの熱き想いが私は好きである。

日生劇場にもその熱い想いが底流にある。「子どもたちによい作品を観てもらい心豊かな社会の実現に貢献したい」という日本生命元社長の弘世現氏。「"生きることは素晴らしい" "命は尊い"と思える作品でなければ演劇ではない」と一貫して主張した演出家の浅利慶太氏。人の心によい影響を与える建築をという信念の下、日生劇場を設計した村野藤吾氏。こうした想いから生み出された数々の名作が街に彩りを添えてきた。

ふと、越路吹雪のマネージャーだった岩谷時子さんの手記に目が留まった。「東京でいちばんお気に入りの風景は日比谷公園側から見た夜の日生劇場」だと。日生劇場は今も昔と変わらぬ姿で、日比谷の街に凛と佇んでいる。

そして、新たな想いを乗せて東京ミッドタウン日比谷が生まれた。これから街にどのような彩りが加わり、どのように街ゆく人の心に響いていくのか、楽しみは膨らむ。

Nissay Theatre and Hibiya

Yoshitsugu Matsumoto
［**Nissay Theatre**］

A town called Hibiya is magically attractive. It brilliantly boosts mood as a mature town, but at the same time, we can get a buzz under a girder bridge with an atmosphere of the Showa Period. Trees and greenery in Hibiya Park which have grown thickly are a kind of refrigerant. I like passions of many forerunners that have formed the town of Hibiya. The passions also underlie Nissay Theatre. "I want to show children good works to contribute to the realization of spiritually rich society" said Gen Hirose, the former president of Nippon Life. Keita Asari, a stage director consistently insisted, "A theatrical show must be a work which makes audiences think 'life is great' and 'life is important.'" Tougo Murano designed Nissay Theatre under the conviction that he should design a building which had a good influence on people's minds. Many masterpieces produced by such passions have added a touch of color to the town.

A note written by Tokiko Iwatani, who was an agent of Fubuki Koshiji, caught my eyes. She said, "My favorite scenery in Tokyo is Nissay Theatre seen from Hibiya Park at night." Nissay Theatre is as dignified as ever in the town of Hibiya.

Tokyo Midtown Hibiya was born with new passions. I am looking forward to seeing what color will be added to the town in the future and how they will resonate with people walking down a street.

千代田区第1号地区計画（1985年）

The first Chiyoda district plan (1985)

■ 日比谷シャンテ建設でつくられた 千代田区第1号地区計画

日比谷映画劇場・有楽座跡地の再開発として、1987（昭和62）年に竣工した日比谷シャンテは、その計画時に新たな地区計画がつくられた。

当時の日比谷は大・中規模映画館と劇場計8館、客席数約1万席の興行場が集中していたが、映画興行の質的変化や施設の老朽化を抱えてい

た。また地元商店街の敷地も細分化と道路幅員狭小が課題となっており、共同化の機運が高まってきていた。

そこで街づくり計画の基本として、人車分離、街路のモール化とポケットパークの創出、公道を隔てた敷地の一体的開発による地下のネットワーク化と高層化・容積移動、映画館に代わる集客効果として店舗とオフィスを想定することなどが方針として取られることになった。

東宝・地元商店街、事業主、行政との折衝の末にこれらを実現した手法は、地区全体に地区計画制度を設けること、既存の3敷地一団地申請および総合設計制度である。地権者負担だけでなく区のコミュニティ道路の指定まで得ることができ、安全な歩行者空間が確保された。また3敷地間で容積移動を行って公開空地が設けられた。さらに、地下でそれぞれ車と人のネットワーク化が実現した。

■ The first Chiyoda district plan developed for building the Hibiya Chanter

When the Hibiya Chanter, completed in 1987 , was planned for a redevelopment of the former sites of the Hibiya Movie Theater and Yurakuza, a new district plan was developed.

At that time, Hibiya had a total of eight large- and medium-sized movie theaters and performance theaters, and performance facilities that accommodated about 10,000 seats, however, they were facing qualitative changes and

deterioration of the facilities. In addition, due to the issues with the subdivision of the local shopping district site and narrow road width, the momentum for unification was on the rise.
As the fundamentals of a town planning, separating cars from people, promenading streets, creating small parks, networking through underground passages by an integration development of sites separated by public roads, building high-rises for transferring capacity, and building shops and offices for replacing movie theaters were all planned to enhance customer attraction.
The solutions for putting those plans into

practice after negotiations with TOHO including the local shopping district, entrepreneurs, and administration were: establish a district planning system for the whole area, application of the site platting for the existing three sites, and a comprehensive design system. With these solutions, we could designate community roads in the district and secure a safe pedestrian space instead of involving only property owners. In addition, as the result of transferring capacity within three sites, an open space was created. Furthermore, networking of cars and people via underground has been achieved.

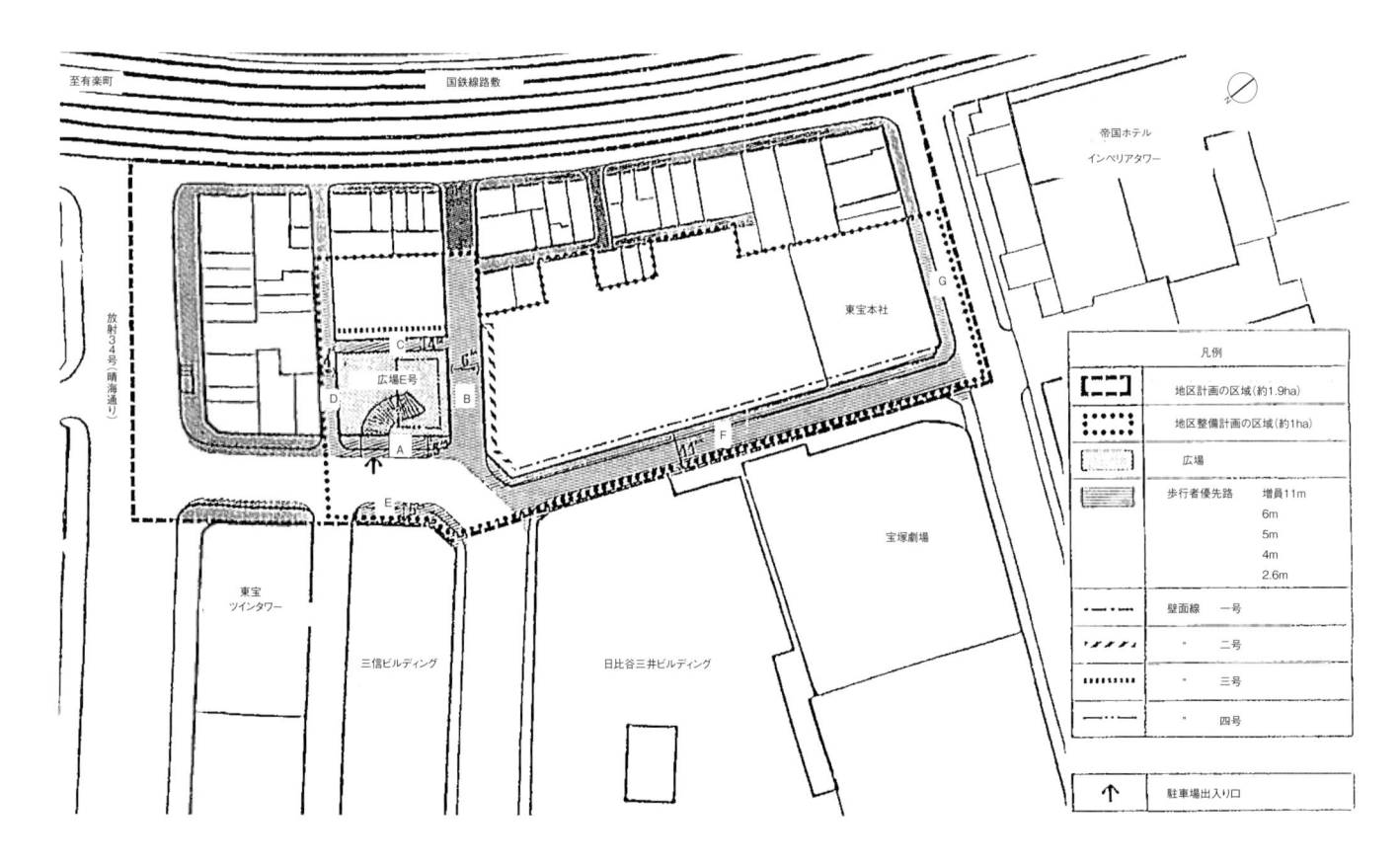

左頁：1985年当時の東京都市計画地区計画・有楽町日比谷地区地区計画図（千代田区決定）。

本頁上：日比谷シャンテ前、合歓の広場見下ろし。右奥に帝国ホテルへと続く。
本頁下：合歓の広場。左に日比谷シャンテ、正面奥に日比谷三井ビルディング、右に三信ビルディング。［写真2点：1987年撮影］

Left page: Drawing of Yurakucho and Hibiya district planning of Tokyo city and district planning in 1985 (decided by Chiyoda Ward).
Top of this page: Overhead view of Nemu Square in front of Hibiya Chanter. The road on the right is led to

Imperial Hotel.
Bottom of this page: Nemu Square. Hibiya Chanter on the left, Hibiya Mitsui Building at the back of the center, and Sanshin Building on the right (2 pictures: Photographed in 1987).

日比谷パティオ（2008年12月〜2011年6月）

Open space demonstration experiment

Hibiya Patio (Dec. 2008 - Jun. 2011)

■ 日比谷パティオによる 広場の可能性の実験

日比谷パティオは三信ビルディングの解体に伴い生まれた約2,800m²の土地活用プロジェクトである。三信ビルディング解体後、「三信ビルディング跡地開発計画」（後の「[仮称]新日比谷プロジェクト」、現「東京ミッドタウン日比谷」）着工までの暫定利用として2008年から約2年半（平成20年12月〜平成23年6月）の間設置された。日比谷パティオでは、日比谷エリアのさらなる活性化・発展に繋げるための情報発信の場として、アートインスタレーションやライブパフォーマンス、移動式のフードワゴンなど、"日比谷に、日々新たなアカリを灯す"という願いを込めた「ヒビアカリ プロジェクト」を実施した。

その後、周辺地権者との検討や地区計画の検討において、この日比谷パティオの開催実績が参考となり、街の賑わいの核となる広場空間の設置に繋がっていくこととなった。　　　　［MF］

■ Experiment a potential of open space by Hibiya Patio

The Hibiya Patio was opened following the demolition of the Sanshin Building as a project for utilizing approximately 2,800m² of land. After the Sanshin Building was demolished, the Hibiya Patio was developed for provisional use for about two and half years (Dec. 2008 - Jun. 2011) until construction work of the "Sanshin Building site development plan" (later changed to "New Hibiya project (tentative name)", the current name of "Tokyo Midtown Hibiya") could start. At the Hibiya Patio, the "Hibi Akari Project (hibi meaning daily and akari meaning light in Japanese)" was held with hopes to shine new light daily on Hibiya. Art installations and live performances, and mobile food wagon events were held for further revitalization and development of the Hibiya area.

After that, during the discussions on district planning with property owners of said area, the experience we gained in these initiatives led to urban development of the open space. [MF]

上3点：三信ビルディング跡地開発計画で生まれた日比谷パティオ。
下：2011年3月11日の東日本大震災発生時には、日比谷パティオに多くの人びとが避難した。

3 pictures at the top: Hibiya Patio built on the site where Sanshin Building once stood.
Bottom: Many people evacuated to Hibiya Patio at the time of the Great East Japan Earthquake on March 11, 2011.

地元の人たちとイベントを行い、日比谷の地熱を上げる

MF 1987(昭和62)年に東宝が日比谷シャンテを建設した際に、東京宝塚劇場との間の区道を管理する組織として、モール協議会という地元の団体がつくられました。それを引き継ぐかたちで、東京ミッドタウン日比谷の広場や周辺の区道を、地元

で構成された法人で一体的に管理する新しい仕組みをつくることを千代田区と検討していました。

NS 街づくりコンセプトの検討段階から、ずっと地元の方と検討を行う組織が続いていました。また、日比谷パティオでは三井不動産がさまざまなイベントを実施されていて、地元の人たちにとっても街の賑わいをアップさせるよいイメージが浸透していました。通常は、まずエリアマネジメントの必要性の

議論から入らないといけないのですが、賑わいを継続するためには、全体で管理・運営をする必要があるという認識を共有できたので、エリアマネジメントの準備は比較的スムーズにいきました。

MF 工事中は、どうしても街の活動が止まってしまいます。その間にも外から来る人に日比谷を好きになってもらうために、さまざまなイベントを行い、日比谷の地熱を上げていくことを大切にしていきました。

Raise enthusiasm of the locals through events

MF When TOHO built the Hibiya Chanter in 1987, a local organization called Mall Council was created to manage the district road between the Tokyo Takarazuka Theater. By succeeding the organization, we were examining with Chiyoda city to create a new system to manage district roads around the Tokyo Midtown Hibiya open space and surrounding area by a corporation consisting of locals.

NS The organization which discusses with locals has been continued since the initial stage of town planning. Also, the Mitsui Fudosan held various events at the Hibiya Patio and made positive impressions for the town's prosperity to the locals. Normally, we would discuss the necessity of area management first. However, the process went smoothly because we all had the same opinion on the responsibilities of managing the organization as a whole.

MF Activeness of the town subsided during construction regardless of any efforts. So, in the meantime, in order to make a good impression of Hibiya for visitors, we held various events and tried keeping the enthusiasm of Hibiya high.

左3点：日比谷シャンテ前の合歓の広場で行われたイベント。地元町会、商店会と連携して行われることもある。

右3点：日比谷公園。さまざまなイベント開催が行われ、家族連れなど幅広い層が訪れている。

3 pictures on the left: Events held in Nemu Square in front of Hibiya Chanter. Some events are held in cooperation with the town assembly or a store association.

3 pictures on the right: Hibiya Park. Various events are held and various people including families visit the place.

土地区画整理事業、地区計画、都市再生特別地区

Urban planning for realization of open space

Land readjustment project, district planning, special urban renaissance districts

■ 道路を付け換え、広場を創出する（土地区画整理事業認可・2012年8月）

2011（平成23）年8月に国家戦略総合特区法案が決定してから、東京都ではアジアヘッドクォーター特区として当計画地を含む都心エリアが区域指定された。また翌年には日比谷地区が都市再生緊急整備地域および特定都市再生緊急整備地域に指定された。

そんな中で、地元地権者間で開催された「まちづくり勉強会」では、かつての日比谷の賑わいを街の課題や街づくりの方向性を議論・共有し、日比谷の賑わいを取り戻すため、街の中心に求心力のある賑わいの広場空間を創出することで合意した。

これを受け、日比谷シャンテ前の合歓の広場と連続するよう三信ビルディングと区道131号の位置を入れ替えて広場空間を創出することが議論された。これにより千代田区道（一部都道）と三井不動産所有の2敷地による敷地整序型土地区画整理事業を用いることで、区道を区域変更（廃道）し、広場へ用途転換した区有地と計画地の公開空地を一体的に整備することが決まった。

■ Renew the roads and create an open space (Land readjustment project - Aug. 2012)

After the National Strategy Comprehensive Special Zone bill had passed on Aug. 2011, a section from the applicable area to Uchisaiwaicho was designated as the Asia Headquarter Special District in Tokyo. In the following year, the Hibiya district was designated as an urban revitalization urgency area and specific urban revitalization urgency area.

Under such circumstances, a "town planning study meeting" was hosted among the local property owners. We discussed the prosperity in the past, challenges, and development direction of Hibiya, and in order to revitalize the town, we all agreed on creating an open space that has an inviting atmosphere. Following this meeting, in order to continue with the Nemu Square in front of the Hibiya Chanter, we discussed the creation of an open space by exchanging the sites between the Sanshin Building and city road no. 131. As the result of the discussion, Chiyoda city road (partially Tokyo road) and two sites owned by Mitsui Fudosan would be redeveloped in accordance with the site rearrangement model - land readjustment project. The city road would be removed and turned into an open space along with said sites.

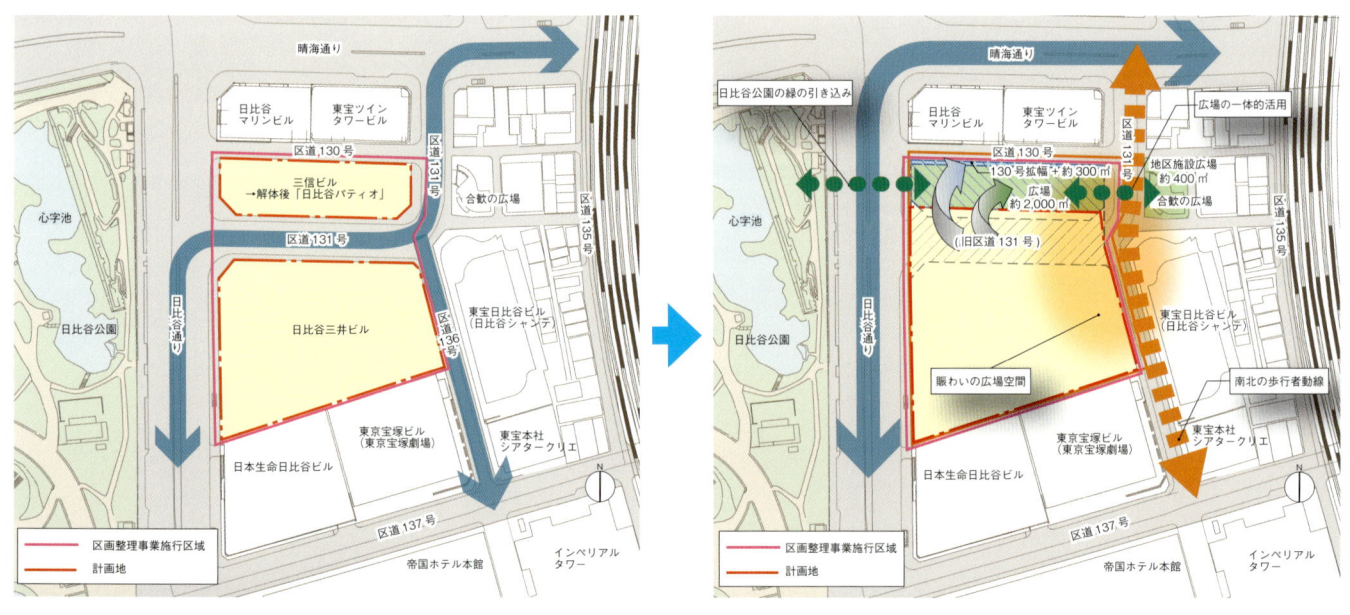

左上：三信ビルディング・日比谷三井ビルディングがあった頃の街区配置。[2007年]
右上：東京ミッドタウン日比谷竣工後の街区配置。[2018年]
左下：三信ビルディング・日比谷三井ビルディング解体後の俯瞰。[2011年撮影]

Top left: Town layout when Sanshin Building and Hibiya Mitsui Building existed.
Top right: Town layout after the completion of Tokyo Midtown Hibiya.
Bottom left: Overhead view after the demolition of Sanshin Building and Hibiya Mitsui Building (photographed in 2011).

▌地区計画が広がる（地区計画 都市計画変更・2012年12月）

2012（平成24）年12月、千代田区によって有楽町・日比谷地区の地区計画を変更する都市計画が決定した。日比谷エリアの街づくりの方針を定めるためのものであり、都市的広場の創出、歩行者中心の街づくりを推進するネットワークづくり、日比谷公園から繋がる緑化空間の整備といった地区施設整備方針が改めて記された。

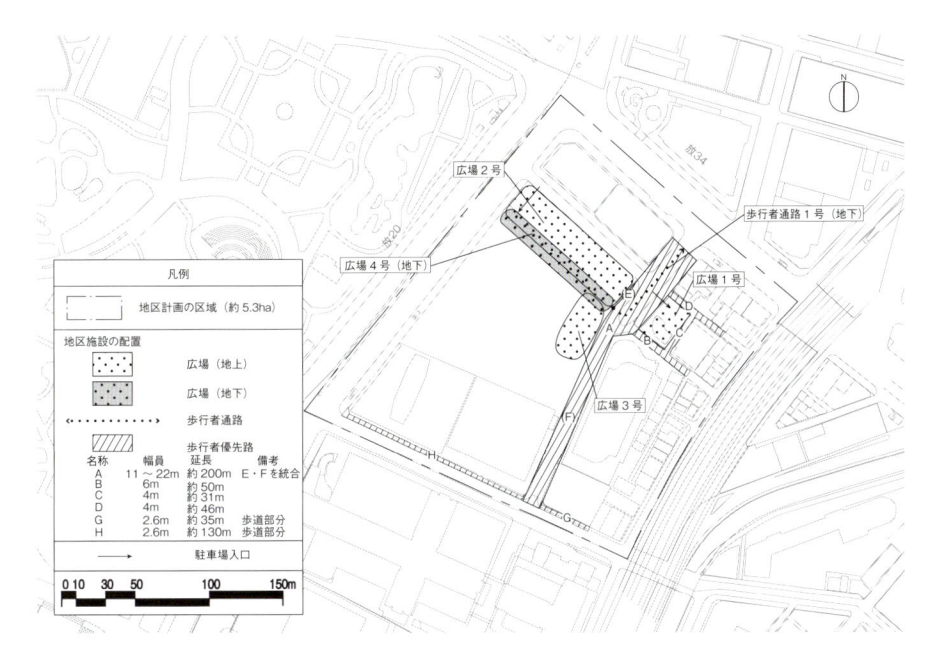

▌街の機能を高めていく（都市再生特別地区都市計画決定・2013年12月）

2013（平成25）年12月、東京都によって都市再生特別地区の都市計画決定が行われた。都市再生貢献の内容としては、歩行者中心の基盤整備、ビジネスの連携や文化発信拠点としての都市機能の導入、防災機能の強化と環境負荷低減への取り組みである。

▌Expansion of district planning (Change in urban planning of district planning - Dec. 2012)

In Dec. 2012, Chiyoda ward created an urban plan to change the district plan of Yurakucho and Hibiya districts. It was intended to determine the policy for town planning in the Hibiya area. The policy described district facility development, such as the creation of an urban open space, creation of a network to promote pedestrian-centered town development, and development of green space continued from Hibiya Park. In addition, for the sites of Sanshin Building and Hibiya Mitsui Building, we believed unification of the two sites was beneficial to the town redevelopment since they shared the same geographic history and it was advantageous on business. As a result, enforcement of the land readjustment project was authorized by Chiyoda ward upon the sites.

▌Increase the functionality of the town (Decision on city planning for urban revitalization special district - Dec. 2013)

In Dec. 2013, the city planning for urban revitalization special district was decided by the Tokyo Metropolitan Government. Contents of the urban revitalization contributions are: pedestrian-centered infrastructure development, introduction of urban functions as business collaboration and cultural initiation base, and efforts to strengthen the disaster prevention function and reduce the environmental burden.

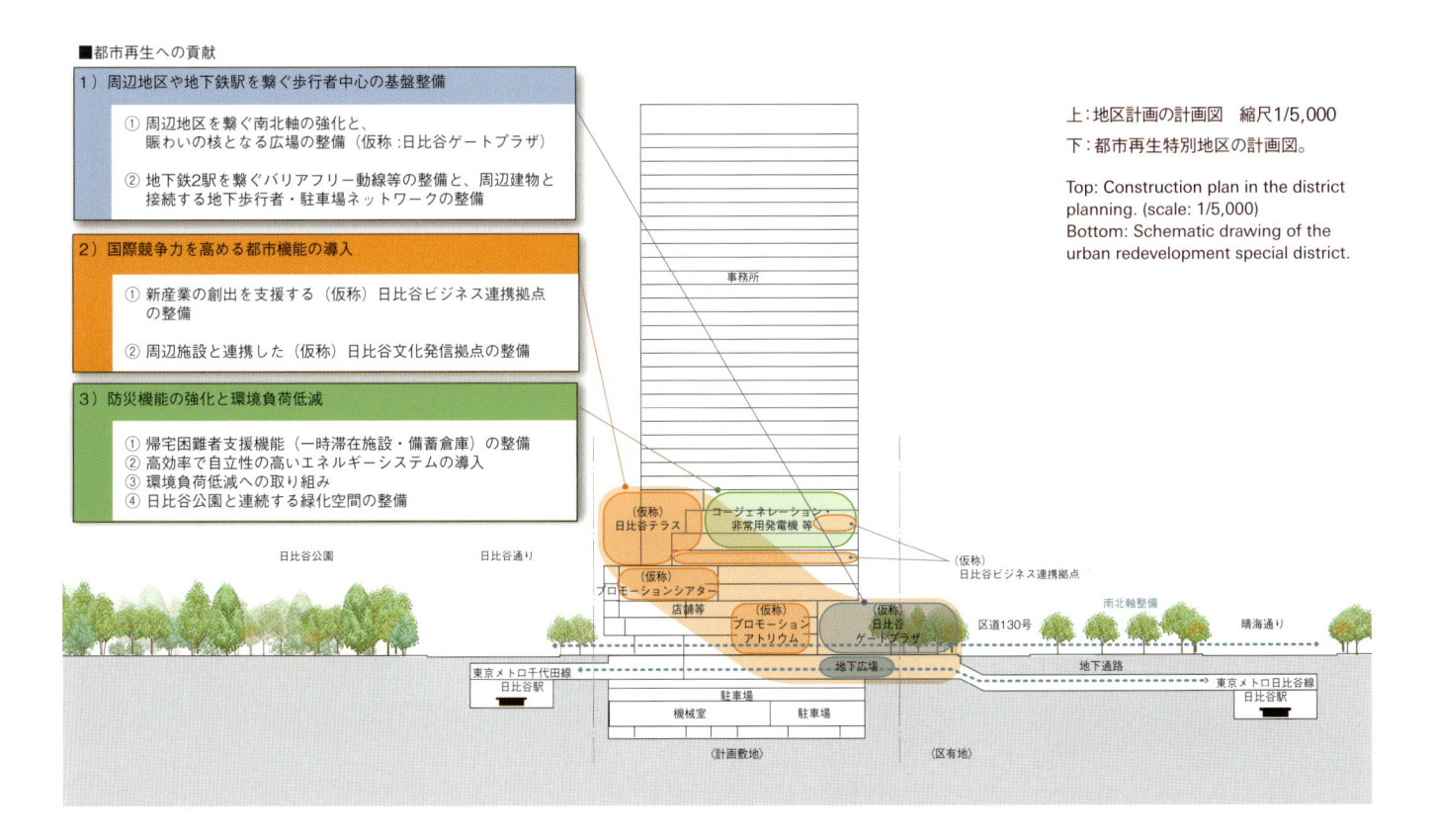

上：地区計画の計画図　縮尺1/5,000
下：都市再生特別地区の計画図。

Top: Construction plan in the district planning. (scale: 1/5,000)
Bottom: Schematic drawing of the urban redevelopment special district.

PHASE 1

「Park Side」から「In the Park」へ

Draft design concept

From "Park Side" to "In the Park"

■ コンセプトを具現化していく

NS　行政や地元の方々と共に策定した「日比谷エリアまちづくり基本構想」という街づくりコンセプトを基に、複合建築に求められる複雑な与件を満足しつつ、エリア全体の価値を最大化する街づくりの骨格を建築として具現化するための検討を開始しました。立地特性を活かし、日比谷エリアを「公園に隣接している街」から「公園の中にある街」にするため、「In the Park」というコンセプトを掲げることにしました。公園の体験を建物内に立体的に積み上げていくようなイメージで、広場やアトリウムや屋上等の公園のようなパブリックスペースを、園路のような回遊性の高い動線で立体的に繋ぐことを提案しています。また、劇場のような階段状の広場空間や、地下の三信ビルディングの記憶を繋ぐ日比谷アーケードも含めて、日比谷特有の空間体験ができる空間を計画しました。

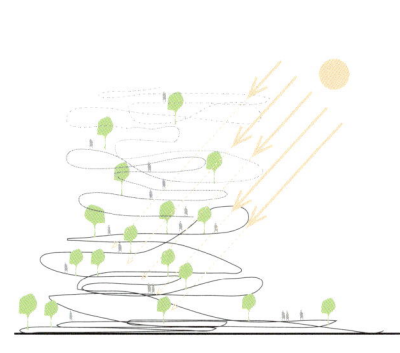
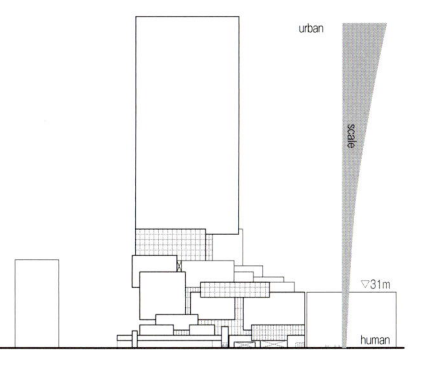

公園の緑が連なる立体的なランドスケープの形成　　　　周辺環境と有機的につながるボリュームの配置　　　　ヒューマンスケールとアーバンスケールの緩やかなつながり

Put concept into practice

NS We began to examine how to design the framework of a town that can maximize the value of the whole area while overcoming complicated challenges which occur during complex construction based on the "basic concept of Hibiya area town planning," which was decided in collaboration with the administration and the locals.

In order to maximize the locational characteristics and change the Hibiya area to "a town located in the park" from "a town beside the park," we composed the concept of "In the Park." As if three-dimensionally piling the experience at the park in the building, we proposed to stereoscopically connect public spaces (open space, atrium, rooftop park, etc.) with flowing lines that have high migratory design like a garden path. We also designed a space where one can experience Hibiya's uniqueness by including a stair-like open space like a theater and an arcade space leading to memories of the Sanshin Building underground area.

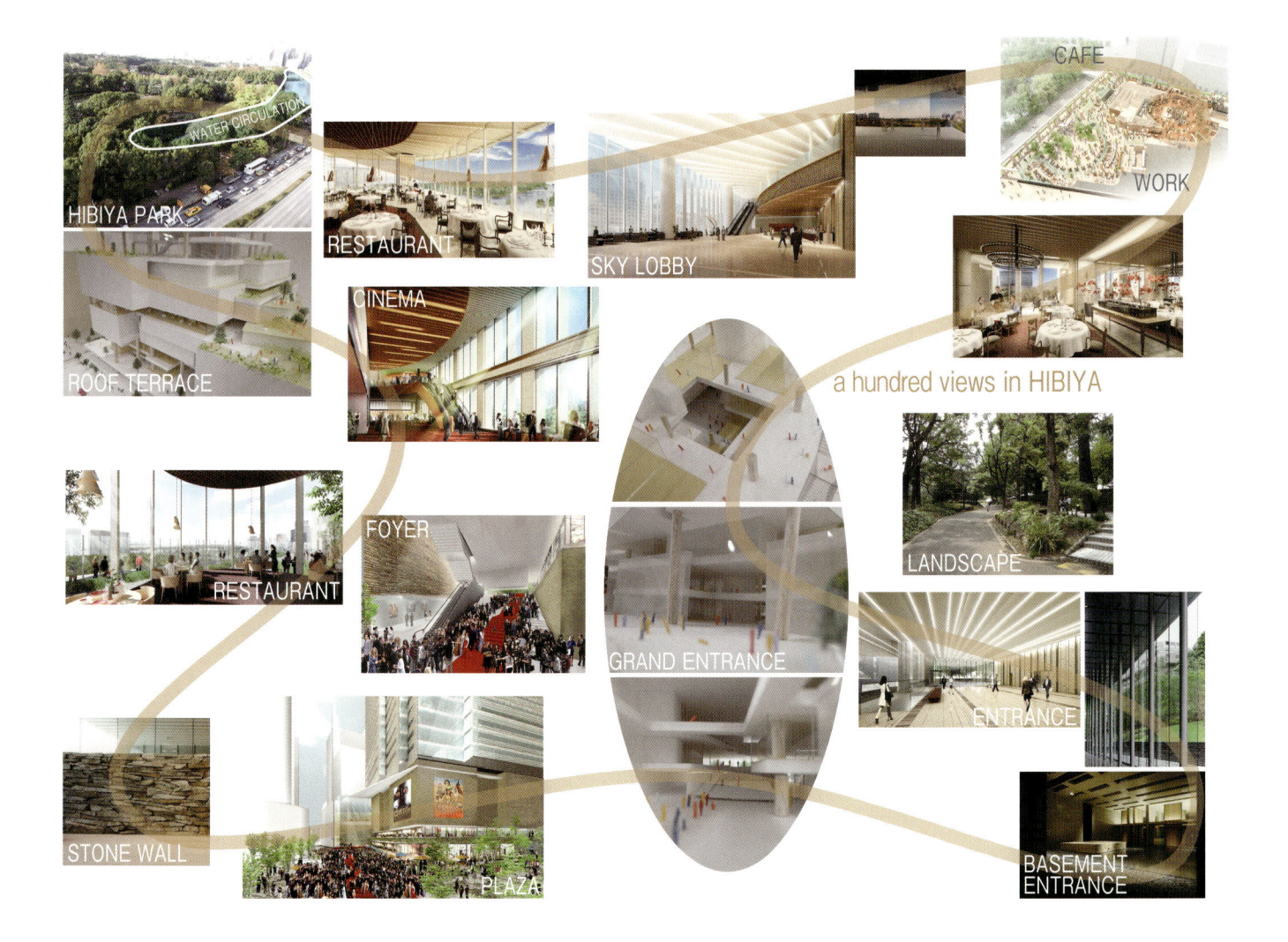

左頁3点：公園が街に広がるイメージを模型やスケッチで表現。[2012年6月、すべて日建設計作成]

本頁上：日比谷公園と一体となる全体構成のコンセプトダイアグラム。
本頁下：それぞれの空間のイメージを共有し、それらの連なりが公園体験となることを表現。[2点、日建設計作成]

3 items on the left page: Images of the park spreading to the town expressed as a diagram, a model, and a sketch. [June 2012, created by Nikken Sekkei] Top on this page: Diagram of the exterior concept. Examination of a city landscape united into Hibiya Park.

Bottom on this page: Sharing the image of each space and showing that a series of images becomes an experience in the park. [2 items, created by Nikken Sekkei]

PHASE 2

街づくりのビジョンを
デザイン・計画として具現化する

Embodiment of urban development as design/plan

都市再生緊急整備地域

都市再生緊急整備地域（拡大）

特定都市再生緊急整備地域

2012.1

都市再生緊急地域指定

Urban revitalization emergency preparation region designation

2012年時点の東京都心・臨海地域の都市再生緊急地域（「都市再生緊急整備地域及び特定都市再生緊急整備地域の一覧(首相官邸ホームページ）を元に編集部作成)

都市再生の拠点として、都市開発事業等を通じて緊急かつ重点的に市街地の整備を推進すべき地域として、内閣府により2012年特定都市再生緊急整備地域に指定された。

As a base for urban revitalization, focusing on an urgency and importance through urban development projects, urban revitalization emergency preparation regions were designated by Cabinet Office as "2012 specified urban revitalization emergency preparation regions."

As of 2012, metropolitan Tokyo and waterfront area emergency revitalization regions (see "urban revitalization emergency preparation region and creation of specific list of areas (Prime Minister's official website) to create."

2012.8

土地区画整理事業認可

Division readjustment project authorization

2012.12

地区計画 都市計画変更

Change in urban planning of district planning

街づくり・都市計画 | Town Development and Urban Planning

建築設計 | Architectural Design

2012.1

グランドデザイン会議スタート

Start of Grand Design Conference

2012.4

基本計画書とりまとめ(「In the Park」の共有)

Basic plan arrangement (sharing "In the Park")

2012.5-

マスターデザイン検討

Master design review

2012.9

ワークセッション1

Work session 1

2012.10

ワークセッション2

Work session 2

2012.11

ワークセッション3

Work session 3

PHAE 2は、PHASE 1で共有しつくり上げた、日比谷にふさわしいプロジェクトのあり方・ビジョンをデザインへと具現化したフェーズ。
事業者や設計者、施工者、デザイナーまで、関係者が一堂に会して検討・議論を行う「ワークセッション」という会議体で、
ビジョンがどのようにデザイン・計画へと具現化されていったかを紹介する。

PHASE 2 was formed based on PHASE 1 and functions to realize vision of project suitable for Hibiya.
Officials including developers, architects, contractors and designers gather in the study and participate
in discussions called "work sessions" and give a brief description of how the vision is embodied in design plans.

2012.2
区道131号線廃道

Ward road Route
131 waste road

千代田区道の一部を北側道路と一体的な
形状になるよう付け替えを行った。

Portion of Chiyoda ward roads replaced
to form unit with North side roads.

2013.12
都市再生特別地区
都市計画決定

Urban revitalization specific
region urban plan decision

2013.5
基本設計書
とりまとめ

Basic design
arrangement

2013.6
Design
Development
Document（DD図）
発行

Design
Development
Document (DD
document)
issue

2013.2
ワークセッション4

Work session 4

2013.4
ワークセッション5

Work session 5

2013.6
ワークセッション6

Work session 6

2013.10
ワークセッション7

Work session 7

PHASE 2

「Dancing Tower」で実現する日比谷らしさ

Hibiya-style realization of "Dancing Tower"

■ マスターデザインアーキテクトのホプキンス・アーキテクツと共に「日比谷らしさ」を考える

MF 日比谷の街づくりコンセプトとして「In the Park」がわれわれチームの中で浸透してきた頃、このコンセプトを具現化するためにマスターデザインアーキテクトとしてホプキンス・アーキテクツに参加していただくことを考えました。われわれが考える、「In the Park」(=公園の中の街づくり)を共有し、建築デザインやランドスケープデザインとして表現・提案していただきたいという思いがありました。

NS われわれは、ビジョンメイキングをしていたということもあり、基本設計者としてホプキンス・アーキ

テクツのみなさんと一緒にマスターデザインを考えました。提案をつくるというよりは、お互いの価値観をすり合わせることをたくさん行いました。それは、机上の言葉を共有するのではなく、たとえばこれくらいの大きさの空間でこういう人の集まり方をした時の感覚を日比谷にあてはめるとどうだろうか、という体験の共有でした。

HA 三井不動産からの要望は、「日比谷らしさ」であると理解していました。有楽町・銀座や霞が関、丸の内などの他の場所とは違う、日比谷らしさをしっかりと読み込み、マスターデザインとして表現することにしました。われわれが以前コンセプトデザインを手掛けた「新丸の内ビルディング」(2007[平成19]年)の丸の内はどちらかと言うとずっしりとした男

性的な建築が合っていたのですが、日比谷ではもう少し柔らかい、女性的な建築が合っているのではないかと思いました。そこで、かつて鹿鳴館が建っていた場所のイメージから、「Dancing Tower」というストーリーをつくり出したのです。

MF 「Dancing Tower」という提案は非常に分かりやすくてよいと感じました。日比谷の価値を、非常に共有しやすい表現としてデザインされていて、誰に対しても説明しやすい。他のエリアとの違いも明確だったため、このデザインで進めることになりました。

■ Consideration of "Hibiya style" together with master design architects of Hopkins Architects

MF When our team became permeated with "In the Park," we thought it would be a good idea to ask master design architects of Hopkins Architects to participate in embodiment of the concept of urban revitalization for Hibiya. We felt they would share our vision of "In the Park" (urban revitalization in the park) and we wanted them to offer expressions and proposals for architectural and landscape design.

NS We were also involved in vision making, so we were thinking about master design together with Hopkins Architects as

basic designers. Rather than vision making, we compared and adjusted our mutual sense of values. This did not mean sharing words on the desk, but rather sharing experience in, for example, how to fit the feeling of people gathered in such a large open space with Hibiya.

HA Mitsui Fudosan expressed a desire for an understanding of "Hibiya style." They wanted to get a deep understanding of how Hibiya style differs from other locations such as Yurakucho, Ginza and Marunouchi and express it as master design. Although it resembled our previous concept design of the heavily masculine architecture of the "Shin Marunouchi Building" (2007), we thought Hibiya should be a softer feminine

architecture. We therefore created the story of "Dancing Tower" from the image of the place where the Rokumeikan once stood.

MH We felt "Dancing Tower" would be very easy to understand. It would be easy to explain the value of Hibiya as design by an easy to share expression. Because the difference with other areas is clear, we decided to proceed with this design.

イギリス・ロンドンの街の多種多様な都市空間を視察。その場で日比谷で参照したい街並みや使い方、体験、設えなどを議論し、価値観を共有した。魅力を感じる場所はヒューマンスケールで、特徴的な空間特性を持っていることが重要であると考えた。[NS]

Observe a wide variety of urban spaces in London, England. We discussed the town scape, way of using, experiencing and arranging with reference to Hibiya and shared our sense of values. Having characteristic spatial features on the human scale is important for places where charm can be sensed. [NS]

2012年7月に実施したイギリス・ロンドンでの視察の様子。左がThe Royal Arcade、右がGees Court。

Observations in London, England that were conducted in July 2012. On the left is the Royal Arcade and on the right is Gees Court.

場所とディテールの重要性
—品質と洗練

マイケル・ホプキンス[ホプキンス・アーキテクツ]

The importance of place and detail – quality and sophistication

Michael Hopkins [Hopkins Architects]

私たちが過去40余年にわたり設計してきた建物には、都市におけるあり方と場所、そしてその文化を取り入れてきました。

私たちはまた、建築言語や設計表現を具現化する上で、ディテールや繋がりの表現も優先してきました。

東京ミッドタウン日比谷の設計を始めるにあたり、私たちは日比谷通りに面した他のソリッドな建物と同様に、ディテールに注意して石造の建物として日比谷通りのファサードを強調することにしました。私たちにとってこれがこのプロジェクトの重要なポイントなのです。そこで広場に面した商業エリアの上にガラス張りでメタリックなタワーをつくろうと思いました。

結果として、差異と関係性のディテールを合わせ持ったクオリティと洗練さを表現した「日比谷の新しい特徴」がもたらされました。

Our buildings which we have designed over the past 40 odd years always take inspiration from their position and location within a city and its culture.

We also prioritise the expression of detail and connections in our designs – this informs our architectural language and expression of design.

When we started on the Tokyo Midtown Hibiya project we wanted to emphasise the Hibiya-dori facade as a carefully detailed stone building reinforcing the other more solid buildings facing Hibiya-dori. For us this is a key characterful distinction for the project. We then wanted to set off the tower above and the retail facade facing the plaza as a more glassy and metallic character.

The overall result is a combination of different but related details which gives a 'new Hibiya character' of quality and sophistication.

2012年7月にホプキンス・アーキテクツのロンドン事務所で行われたマスターデザインの検討。

Review of the master design created at Hopkins Architects in London in July 2012.

■ ワルツのステップのような柔らかなラインを描く
Draw a soft line like the step of a waltz

丸の内や銀座や新橋はグリッドで構成された街区だが、日比谷はそのグリッドからずれている。われわれの事務所があるロンドンの街も、ニューヨークのようなグリッドではなくオーガニックで柔らかな曲線で構成されていて、日比谷と印象が近くイメージがしやすかった。[HA]

Marunouchi, Ginza and Shinbashi are laid out as a grid but Hibiya departs from the grid layout. The streets of London, where our office is, are not laid out in a grid like New York, but rather more organic, soft curves. This makes it easy to understand the close impression with Hibiya. [HA]

4点：マスターデザイン検討時のスケッチ。日比谷から着想を得たダンスのステップや踊る女性のスカートのプリーツ。[2012年7月、ホプキンス・アーキテクツ作成]

4 items: Sketch of pleats of the skirt of a dancing woman or steps of a dance that yields the concept from Hibiya when master design was being considered. [July 2012, created by Hopkins Architects]

ELEGANCE

CLASSICAL MUSIC   WALTZ DANCE   SWEEPING CURVES.... SMOOTH MOVEMENT

"A WALK IN THE PARK"

A MEANDERING PATH

マスターデザイン検討時に作成された日比
谷公園から見た外観CGパース。[2012年8
月、ホプキンス・アーキテクツ作成]

Appearance CG perspective from
Hibiya Park created when master
design was being considered. [August
2012, created by Hopkins Architects]

PHASE 2

左：マスターデザイン検討時のスケッチ。街の趣を代表するファサードを模索した。[2012年7月、ホプキンス・アーキテクツ作成]

Left: Sketch when master design was being considered. We were looking for a facade that would be representative of the elegance of the city. [July 2012, created by Hopkins Architects]

この敷地にかつてあった三信ビルディングのエレガントさや柔らかなデザインを、新しいマスターデザインへ結び付けたいと考えた。[HA]

We wanted to incorporate the elegant, soft design of the Sanshin Building that once stood on the property to the master design. [HA]

下2点：マスターデザイン検討時のスケッチ。三信ビルディングからファサードデザインの要素を引き出す試みがなされた。[2012年7月、ホプキンス・アーキテクツ作成]

Bottom 2 items: Sketch when master design was being considered. We attempted to bring out the facade elements from the Sanshin Building. [July 2012, created by Hopkins Architects]

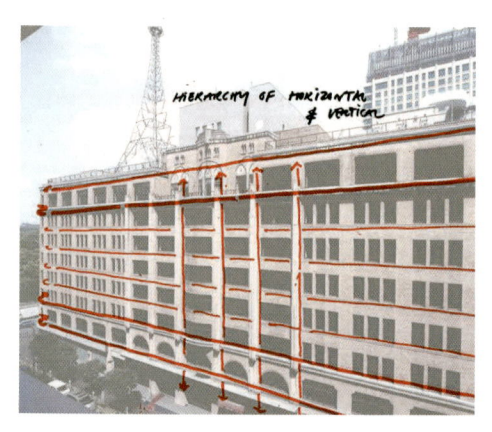

▌広場が公園の緑へと繋がる日比谷ならではの賑わい空間
Bustling space where the plaza leads to the park greenery that connects Hibiya

海外から訪れる人たちのガイドブックに写真が載るような場所をつくりたいという思いがあった。そこで、スペイン広場のようなイメージで、特徴的な階段に人が集まり賑わいのある広場をつくりたいと考えた。[HA]

We wanted to create a space such as those seen in guide books of people who have visited from abroad. We thought of a Spanish plaza full of people gathering in characteristic stairway. [HA]

102〜103頁：マスターデザイン検討時に作成された1階日比谷ステップ広場CGパース。[2012年8月、ホプキンス・アーキテクツ作成]

pp. 102-103: Appearance 1st floor Hibiya Step Square CG perspective. [August 2012, created by Hopkins Architects]

▌日比谷シャンテの広場と一体となる円形広場
Hibiya Chanter plaza containing circular plaza

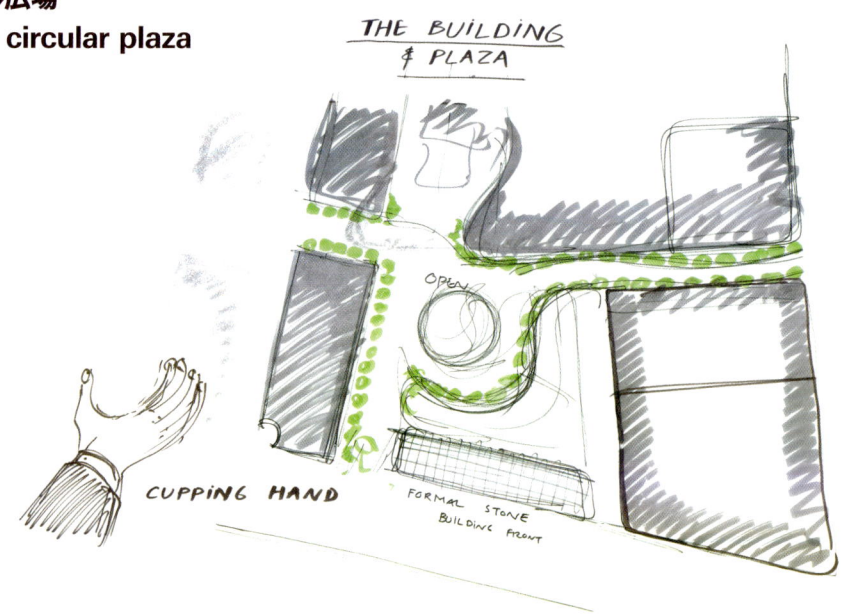

日比谷シャンテの広場と一体となる、人を
キャッチするような円形の広場を最初にイメー
ジした。［HA］
マスターデザイン検討時に周囲に連続する
広場をイメージした。［2012年7月、ホプキンス・
アーキテクツ作成］

Initial image of circular plaza that would
catch people contained in Hibiya
Chanter plaza. [HA]
Image of nature of plaza continuing
around the circumference when master
design was being considered. [July
2012, created by Hopkins Architects]

柔らかさのデザイン

サイモン・フレーザー［ホプキンス・アーキテクツ］

Design of softness

Simon Fraser [Hopkins Architects]

この場所の思い出と歴史─三信ビルディングと鹿鳴館

東京メトロ千代田線の出口から三信ビルディングへ入ると、プロ
ポーションとディテールの美しいアーケードや、丸みのある手すりとド
アの取っ手、そして映画館や店舗の建ち並ぶ賑やかな日比谷仲
通りへの接続が印象的でした。これは今から25年以上も前の私
の最初の日比谷エリアの思い出で、今でも心に残っています。この
柔らかな印象が、今回の東京ミッドタウン日比谷へのビジョンに繋
がっています。

また、約140年前、このエリアには鹿鳴館が建ち、外国人と日本人
が交流し踊っていました。私はダンスをする女性の小さなスケッチ
から、その女性のスカートのプリーツのような柔らかな曲線を描くファ
サードを考えました。さらにこの丸みのある形状は、人を優しく迎え
入れ、都市の中で動きのある建物となることを期待しました。

このように、歴史を取り込みつつ、先進的な建築にしたいと考えまし
た。たとえば、日比谷通り側のファサードは粗目の花崗岩仕上げと
し、三信ビルディングを踏襲して、日生劇場のファサードと連続さ
せています。石のファサードは曲線を描いて日比谷ステップ広場
へと繋がり、商業エリアの入口ではガラス張りのファサードへと変化
します。

オーガニックさ─日比谷公園と自然のインスピレーション
柔らかさのデザイン─縁どり、曲線と入口

日比谷エリアは丸の内や銀座とは異なり、より女性的かつオーガ
ニックで優雅さがあると私たちは感じていました。もちろんこれには
日比谷公園が起因しているため、「建物内に公園を持ちこむ方
法」を追求しました。自然の持つオーガニックさを感じるにはどうす
ればよいか、緑あふれる快適な場所をつくるにはどうすればよいか。
ワルツのダンスの動きから、オーガニックな形状を採用し、水が脇
を流れ落ち、緑であふれる場所として日比谷ステップ広場をデザ
インしました。さらに、6階パークビューガーデンと9階スカイガーデ
ンは、小さな公園のように感じられるよう設計しています。

コンセプトの構築─チームワーク
チームワークにより生み出される建築のディテール

たくさんのメンバーによる貢献と、切磋琢磨。これがよい建築には
不可欠だと思います。同時に、コンセプトを共有し、問題を解決し
て進めていくためには、お互いをサポートし合うチームワークが必
要です。三井不動産、日建設計、KAJIMA DESIGN、その他多く
のチームメンバーたちと協働できたことは、われわれにとって素晴ら
しい経験でした。それらの協働の先に、細部まで美しく仕上がった
建築ができ上がりました。

■ 賑わいの中心となる劇場空間のような商業エリアのアトリウム
Atrium like commercial zone like theater space that is center of bustling area

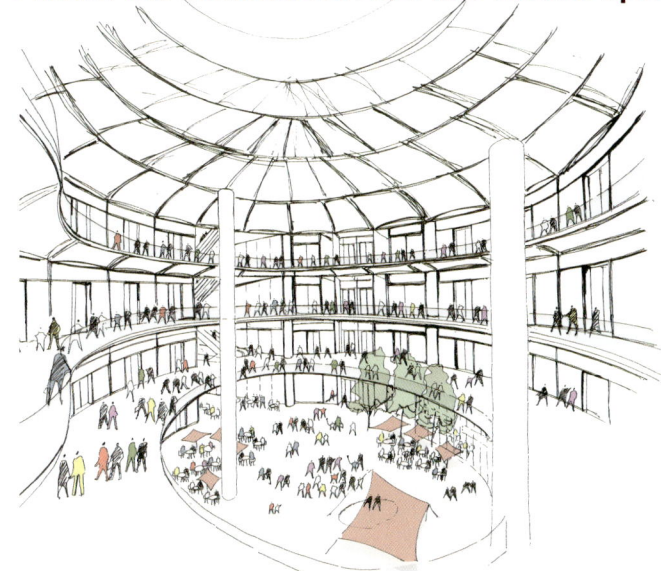

劇場文化の中心であった日比谷の歴史から、エンターテインメントの街を可視化することを考え、商業エリアの中心に劇場をイメージしたアトリウムを提案。外部に広がる日比谷ステップ広場と連続したイベント広場であると同時に屋内外シアターになるようにデザインした。[HA]
劇場空間のような商業エリアのアトリウムスケッチ。[2012年7月、ホプキンス・アーキテクツ作成]

The history of Hibiya, which was the center of theater culture, gave us the idea of making the center of the commercial zone like a theater to make the image of Hibiya as an entertainment town visible. The design was that of an outdoor theater which at the same time was an event plaza connected the Hibiya Step Square that spread out. [HA]
Sketch of commercial zone Atrium like theater space. [July 2012, created by Hopkins Architects]

Memories and history of the site
Sanshin Building and Rokkumeikan

My first memories of the Hibiya district were of coming into the old Sanshin building over 25 years ago I used to go into the building from the Chiyoda-sen exit and walk through the well proportioned and detailed arcades of the building, running my hands over rounded handrails and door handles and finally exiting into the busy surrounding streets with the many cinemas and shops. This memory still remains with me today and it is this feeling of softness that inspired our vision for the Tokyo Midtown Hibiya.

We were also inspired by the dancing in the old Rokkumeikan – this was a place for foreigners and Japanese people to meet and dance over 140 years ago. I drew this little sketch of a lady dancing and the pleats of her skirt inspired the form of the facetted curve on the façade as it turns the corners and creates soft edges. We wanted to create a building that had a spirit of welcome and movement (the entrances, the rounded forms etc.)

So in this way, we wanted to make the new building design to have echoes of the past but also be modern and look to the future. The Hibiya-dori facade for example is more solid and made from a rough finished granite and has some echoes of the proportions similar to the Sanshin building base and also the Nissay Theatre facade. It has soft edges to the stone detailing and it curved into the main plaza area changing to a glass facade as it faces the plaza and entrance to the shopping atrium.

An Organic character – inspiration of Hibiya park and nature
Design of Softness – edges, corners and entrances

The Hibiya district is different from Marunouchi and Ginza. We felt it was more feminine and organic in nature – somehow more elegant. Of course it also has a more direct relationship with Hibiya Park, so we asked, 'how can we bring the park into the building?' How can the new project feel more natural and organic – a place that is welcoming and green. Following on from the idea of dancing we sketched the dancing moves of a waltz. We also designed the streets to have natural forms and the 'Hibiya Step Square' to be sensual in design with water and plants cascading down it's sides.

The terraces on the 6th to 9th floors are designed to feel and work like a small park and these are organic in form and shape.

Building the concept – teamwork
A Spirit of collaboration and great teamwork produces the final building detail

To do a good building – you need many people all contributing and challenging each other to do better. At the same time, to take a concept sketch and address and solve problems as you progress along the way, requires a team that is supportive of each other. What a very enjoyable experience it was working alongside my fellow team members from Mitsui Fudosan, Nikken Sekkei and KAJIMA DESIGN and many others. We experienced a true spirit of collaboration and the final building product that is beautifully made and detailed.

全関係者が一堂に会する
重要な会議体「ワークセッション」

2012.9–
Start of work sessions

"Work sessions" were important meetings of concerned individuals in one place

■ 全16回のワークセッション
Total of 16 work sessions

ロンドンを拠点とするホプキンス・アーキテクツとの協働のため、全関係者が一堂に会するワークセッションという会議体を開催することとし、各段階での検討事項をまとめた計画を立てた。これは、ゴールが見えやすく、大きなプロジェクトでは効果的な方法である。[NS]

To collaborate with Hopkins Architects with London as the base, a plan was drawn up to include things to consider at each stage and when and how many times work sessions would be held. This would make the goal more visible and would be an important method when implementing a large project. [NS]

ワーク セッション/WS	年 月/Year, Month		内容/Theme
1	2012	9	外装、広場、ボリューム構成等の方針検討 — Considering course including exterior, plaza, volume configuration, etc.
2	2012	10	タワー部の跳ね出しのあり方とタワー形状のデザイン検討/リーフガーデン側低層部外装取り合い検討 — Consideration of tower design and concept of tower overhang / consideration of exterior balance of lower-rise on the leaf garden side
3	2012	11	タワー部の跳ね出しのあり方とタワー形状のデザイン検討/商業エリアのアトリウムインテリアデザイン提案/日比谷ステップ広場提案/パークビューガーデンのランドスケープデザインコンセプト提案 (リーフガーデンの原型) — Consideration of tower design and concept of tower overhang / commercial area atrium interior design proposals / Hibiya Step Square proposals / park view garden landscape design concept proposals (leaf garden model)
4	2013	2	タワー部の長柱の外装デザイン検討/タワー外装フィンディテールデザイン検討/オフィスエントランス、商業エリアのアトリウム、地下日比谷アーケードインテリアデザイン提案/日比谷ステップ広場提案/パークビューガーデンランドスケープデザインコンセプト提案 — Consideration of exterior design for tower pillars / consideration of tower exterior fin detail design / office entrance, commercial area atrium, underground Hibiya Arcade interior design proposals / Hibiya Step Square proposals / Park View Garden landscape design concept proposals
5	2013	4	タワー部とパークビューガーデンの取り合い検討/日比谷ステップ広場とパークビューガーデンのランドスケープデザイン提案 — Consideration of balance of tower portion and view garden / landscape design proposals for Hibiya Step Square and Park View Garden
6	2013	6	タワー頂部デザイン提案/低層部日比谷通りファサードデザイン検討/パークビューガーデンデザイン検討 — Tower top design proposals / consideration of low stories of Hibiyadori street facade design / consideration of Park View Garden design
7	2013	10	日比谷通りファサード提案 (3案提示)/タワー頂部デザイン提案→現状のシルエットに変更/パークビューガーデン検討→現状プランの原型を提案 — Facade of Hibiya-dori side proposals (3 proposals) / tower top design proposals --> current silhouette change / consideration of Park View Garden --> current plan model proposals
8	2014	5	ランドスケープ提案→方針決定/ソフトランドスケープ[MB]/商業共用部インテリア提案→方針決定[NK]/グランドデザインとりまとめ[NS]/共用部インテリア提案まとめ[NS] — Landscape proposals --> course decision / soft landscape [MB] / commercial shared interior proposals --> course decision [NK] / grand design summary [NS] / summary of shared interior proposals [NS]
9	2014	10	全体コンセプト確認/外観方針決定 (頂部クラウン案、オフィスエントランスゲート設置、低層部日比谷通りファサードディテール)/パークビューガーデンとスカイガーデンランドスケーププラン議論[NK]/商業インテリア議論[NK]/オフィスエントランスインテリア議論[NS] — Overall concept confirmation / appearance course decision (crown plan of tower top, office entrance gate installation, low rise facade of Hibiya-dori side details) / Park View Garden and Sky Garden landscape plan discussion / commercial interior discussion [NK] / office entrance interior discussion [NS]
10	2015	1	外観照明デザインイニシャル提案[DHA]/オフィスエントランスインテリアデザイン提案[NS]/ランドスケープデザイン/タワー外装モックアップ確認 — Outer appearance illumination initial proposals [DHA] / office entrance interior design proposals [NS] / landscape design / tower exterior mock-up confirmation
11	2015	3	タワー外装モックアップ確認 (バックパネルの色確認)/オフィス外装検討 (2ラップ→1ラップ)/石柱モックアップ確認、石種確認/オフィスエントランスインテリアデザイン提案[NS] — Tower exterior mock-up confirmation (back panel color confirmation) / consideration of office exterior (2 lap --> 1 lap) / stone pillar mock-up confirmation, stone type confirmation / office entrance interior design proposals [NS]
12	2015	5	低層外装石種決定/地下広場デザイン提案[NK]/植栽計画提案/低層部オーニング色確認 — Low rise exterior stone type decision / underground plaza design proposals [NK] / plant plan proposals / low rise awning color confirmation
13	2015	8	オフィスインテリアデザイン提案[IL]/低層外装モックアップ確認/ソフトランドスケープデザイン提案、方針決定[MB]/区道のシケイン化/低層部日比谷通りファサード照明モックアップ確認 — Office interior design proposals [IL] / low rise exterior mock-up confirmation / soft landscape design proposals, course decision [MB] / ward road chicane / low rise Hibiyadori street facade illumination mock-up confirmation
14	2015	10	日比谷ステップ広場ランドスケープデザイン提案、方針決定[MB]/照明デザイン提案[DHA]/和泉氏作品 石材視察[IZ] — Hibiya Step Square landscape design proposals, course decision [MB] / illumination design proposals [DHA] / stone material observation for Mr. Izumi's creation [IZ]
15	2016	5	和泉正敏氏作品提案[IZ, NS]/植栽実査/ランドスケープモックアップ確認/TOHOシネマズ日比谷インナースキンデザイン検討/堀木エリ子氏作品提案[HO] — Mr. Izumi's creation proposals [IZ, NS] / plant inspection / landscape mock-up confirmation / consideration of TOHO Cinemas Hibiya inner skin design / Ms. Horiki's creation proposals [HO]
16	2016	11	タワー部照明確認/TOHOシネマズ日比谷インナースキンデザイン検討 — Tower illumination confirmation / consideration of TOHO Cinemas Hibiya inner skin design

全16回実施されたワークセッションの開催時期と検討内容。

Period and consideration results of 16 work sessions.

■ 合宿のように一度に参加者全員が集まり、ものを決めるワークセッション
Work session to decide with all participants meeting at one time like training camp

ワークセッションは、重要な意思決定を行う場と捉えていた。それは、デザイナーや意思決定権者など全関係者が一堂に会し、ここで決めたことを与件として次に繋げる大事な結節機能を持った会議体だったからである。回を重ねるごとにコンセプトが具体化し、よりよくなっていく実感があり、非常に有効だと感じていた。[MF]

Work sessions provided an opportunity to catch important ideas. Work sessions provided an opportunity for all pertinent parties including designers and decision-makers to meet at one place to make decisions and are connected to next important node function. With each meeting, concepts become clearer with sensation of progress and were found to be extremely effective. [MF]

ワークセッションの参加企業とそれぞれの役割。

Work session participating companies and their roles.

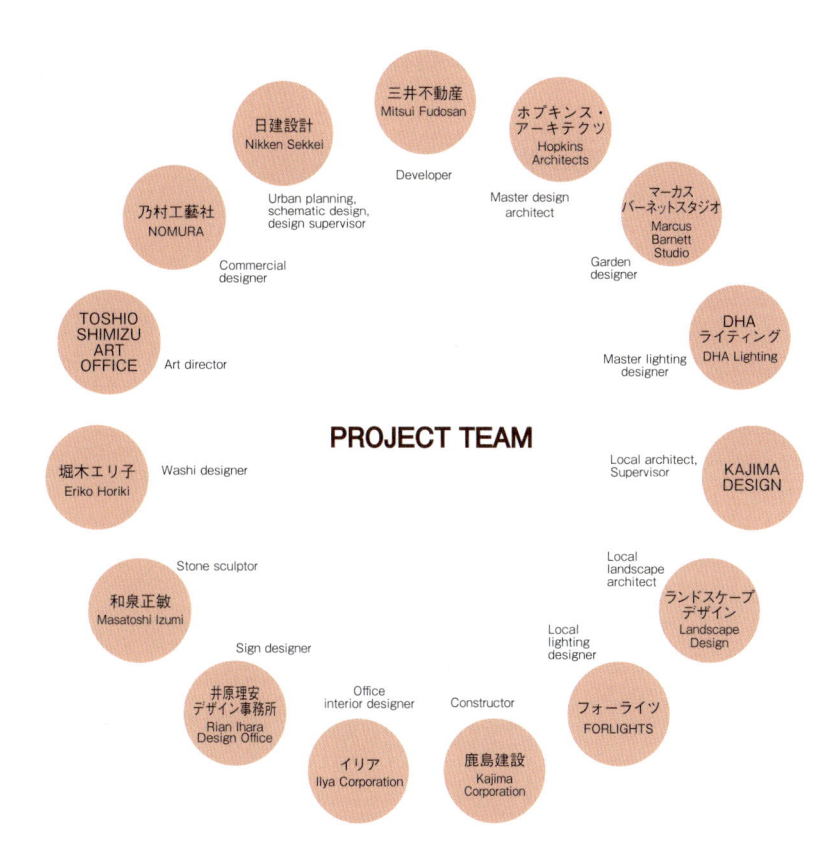

PROJECT TEAM

- 日建設計 Nikken Sekkei — Urban planning, schematic design, design supervisor
- 三井不動産 Mitsui Fudosan — Developer
- ホプキンス・アーキテクツ Hopkins Architects — Master design architect
- マーカスバーネットスタジオ Marcus Barnett Studio — Garden designer
- 乃村工藝社 NOMURA — Commercial designer
- DHA ライティング DHA Lighting — Master lighting designer
- TOSHIO SHIMIZU ART OFFICE — Art director
- KAJIMA DESIGN — Local architect, Supervisor
- 堀木エリ子 Eriko Horiki — Washi designer
- ランドスケープデザイン Landscape Design — Local landscape architect
- 和泉正敏 Masatoshi Izumi — Stone sculptor
- フォーライツ FORLIGHTS — Local lighting designer
- 井原理安デザイン事務所 Rian Ihara Design Office — Sign designer
- イリア Ilya Corporation — Office interior designer
- 鹿島建設 Kajima Corporation — Constructor

3点：ワークセッションの様子。左上：低層部商業エリアの空間構成の検討。[2012年9月]　左下：タワー形状の検討。[2012年10月] 右：ランドスケープデザインの検討。[2014年10月]

3 pictures: Scene of work sessions Upper left: Consideration of space configuration of low rise commercial zone. [September 2012]

Lower left: Consideration of tower shape. [October 2012] Right: Consideration of landscape design. [October 2014]

PHASE 2

デザインと並行して進む都市計画の協議

2012.8–
**Land division readjustment
project authorization, district plan
decision, urban plan decision**

Discussion of urban plan in parallel with design

■ 関係者だけでなく地域や行政と 一体となり街のあり方を考える

NS ワークセッションでの事業者・デザイナー・設計者等との検討と並行して、地元の方々との意見交換や、都市計画の行政協議も進めていました。行政や地元の方々が参加された検討会では、このエリアがどのような街となるのがよいか、どういうものが必要なのかを話し合いました。そこで広場をつくるという方向性も見えてきました。これは、三信ビルディング解体後、日比谷パティオを開催していた時の広場空間がよかったという実体験に基づいた意見でした。事業の関係者だけでなく、地元の方々や行政のコンセンサスが得られたからこそ、都市計画の手続きに入ることができたのだと考えています。

土地区画整理事業では、三信ビルディングと日比谷三井ビルディングの間にあった千代田区道131号を廃道し、広場にすることを千代田区から認可してもらいました。(2012年8月) また、地上・地下の広場や歩行者通路等も、地区計画が変更され地区施設に位置付けられました。(2012年12月) ワークセッションでのデザインの検討が進む中、都市再生特別地区の行政協議を並行して進めていたので、デザインが全く変わってしまう可能性のある中での協議は難しいものではありましたが、「In the Park」という分かりやすいコンセプトが共有されていたので、きっと大きなデザイン変更となることはないだろうなという確信もありました。
デザイン検討と都市計画協議を並行して進めて行く中で、特に重要となったのが、「都市景観」と「建築デザイン」の融合でした。都市計画的な目線で、

周辺と調和した都市景観として語れなければ、今回のデザインを実現することはできません。ワークセッションでは、都市計画的な視点から検討が必要なポイントを提示し、手戻りなくデザイン検討が進むように心がけました。逆に都市計画協議では、デザインで大切にしてきたコンセプトを都市計画・都市景観の言葉に置き換えてしっかりと説明しきりたいという思いで進めて行きました。
都市計画決定後に詳細なデザイン検討を行うプロジェクトもありますが、このようなさまざまな検討を行った上で、都市再生特別地区の都市計画決定(2013年12月)を迎えられたことは、日比谷プロジェクトの特徴であり、まちづくりを大きく飛躍させたと考えています。

■ Taking into consideration the entire city district rather than just the commercial stakeholders

NS With the land division readjustment, authorization to eliminate Chiyoda ward route 131 running between the Sanshin Building and the Hibiya Mitsui Building and replace it with a plaza was obtained. Prior to authorization, we held discussions on what sort of environment would be good for the area and what would be needed to achieve that. This involved Mitsui Fudosan as the key developer, Chiyoda ward and all the people in the surrounding areas who participated in the conference. It was during this discussion that the idea for the plaza took shape. After demolishing the Sanshin Building, we

embarked on an urban planning process in keeping with opinions based on actual experience that a plaza would be a good idea and reaffirmed during the Hibiya Patio events (see p. 90). Progress then proceeded based on a consensus of the local people rather than the team engaged in the project.
Because urban planning had proceeded in parallel with proposed designs, there was a chance that the design would need to be completely transformed, resulting in difficult negotiations with the administrative council. The shared concept was however easily understood by all parties, so we were convinced that design would not be changed significantly. Landscape and public space (plaza) were the most important components as design and urban planning proceeded simultaneously. Public space is related to the favorable impact

of building appearance on the space. On the other hand, there needed to be an understanding with the administrative council concerning space that offered benefits to the area in terms of urban planning. Using a soft curved surface was a strong design concept, but in discussions concerning landscape, Metropolitan Tokyo and its advisers took the view that other buildings facing Hibiya-dori were all rectangular, so this development should also be rectangular. We therefore proceeded by attempting to explain the concept had been carefully designed with urban planning in mind by creating various scenarios whereby, in relation to Hibiya-dori, some of the buildings employed a curved surface, which would morph into a rectangular shape when seen up close.

2012.9–11
Work sessions 1 - 3:
Consideration of tower shape
and landscape

景観と事業性を両立させる
曲面のタワー形状

Curved tower shape that offers
both scenic view and commercial potential

▮ 周囲に圧迫感を与えないタワー形状
Tower shape that does not overwhelm the surrounding area

タワー部のオーバーハング（跳ね出し）の形状が不安定で、日比谷公園側へ圧迫感を与えているのではないかという懸念があった。考えられる形状をいくつも並べ、日比谷にふさわしい形状を検証した。[NS]

The shape of the tower overhang is unstable and there is concern that it will have an overwhelming presence on the Hibiya Park side. Several other possible shapes were offered that proved to be suitable for Hibiya. [NS]

3点：タワー部のオーバーハングの形状と日比谷公園側からの見え方の検討。[2012年10月、ホプキンス・アーキテクツ作成]

3 items: Consideration of how the tower overhang shape is viewed from the Hibiya Park side. [October 2012, created by Hopkins Architects]

オーバーハングの形状検討スケッチ。[2012年10月、ホプキンス・アーキテクツ作成]

Study sketch of overhang shape. [October 2012, created by Hopkins Architects]

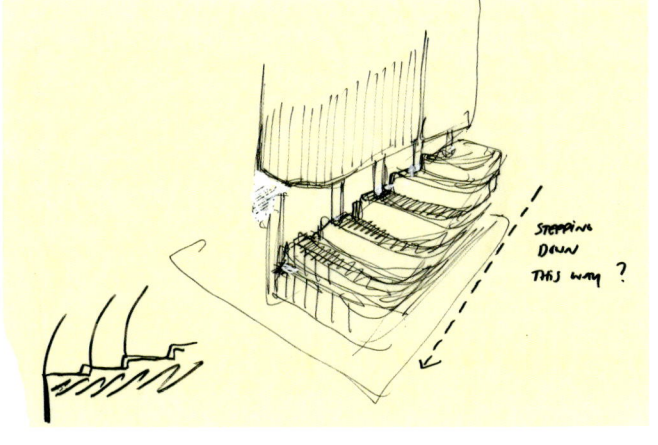

オーバーハング部とテラスの関係検討スケッチ。[2012年10月、ホプキンス・アーキテクツ作成]

Study sketch of the relation between overhang and terrace. [October 2012, created by Hopkins Architects]

▌「日比谷らしい」タワー形状とオフィス平面をすり合わせる
Reconcile "Hibiya-style" tower shape and office plane

日比谷公園への圧迫感の低減を図りつつ、「Dancing Tower」のイメージを具現化できているかという観点で、考えられる限りのバリエーションを検討した。この検討を経て、当初の提案に最も近い構成をベースとして進めていくこととなった。[NS]

Possible variations were considered from the standpoint embodiment of the "Dancing Tower" image and reducing pressure on Hibiya Park. Through this study, it was decided to base the image on the configuration that most closely resembled the initial proposal. [NS]

3点：タワー形状検討パース。左からA案、B案、C案。[2012年11月、ホプキンス・アーキテクツ作成]

3 items: Tower shape study perspective. From the left, Proposal A, Proposal B and Proposal C. [November 2012, created by Hopkins Architects]

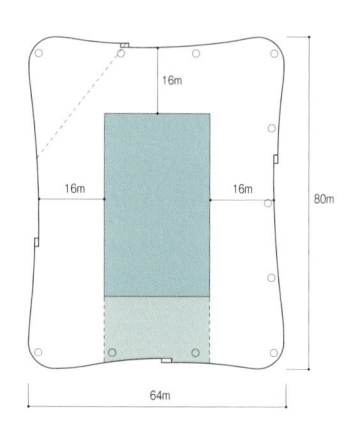
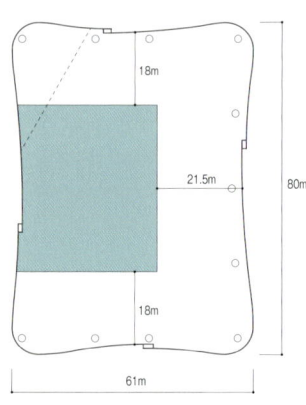
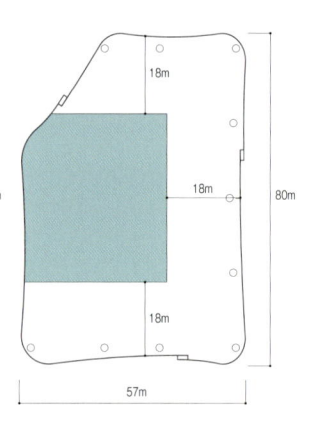

A案
ワンフロアの貸室面積：約950坪
基準階フロア数：23層（約22,000坪）

Proposal A
One floor rental office area: Approx. 950 tsubo
Number of typical floors: 23 (approx. 22,000 tsubo)

B案
ワンフロアの貸室面積：約840坪
基準階フロア数：26層（約22,000坪）

Proposal B
One floor rental office area: Approx. 840 tsubo
Number of typical floors: 26 (approx. 22,000 tsubo)

C案
ワンフロアの貸室面積：約840坪
基準階フロア数：26層（約22,000坪）

Proposal C
One floor rental office area: Approx. 840 tsubo
Number of typical floors: 26 (approx. 22,000 tsubo)

タワー形状は、見た目の印象はもちろんのこと、商品企画的に問題がないかの確認も重要だった。オフィス基準階の貸室面積（有効面積）と、タワー部の高さと幅をパラメトリックに検討し、オーバーハングの形状を決めていった。[NS]

われわれ事業者も曲面の平面形状は変更するつもりはなかったので、その中で利用しやすいオフィスとはどういうものかを踏まえながら、だんだんとタワー形状を確定していった。[MF]

It was important to take whether the tower shape posed any problems for the real estate business as well as the visual impression into account. The shape of the overhang was decided taking into consideration parametric office floor rental space area (effective area) on the office floors, height and width of the tower. [NS]

We did not intend to alter the plane shape of the curved surface, so we gradually ascertained the tower shape based on what kind of offices would be convenient. [MF]

3点：A～C案のオフィス平面検討。[2012年12月、日建設計作成]

3 items: Office plane study of Proposals A - C. [December 2012, created by Nikken Sekkei]

日比谷公園の大噴水越しに見るタワー部。
Tower as seen through the fountain water in Hibiya Park.

2013.2–10
ワークセッション4~7 =
外装ディテール(景観)の検討

2013.2–10
Work sessions 4 - 7:
Exterior detail (scenic) study

景観を決定付ける外装ディテール

Exterior details with decided scenery

■ 景観を左右するタワー部外装カーテンウォールのフィン
Fin of tower exterior curtain wall influences scenery

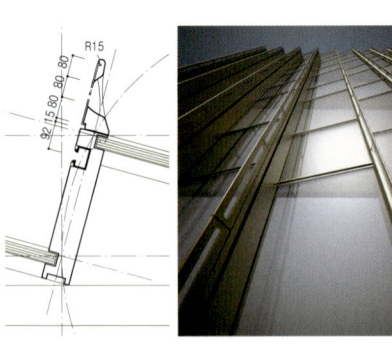
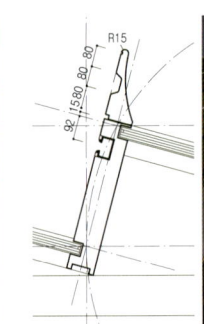

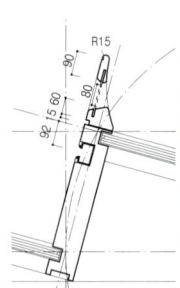

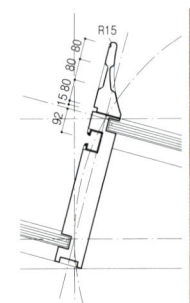

左：タワー部のプリーツ状の外装フィンのディテール検討。開口やリブの有無で印象をスタディしている。[2013年2月、ホプキンス・アーキテクツ作成]

ラップ部分を表現するために柔らかく軽やかな表情が感じられるような形状を検討しつつ、風切音や着雪対策についても考慮し、実現可能なデザインとした。[NS]

Left: Detail study of pleat-shaped exterior fin of tower. Study of impression with/without opening or ribs is being conducted. [February 2013, created by Hopkins Architects] A shape that provides a soft impression is being considered to express pleats. The practical design also takes wind noise and snow countermeasures into account. [NS]

■ 三信ビルディングを踏襲し、
石を用いた柔らかな外装をつくる
Create soft exterior using stone in the tradition of the Sanshin Building

マスターデザインと構造的な検証が何度も必要となった。マスターデザインのコンセプトと変わらない部分もあったり、シンプルなディテールへの変更を行うこともあった。[HA]
ディテールは細かい検討の繰り返しだった。たとえば低層部のベイウィンドウの庇の張り出し方ひとつにしても、たくさんのパターンを提案してもらった。[MF]
デザイナーにとってはネガティブな要素にも取れる景観協議からのさまざまな意見に対しても、それを超えて多くの提案を出し最適な案が見出せた。[NS]

Verification of master design and structural design had to be conducted over and again. Some of the concept of the master design did not change, but some parts were changed to simple detail. [HA]
Details were considered repeatedly. For example, lots of pattern suggestions were received eve concerning the eaves of the bay windows of the low rise part. [MF]
Despite there being various opinions from landscape discussions involving negative elements for designers, there were many positive proposals resulting in determining the best idea. [NS]

日比谷通り側低層部外装のコンセプトスケッチ。[2013年6月、ホプキンス・アーキテクツ作成]

Concept sketch of Hibiya-dori side low rise exterior. [June 2013, created by Hopkins Architects]

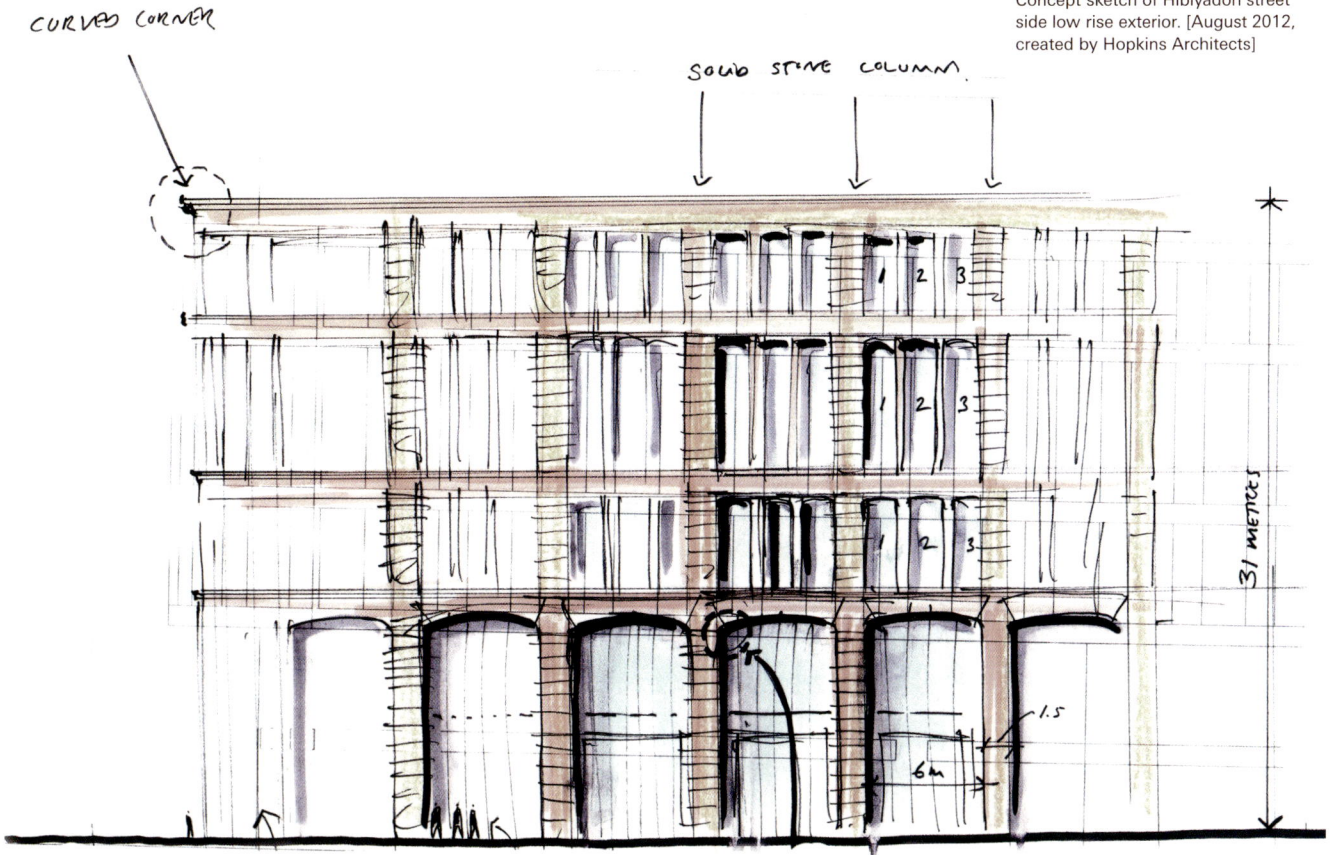

CURVED CORNER

SOLID STONE COLUMN

31 METRES

1.5

6m

1 2 3

下3点：日比谷通り低層部のファサード検討。左からA案、B案、C案。［2013年10月、ホプキンス・アーキテクツ作成］

三信ビルディングをモチーフとするコンセプトに基づいて、日生劇場や日比谷公園との関係性、さらには日比谷通りとしての景観を意識して、石とメタルの配分や形状を検討。最終的には石でありながら、柔らかな印象が日比谷特有のデザインとなるという考えでB案ベースとすることになった。［NS］

Bottom 3 items: Consideration of facade of Hibiya-dori side low rise section. From the left, Proposal A, Proposal B and Proposal C. [October 2013, created by Hopkins Architects] Consideration of stone and metal portions and shape based on the concept employing the motif of the Sanshin Building, the association with the Nissay Theatre and Hibiya Park as well as the landscape of Hibiya-dori side. Ultimately based on Proposal B from the standpoint of Hibiya unique design with soft image despite being stone. [NS]

日比谷ステップ広場からの見上げ。
Looking up from Hibiya Step Square.

2012.9–2013.10
ワークセッション1~7 =
パブリックスペース(広場)の検討

2012.9–2013.10
Work sessions 1 - 7:
Consideration of public space
(plaza)

人が集い賑わう広場

Bustling plaza where people gather

▌アクティビティから広場の性格を導き出す
Nature of plaza brought out by activity

上2点：ランドスケープコンセプトスケッチ。
左：日比谷ステップ広場から階段状の広場
とオフィスエントランスを見る。右：日比谷ス

テップ広場のレストラン・カフェのイメージ。
[2012年11月、ホプキンス・アーキテクツ作成]

Top 2 items: Landscape concept
sketch. / Left: View of stepped plaza
and office space from Hibiya Step
Square. Right: Image of restaurants

and cafes in Hibiya Step Square.
[November 2012, created by Hopkins
Architects]

日比谷ステップ広場は結節機能を持つ拠点
となるように、円形がいちばんよいと考えた。
その広場が屋内の商業エリアのアトリウムと
繋がることで、たとえばレッドカーペットイベント
では、屋内外にレッドカーペットを敷いて連動
した使い方ができ、日比谷ステップ広場に座
り円形の広場で繰り広げられるイベントを眺
めることもできる。[MF]

The circular shape was deemed best
for the plaza to function as a node. By
having the plaza be connected to the
indoor commercial area atrium, it could
be used to lay a red carpet inside/
outside for red carpet events, and could
be used to watch events unfolding in
the amphitheater-shaped Hibiya Step
Square. [MF]

下：日比谷ステップ広場のランドスケープコ
ンセプト検討の模型。[2012年11月、ホプキン
ス・アーキテクツ作成]

Bottom: Model of Hibiya Step Square
landscape concept study. [November
2012, created by Hopkins Architects]

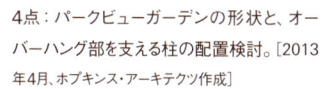

4点：パークビューガーデンの形状と、オーバーハング部を支える柱の配置検討。[2013年4月、ホプキンス・アーキテクツ作成]
タワー部の跳ね出しと圧迫感の低減についての議論は柱1本で不安定感を緩和する方針となった。6〜9階のパークビューガーデン、スカイガーデンの構成は、日比谷公園からの

緑の連続性、タワーとの関係性を考慮して階段状の大地のような表現とするか、タワーの延長上とするかを検討し、最終的には、ステップを多段化して緩やかに緑が駆け上がる構成となった。[NS]

4 items: Consideration of Park View Garden and layout of pillars to support the overhang. [April 2013, created by Hopkins Architects]
Discussion of tower overhang and pressure reduction resulted in deciding to reduce the sense of instability with a single pillar. Taking continuity of green from Hibiya Park and connection with

the tower into account, whether the configuration of the Park View Garden on floors 6 - 9 and Sky Garden should express stage-shaped ground or should be an extension of the tower were considered. It was ultimately decided to use the configuration of steps that gently lead to the greenery. [NS]

■ タワー部の跳ね出し形状とパークビューガーデンからの眺望
Tower overhang shape and view from Park View Garden

上空から日比谷公園や皇居を眺められるような場所は他にないため、パークビューガーデンの価値は高く、どのようにつくり込むかは大きな議論の対象だった。[MF]
パークビューガーデンの検討にあたっては、日比谷公園の緑との繋がりと、タワー部との関係性が大きく影響していた。6階パークビューガーデンと9階スカイガーデンの大きさや段状の形状は、その2点から最善案を導き出した。また、空間構成だけでなく、アクティビティや運営までを視野に入れ、フロア全体でどのようなイメージづくりができるかをアクティビティイメージスケッチでポテンシャルを検証し、回遊性のある動線と公園のようなゾーニングがベースとなった。[NS]

Because there is nowhere else you can get a view of Hibiya Park and the Imperial Palace from above, the Park View Garden is very valuable and was the subject of much discussion as to how it should be created. [MF]
When considering the Park View Garden, connection with greenery of Hibiya Park and relation with the tower portion had a significant impact. The large step-like shape of the Park View Garden on the 6th floor and Sky Garden on the 9th floor lead to proposals from those 2 points. The proposals included not only spatial composition but aspects of activities and business operation as well. Activity image sketches verified the overall potential of the floors. The proposals were based on accessible traffic line and park-like zoning. [NS]

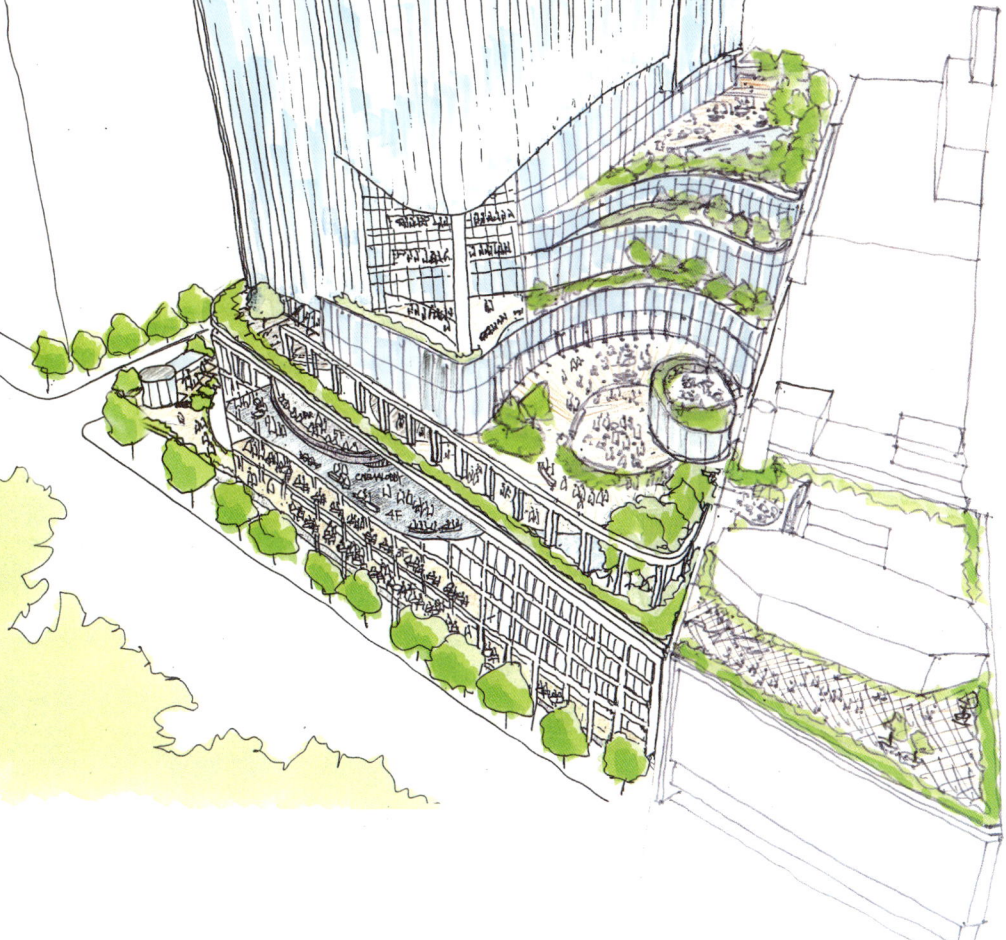

下：パークビューガーデン、スカイガーデンの検討スケッチ。[2013年4月、日建設計作成]

Bottom: Study sketches of Park View Garden and Sky Garden. [April 2013, created by Nikken Sekkei]

日比谷ステップ広場の検討CGパース。
［2014年5月、ホプキンス・アーキテクツ作成］

Study CG perspective of Hibiya Step Square. [May 2014, created by Hopkins Architects]

■ ペーブメントのパターンで柔らかな広場をつくる
Soft plaza created by pavement patterns

ペーブメントの詳細な検討を基本設計段階でスタートし、イメージを具現化する石の割り付けや配色など技術的な課題を抽出しながら、ブラッシュアップしていった。分かりやすいモチーフが広がっていくイメージで表現するA、B案（下部左2点）をベースにして合理化を進めた。[NS]

The detailed study of pavement started at the basic design stage. The design was brushed up while extracting technical issues such as stone layout and color scheme to embody the image. Design was streamlined based on proposals A and B (2 items on the bottom left) that express the image spreading out in easy to understand motif. [NS]

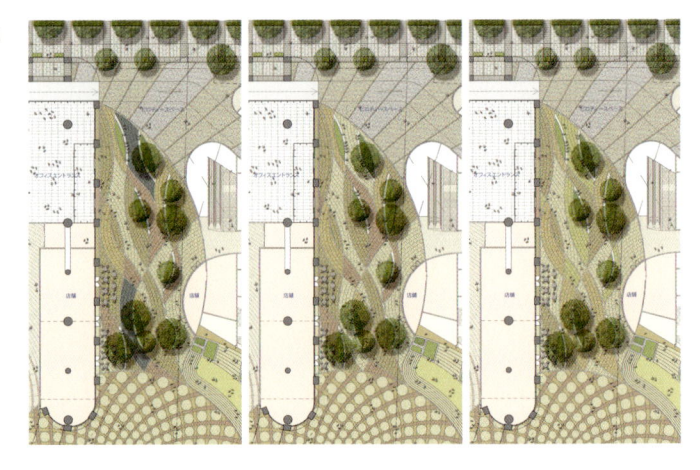

3点：リーフガーデンのペーブメント検討。
［2013年4月、ホプキンス・アーキテクツ作成］

3 items: Leaf garden pavement study. [April 2013, created by Hopkins Architects]

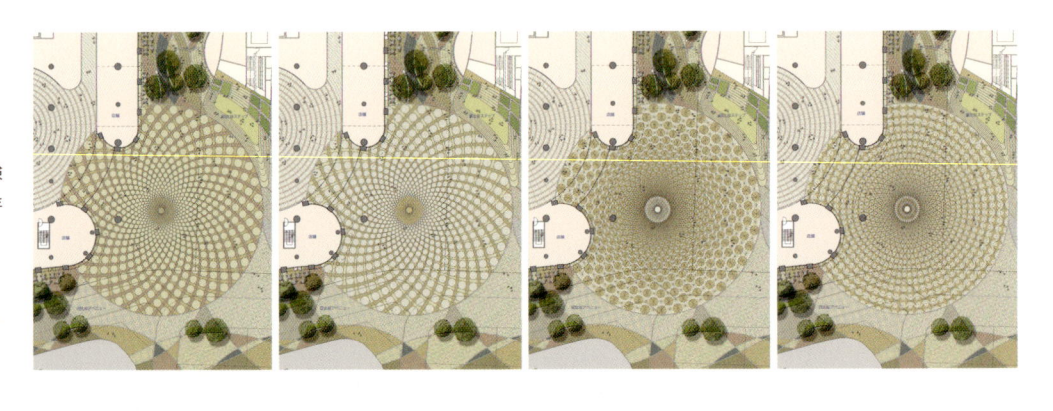

4点：日比谷ステップ広場のペーブメント検討。左からA案、B案、C案、D案。［2013年4月、ホプキンス・アーキテクツ作成］

4 items: Hibiya Step Square pavement study. From the left, Proposal A, Proposal B, Proposal C and Proposal D. [April 2013, created by Hopkins Architects]

日比谷ステップ広場夕景。
Night view of Hibiya Step Square.

6階パークビューガーデン。
6th floor Park View Garden.

日比谷ステップ広場。2階レベルで日比谷三井タワーと接続する。
Hibiya Step Square. Connects to Hibiya Mitsui Tower at 2nd floor level.

初心を確認するための
グランドデザイン会議

Grand design conference to confirm the original intention

■ ビジョンメイキングで決めた
価値観を検証し続ける

NS　ビジョンメイキングの頃からずっと続けてきたグランドデザイン会議（70-71頁参照）。当時は街づくりや建築の骨格づくりが、進んでいるデザインや都市計画においても価値観がちゃんと落とし込まれているかを検証する基準になっていました。ここでいう価値観は、ビジョンメイキングで決めた3つの言葉「公園をまちへ、まちを公園へ」、「歴史をつむぐ、文化をはぐくむ」、「日比谷に集う、日比谷から広がる」に現れています。

■ Continuing to verify the
sense of values of vision
making

NS　Concerning the grand design conference (see pp. 70 - 71) that continued since the stage of vision making was originally urban planning and architectural design. The developing design and urban planning were based on verification of whether sense of values was properly incorporated. This sense of values is expressed in the three phrases decided in vision making, i.e., "town in park, park in town," "spin history, foster culture" and "meet in Hibiya, spread from Hibiya."

グランドデザイン会議で共有された、このプロジェクトで実現すべき新たな価値創造。
[2012年6月、日建設計作成]

New value creation that should be expressed by the project shared at the grand design conference. [June 2012, created by Nikken Sekkei]

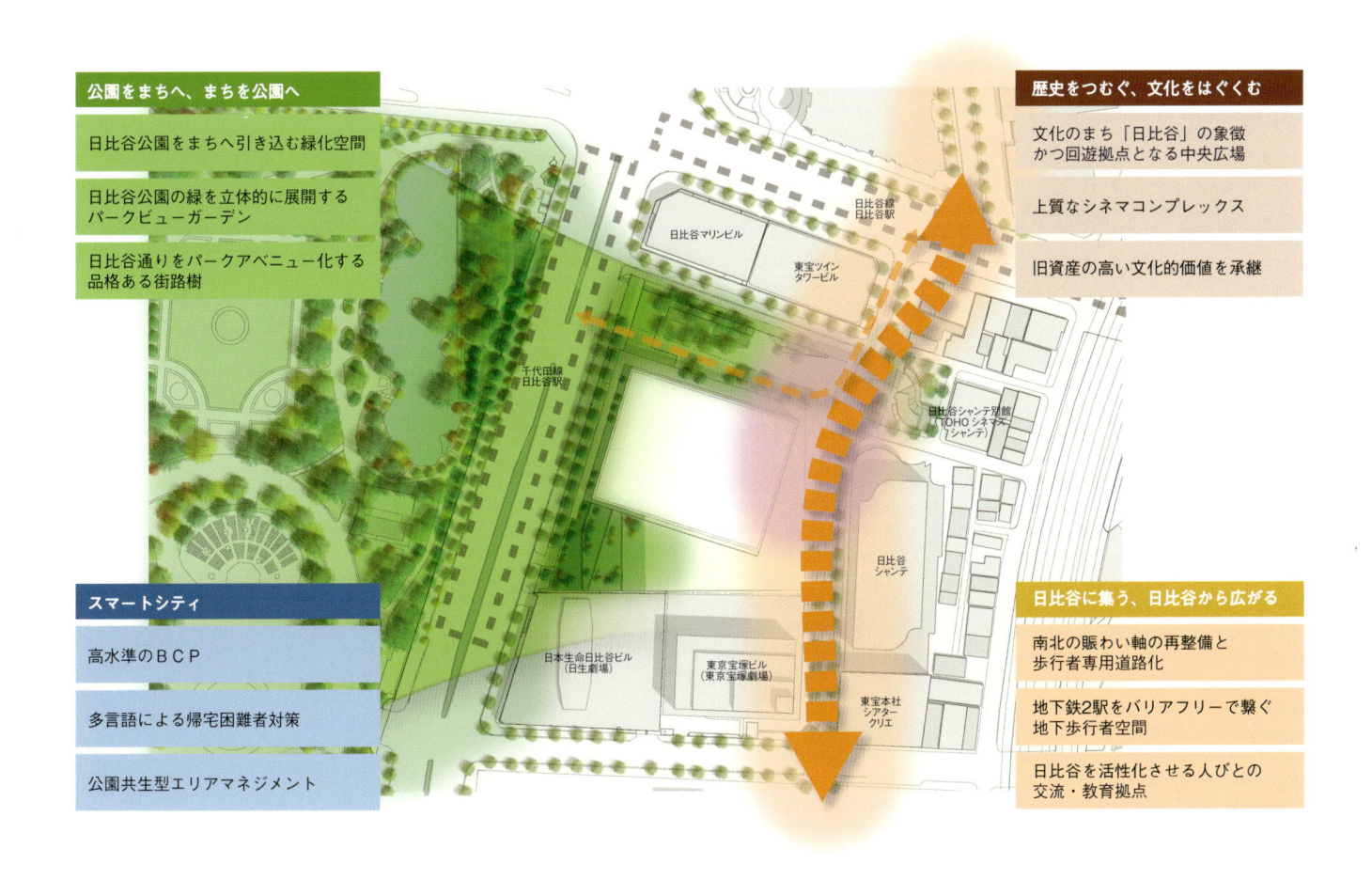

公園をまちへ、まちを公園へ
- 日比谷公園をまちへ引き込む緑化空間
- 日比谷公園の緑を立体的に展開するパークビューガーデン
- 日比谷通りをパークアベニュー化する品格ある街路樹

スマートシティ
- 高水準のBCP
- 多言語による帰宅困難者対策
- 公園共生型エリアマネジメント

歴史をつむぐ、文化をはぐくむ
- 文化のまち「日比谷」の象徴かつ回遊拠点となる中央広場
- 上質なシネマコンプレックス
- 旧資産の高い文化的価値を承継

日比谷に集う、日比谷から広がる
- 南北の賑わい軸の再整備と歩行者専用道路化
- 地下鉄2駅をバリアフリーで繋ぐ地下歩行者空間
- 日比谷を活性化させる人びとの交流・教育拠点

日比谷マリンビル
東宝ツインタワービル
千代田線日比谷駅
日比谷線日比谷駅
日比谷シャンテ別館TOHOシネマズ〔シャンテ〕
日比谷シャンテ
日本生命日比谷ビル〔日比劇場〕
東京宝塚ビル〔東京宝塚劇場〕
東宝本社シアタークリエ

PHASE 3

実現に向けた
デザインの深化と検証

Detailing and verification of design oriented for implementation

[メンバー]

MF 三井不動産［事業主］
Mitsui Fudosan [Developer]

NS 日建設計［都市計画・基本設計・デザイン監修］
Nikken Sekkei [Urban planning, schematic design, design supervisor]

HA ホプキンス・アーキテクツ［マスターデザインアーキテクト］
Hopkins Architects [Master design architect]

MB マーカスバーネットスタジオ［ガーデンデザイナー］
Marcus Burnet Studio [Garden designer]

KD KAJIMA DESIGN［実施設計・監理］
KAJIMA DESIGN [Local architect, Supervisor]

LD ランドスケープデザイン［外構実施設計協力］
Landscape Design [Local landscape architect]

NK 乃村工藝社［商業環境デザイン］
NOMURA [Commercial designer]

街づくり・都市計画 | **Town Development and Urban Planning**

建築設計 | **Architectural Design**

2014.4—
実施設計1
スタート
Start of the
execution
design 1

2014.5
グランドデザイン
とりまとめ
Compilation of grand
design

2014.5
最終DD図
発行
Final Design
Development
Document (DD
document)
issue

2014.6—
実施設計2
スタート
Start of the
execution
design 2

施工 | **Construction**

2014.10—
基準階ACW
モックアップ
Standard floor
aluminum
curtain wall
mock-up

2014.5
ワークセッション8
Work session 8

2014.10
ワークセッション9
Work session 9

PHASE 3では、チーム全体で具現化したデザインを、
着工へ向けてさらに解像度を上げていくプロセスを紹介する。
より専門的で詳細な検討を行うため、デザインチームへの参加者がどんどん増えていった。

PHASE 3 introduces the process of refining the design idea materialized by the whole team toward the start of the construction.
As the process required more technical and detailed study,
the number of members participating in the design team rapidly increased.

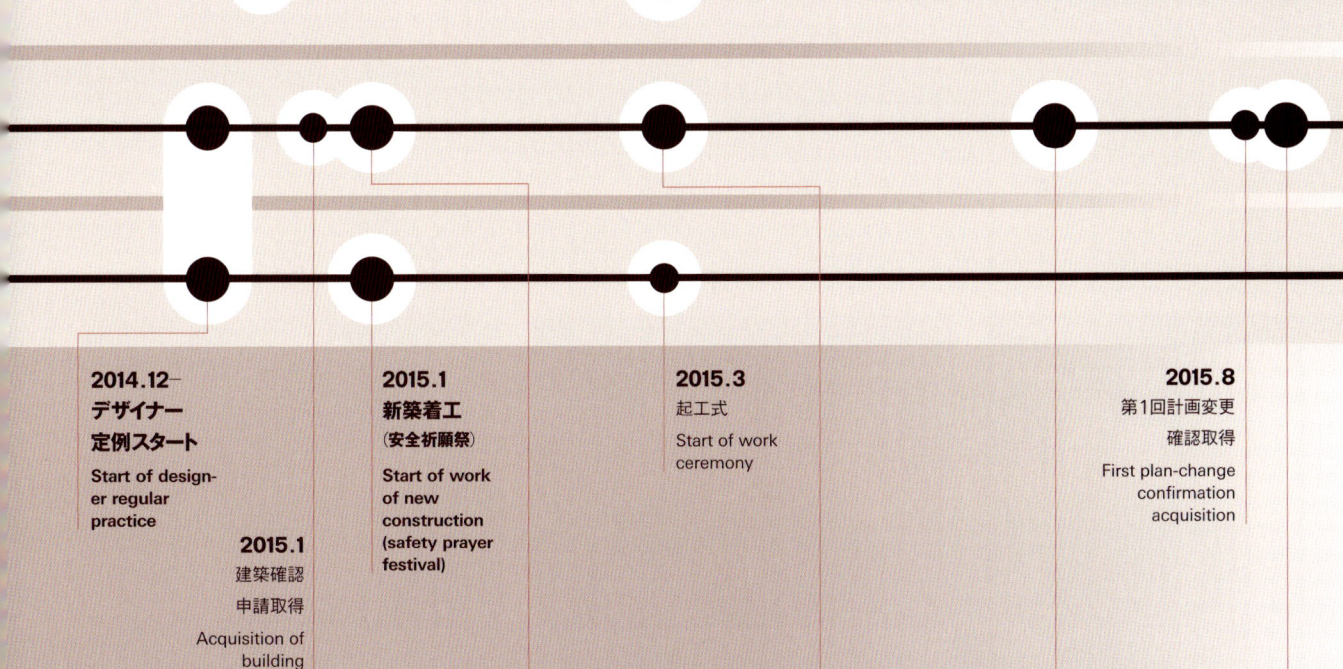

DHA DHAライティング［照明デザイナー］
DHA lighting [Master lighting designer]

FL フォーライツ［外構・外観照明実施設計協力］
FORLIGHTS [Local lighting designer]

IL イリア［オフィス共用部環境デザイン］
Ilya Corporation [Office interior designer]

和泉正敏／堀木エリ子／TOSHIO
SHIMIZU ART OFFICE／井原理安デザ
イン事務所［各種アーティスト・デザイナー］

Masatoshi Izumi / Eriko Horiki / Toshio
Shimizu Art Office / Rian Ihara Design
Office [Various artists and designers]

2014.12
国家戦略特区認定

National Strategic
Special Zone
Certification

2015.3
エリアマネジメント法人設立
（一般社団法人日比谷エリアマネジメント）

Establishment of area management
corporation (Hibiya Area
Management)

2014.12−
デザイナー
定例スタート

Start of design-
er regular
practice

2015.1
建築確認
申請取得

Acquisition of
building
confirmation
application

2015.1
新築着工
（安全祈願祭）

Start of work
of new
construction
(safety prayer
festival)

2015.3
起工式

Start of work
ceremony

2015.8
第1回計画変更
確認取得

First plan-change
confirmation
acquisition

2015.1
ワークセッション10
Work session 10

2015.3
ワークセッション11
Work session 11

2015.5
ワークセッション12
Work session 12

2015.8
ワークセッション13
Work session 13

PHASE 3

新たなデザイナーの参画

Participation of new designers

■ デザイン案の解像度を
　上げるためにチームを拡大させる

MF　これまで具現化してきたデザイン案を実際につくるためには、早期に施工を踏まえた検討が必要だと考えました。また、デザイン案は絶対に実現させたいと同時に、コストをいかに抑えるかという事業者としての使命もありました。そこで当敷地に建っていた日比谷三井ビルディングの施工者というゆかりがある鹿島建設に設計施工で参画してもらうことになりました。

NS　デザインの解像度を上げていくために、さまざまなデザイナーに参画してもらいました。商業インテリアには乃村工藝社、オフィスインテリアはイリア、ランドスケープデザインにはマーカスバーネットスタジオとランドスケープデザイン、照明デザインにはDHAライティングとフォーライツ、サインデザインには井原理安デザイン事務所。また、アートでは和泉正敏氏、堀木エリ子氏、TOSHIO SHIMIZU ART OFFICEに参画いただきました。チームの中に新しいメンバーが入ってくる度に、われわれはみんながひとつにまとまれる場所を提供し、当初からのコンセプトやビジョンを共有してもらうことを意識しました。

■ Expand the team to
increase the resolution of
the design plan

MF　For the actual implementation of the design plan realized till now, we thought that review to consider early construction is necessary. Again, while we thought that we should certainly implement the design plan, as business operators, we also had the mission of reducing the cost. At that point, Kajima Corporation, the constructor of Hibiya Mitsui Building in the same premise, was requested to participate in the design and construction.

NS　To increase the resolution of each design, various designers were also made to participate - NOMURA for commercial interiors, Ilya Corporation for office interiors, Marcus Barnett Studio and landscape design for landscape design, DHA Lighting and Forlights for illumination design and Rian Ihara Design Office for sign design. Also, for art, Mr. Masatoshi Izumi, Ms. Eriko Horiki and Toshio Shimizu Art Office participated. As more and more new members joined the team, we provided a place for everyone to gather together and consciously shared the concepts and vision of our company with them.

3点：新たなデザイナーが参画し、メンバーが増える議論の様子。左：イリアによるオフィスインテリアのプレゼンの様子（ワークセッション13）。中：マーカスバーネットスタジオによるランドスケープの検討（ワークセッション13）。右：堀木エリ子氏によるアートの検討（ワークセッション15）。

Three: State of discussion where the members are increasing due to participation of new designers. On the left, presentation by Ilya Corporation on office interiors (Work session 13). In the middle, consideration of landscape by Marcus Barnett Studio (Work session 13). On the right, consideration of art by Eriko Horiki (Work session 15).

2014.5
ワークセッション8 =
商業インテリアの検討

2014.5
Work session 8 =
Consideration of commercial
interiors

記憶を継承しながらも
先進性のある商業インテリア

Commercial interiors that are advanced,
at the same time inheriting memories

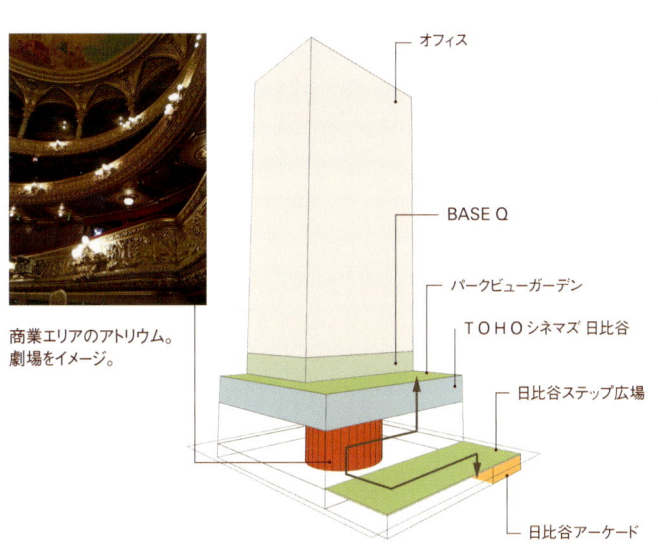

商業エリアのアトリウム。
劇場をイメージ。

オフィス
BASE Q
パークビューガーデン
ＴＯＨＯシネマズ日比谷
日比谷ステップ広場
日比谷アーケード

左：商業エリアのアトリウムの位置付け検
討。広場やテラス、地下1階日比谷アーケー
ドなど公共空間の中心となる場所と考えてい
た。[2014年5月、乃村工藝社作成]

Left: Consideration of position of
Atrium of commercial zone. Square,
terrace or basement first floor Hibiya
Arcade was thought to become the
center of public space. [May 2014,
created by NOMURA]

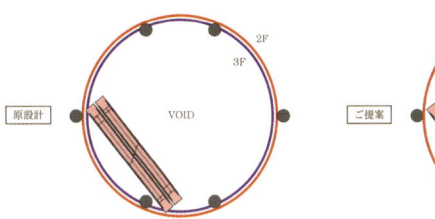

上：円形劇場とその特別席をモチーフとして
アトリウム形状をデザインした。[2014年5月、
乃村工藝社作成]

Top: Atrium shape was designed, using
amphitheater and its special seats as a
motif. [May 2014, created by
NOMURA]

下：三信ビルディングのアーケードのアーチ
の装飾を現代的に再解釈してアイアンレリー
フをデザイン。[2013年6月、乃村工藝社作成]

Bottom: The decoration of the arch of
the arcade of Sanshin Building,
contemporarily reinterpreted to design
iron relief. [June 2013, created by
NOMURA]

■ 三信ビルディングを再現する
のではなく、「記憶」を継承する

MF 商業空間は特別な空間ですが、かといって
インテリアとエクステリアが乖離しすぎているのはよく
ない。そこで、ホプキンス・アーキテクツにさまざまな
オーガニックなイメージを出してもらいました。その
日比谷らしい要素を活かしながら、さらに商業空間
としての賑わいやテナントが入った時の視認性と

いった具体的な要素を詰めていくため、商業インテ
リアデザインのコンペを行いました。

NK 2013（平成25）年7月にコンペで選定された
後、これまでみなさんが話し合われていた内容を
共有してもらい、およそ1年間かけて日建設計と一
緒にインテリアデザインを練っていきました。
地下1階の日比谷アーケードのインテリアデザイン
に関しては、当初は三信ビルディングのデザイン
を継承し、再現することを考えていました。しかし、

ワークセッションで三信ビルディングをそのまま再現
することが正しいのか、それでは新しいものが出ない
のではないかと議論をし、最終的には、三信ビル
ディングの記憶を継承することで、プロポーションな
どのプリミティブな部分を抽出して先進性を加味す
ることになりました。

MF われわれがいつも考えている「どうやってそ
の土地の持つ歴史を活かしていくか」をデザイン
に反映していただきました。

■ Inheriting the memory of
Sanshin Building, instead
of reproducing it

MF Commercial space is a special space but,
it is not good to have high divergence between
the interiors and exteriors. Therefore, we got
various organic images from Hopkins
Architects. While utilizing those Hibiya-ness
elements, additionally, commercial interior
design competitions were carried out to put in
specific elements such as visibility during

tenant entry and liveliness as a commercial
space.

NK After selecting from the competition
held in July 2013, everyone was asked to share
the contents that they were talking about till
then and over a period of about a year, the
interior design was worked out along with
Nikken Sekkei.
Regarding the interior design of the basement
first floor Hibiya Arcade, it was planned to
initially inherit the design of Sanshin Building
and reproduce it. However, during the work

session, it was discussed if it was right to
reproduce the Sanshin Building as it was or if
it was better to produce a new one. Finally, it
was decided to inherit the memory of Sanshin
Building by extracting the primitive parts such
as proportion and add advanced features.

MF This gives the impression of having
designed well in accordance with "how to
make use of the land's history", which we
always think about.

PHASE 3

126

商業エリアのアトリウム見上げ。
Look up of Atrium of commercial zone.

三信ビルディングのエレベータホール。
地下1階日比谷アーケード脇のエレベータは
三信ビルディングの保存部材を活用。

The elevator hall of Sanshin Building.
The elevator by the side of the
basement first floor Hibiya Arcade
utilizing the preserved material of
Sanshin Building.

地下1階日比谷アーケードの広場CGイメー
ジ。[2014年6月、乃村工藝社作成]
オフィスエントランスと商業施設が並ぶ空間。
ワークセッションでデザイナー同士が直接議
論しながらデザインを統合した。[NS]

CG image of square inside the
basement first floor Hibiya Arcade.
[June 2014, created by NOMURA]
Space where office entrances and
commercial facilities line up. The
designers integrated the design while
directly discussing in the work session.
[NS]

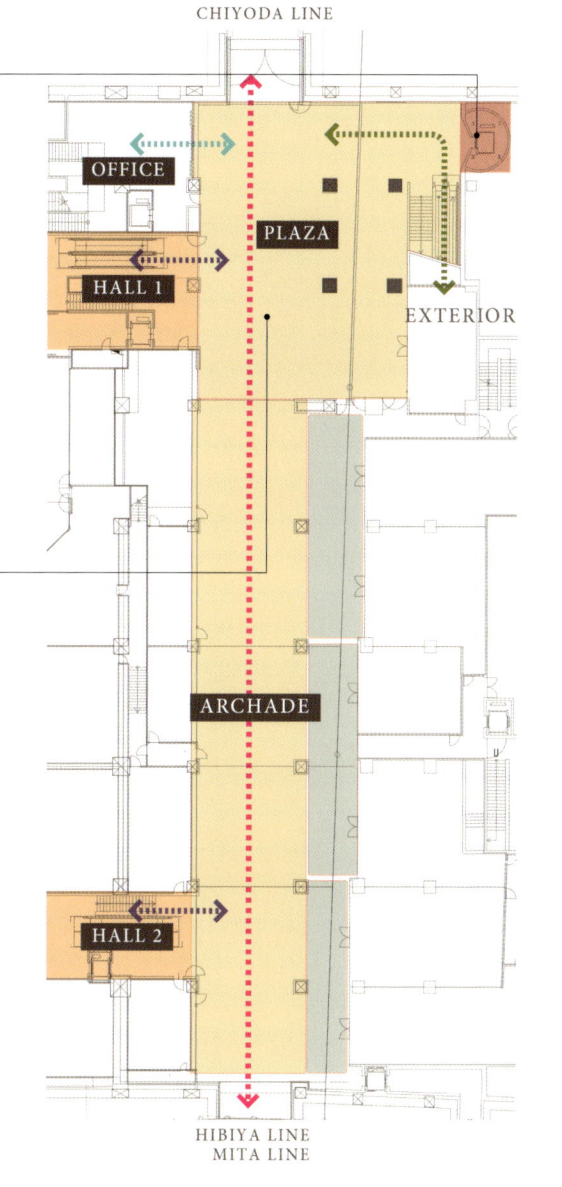

CHIYODA LINE

OFFICE

PLAZA

HALL 1

EXTERIOR

ARCHADE

HALL 2

HIBIYA LINE
MITA LINE

上：三信ビルディングのアーケード天井見上
げ。三信ビルディングの要素を抽出し、リデザ
インすることにより「記憶」としてモダンな空間
へと再生した。

Top: Lookup of Sanshin Building's
arcade ceiling. The concept of
reproducing a memory as a modern
space by extracting the elements of
Sanshin Building and redesigning.

中：地下1階の空間コンセプト。[2015年7月、
乃村工藝社作成]

Middle: Spatial concept of basement
first floor. [July 2015, created by
NOMURA]

三信ビルディングの保存部材の活用やモ
チーフを踏襲するための材料選定など、建築
側の与件との調整によってシュリンクするの
ではなく、よりコンセプトを強化できるよう検討
や議論を重ねた。[NS]

Sanshin Building's utilization of
preserved members and selection of
materials to follow motifs etc., rather
than shrinking by adjusting with the
construction side's data, accumulated a
lot of consideration and discussion to
further strengthen the concepts. [NS]

左：商業エリアのアトリウムCGパース。
右：地下1階日比谷アーケードCGパース。
[2015年10月、乃村工藝社作成]

Left: Commercial zone Atrium CG
Perspective. Right: Basement first floor
Hibiya Arcade CG Perspective. [October
2015, created by NOMURA]

PHASE 3

地下1階日比谷アーケード。
店舗上部の欄干には三信ビルディングの一部を
保存・復元した部材が活用されている。

Basement first floor Hibiya Arcade. Part of the Sanshin Building,
at the railing at the top of the store, saved and restored, is utilized as a design.

上：日比谷アーケードの照明と欄干。
下：地上の日比谷ステップ広場へ繋がるエ
スカレータ。

Top: Illumination and railings of Hibiya
Arcade.
Bottom: View of the escalator
connecting to Hibiya Step Square
above the ground.

2014.5–2015.8
ワークセッション8〜13 =
オフィスインテリアの検討

2014.5–2015.8
Work session 8-13 =
Consideration of office interiors

オフィスワーカーが舞うステージ

Stage where office workers dancing

■ オフィスワーカーが 主役として華やかに舞う（働く） オフィス共用空間

IL　日比谷公園に隣接し、劇場の街としての流れを汲む日比谷に佇むこの建物のコンセプトである「Dancing Tower」を継承し、主役であるオフィスワーカーが"On the Stage"で華やかに舞う（働く）、高揚感とホスピタリティを感じられるホテルのようなオフィス共用部をデザインしました。
1階では、床に施したストーンカーペットが、エントランス前の外構に設置された和泉正敏氏のストーンアートからシャトルエレベータホール、車寄せを

一気に結び付けました。このカーペットは、公園との一体感、内外の繋がりに配慮し、日比谷公園の石畳からイメージを引用しました。
9階スカイロビーへ繋がるシャトルエレベータのかご室は、堀木エリ子氏の和紙アートが映り込む幻想的な空間でゲストを楽しませてくれます。また、9階スカイロビーのエレベータホールにも内へとゲストを導くストーンカーペットを敷き、その先の受付カウンター上部に吊るされたシャンデリアアートが迎えることで、到着時の感動を与えるホテル空間のようなホスピタリティを演出しました。このアートは、ホテル等の商環境アートを手掛けるSTUDIO SAWADA DESIGNに依頼し、緩やかに垂らした

無数の細いステンレスフラットバーが光を受け煌く独創的なアートとなりました。2層吹き抜けのスカイロビー天井には、五線譜をモチーフとした照明や各種設備を納めた窪みを走らせ、「Dancing Tower」の"リズミカルさ"を大空間の中に表現しました。この五線譜は各バンクエレベータホールへ誘う装置にもなっています。
また同フロアにあるカフェや日比谷三井カンファレンス貸会議室ROOM6などは、本プロジェクトの命題であるオフィスワーカーのサード・プレイスの創出の一場面であり、スカイガーデンや公園の景色と融合した開放的な空間を演出しました。

■ Office shared spaces where office workers gaily dance(work) as lead characters

IL　Inheriting the "Dancing Tower" concept of this building standing in Hibiya which hangs over as the theatre city, adjacent to Hibiya Park, designed office shared areas like hotels where office workers who are the leading characters, feel the euphoria and hospitality when gaily dancing(working) " On the stage". On the first floor, the stone carpet on the floor ties, at a stretch, the stone art of Mr. Masatoshi Izumi installed on the outside in front of the entrance, the Shuttle elevator hall and the porch. This carpet, considering the sense of

unity with the park and the connection between inside and outside, has cited its image from the stone pavement of the Hibiya Park. The shuttle elevator cabin that connects to the 9th floor Sky Lobby, is a fantastic space reflecting Ms. Eriko Horiki's washi art and entertains guests. Again, in the 9th floor Sky Lobby's elevator hall also, a stone carpet has been laid leading the guests into the Sky Lobby, and the greeting chandelier art hanging at the top of the reception counter produces hospitality like that of a hotel space, giving an impression at the time of arrival. This art was requested STUDIO SAWADA DESIGN which works on the business environment art of hotels etc., an infinite number of loosely suspended thin stainless-steel flat bars became

creative art inspired by light. In the 2 layered, blown through ceiling of the Sky Lobby, illumination with staff notation as motif and running a hollow(dent) housing various equipment, the "rhythmicalness" of the Dancing tower has been expressed in the large space. This staff notation is also an invitation device to each bank elevator hall.
Also, the café, the rental conference room ROOM 6 of Hibiya Mitsui Conference etc., in the same floor is a scene of creation of the third place of the office worker, which is the proposition of this project and has produced an open space fused with the scenery of the Sky Garden and park.

2点：9階スカイロビーイメージスケッチ。
［2015年7月、イリア作成］

2 pictures: 9th floor Sky Lobby image sketch. [July 2015, created by Ilya Corporation]

9階スカイロビーの動線と眺望、スカイガーデンとの関係を検討したスケッチ。[2015年7月、イリア作成]

Sketch considering the flow line and view of the 9th floor Sky Lobby and the relationship with the Sky Garden. [July 2015, created by Ilya Corporation]

Town Development and Urban Planning | 街づくり・都市計画 |

エリアマネジメント法人（一般社団法人日比谷エリアマネジメント）設立（2015年3月）
Establishment of area management corporation (Hibiya Area Management) (March, 2015)

三井不動産だけでなく、地元企業、町会、商店会など地域の構成員で組織したエリアマネジメント（一般社団法人日比谷エリアマネジメント）と連携し、千代田区有地（日比谷ステップ広場の一部）や区道の維持管理や、賑わいの中心となる日比谷ステップ広場でさまざまなイベントを開催する共に、周辺施設とも連携し、地域と一体になったエリアマネジメントで日比谷の魅力を発信している。[MF]

We do not act alone. We, Mitsui Fudosan, cooperate with Hibiya Area Management which is composed of local companies, the town council and store association to maintain and manage facilities owned by Chiyoda ward (a part of Hibiya Step Square) and the ward roads. We also hold various events in Hibiya Step Square, which is the center of the bustling town, and collaborate with facilities in the vicinity of the area. We promote Hibiya with sustainable area management which is united with the local community using profits of shops in the area owned by Chiyoda ward as activity funds. [MF]

9階スカイロビー。シャトルエレベータホールと床仕上げを連続させている。
9th floor Sky Lobby. Continues the finishing of the shuttle elevator's hall and floor.

9階スカイガーデンに面したスカイラウンジ。カフェやコンビニなどのサービス店舗が設けられている。
Sky Lounge facing the 9th floor Sky Garden. Service shops such as cafe and convenience stores are set up.

9階スカイガーデン。日比谷公園の緑と連続するようランドスケープデザインが施されている。
9th floor Sky Garden. Landscaping has been designed so that it is continuous with the greenery of Hibiya Park.

PHASE 3

2014.5–2015.8
ワークセッション8〜13 =
ランドスケープデザインの検討

2014.5–2015.8
Work session 8-13 =
Consideration of landscape
design

公園のような柔らかなランドスケープ

Soft landscape like that of a park

■ **日比谷らしいオーガニックな柔らかい外構パターン**
Soft, organic outer pattern
like that of Hibiya

外構実施設計協力として途中からワークセッションへ参加したが、既に共有されたコンセプトやビジョンが模型などではっきり示されており、ゴールも明確でそれをどうつくり上げればよいかという検討に集中できた。

ワークセッションでは、チームで各地のランドスケープの事例を見学し、方向性を共有することからスタートした。選択する植栽ひとつにしても、実際にチームで見て決めるという進め方ができた。[LD]

これまでのランドスケープの提案をさらに飛躍させるため、マーカスバーネットスタジオというイギリス・ロンドンのガーデンデザイナーに参加してもらった。日比谷らしい樹木として、ケヤキとアキニレが選定された。ケヤキだけでは街路樹のようになってしまうが、枝が暴れるアキニレを入れることによって、公園らしさを表現できるのではないかと考えた。デザイナーが増えることで、当初のコンセプトに近いランドスケープが実現できた。[HA]

Though we joined the work session midway, since the shared concepts and vision were clearly shown by models etc., the goal was clear, and I was able to concentrate in considering on how to make it.

In a work session, the case of landscape of various places is observed as a team and it is started by sharing the directions. Even if one planting was selected, we could proceed to decide by looking as a team. [LS]

To further make a leap on the landscape proposal so far, participation was sought from Marcus Barnett Studio, Garden designer in London, UK. As trees, as in Hibiya, Zelkova and Ulmus parvifolia were selected. We thought that the likeness of the park could be expressed by putting Ulmus parvifolia where the branches get riotous, along with Zelkova which will be like a street tree. With the increase in designers, implementation of landscape close to the original concept was achieved. [HA]

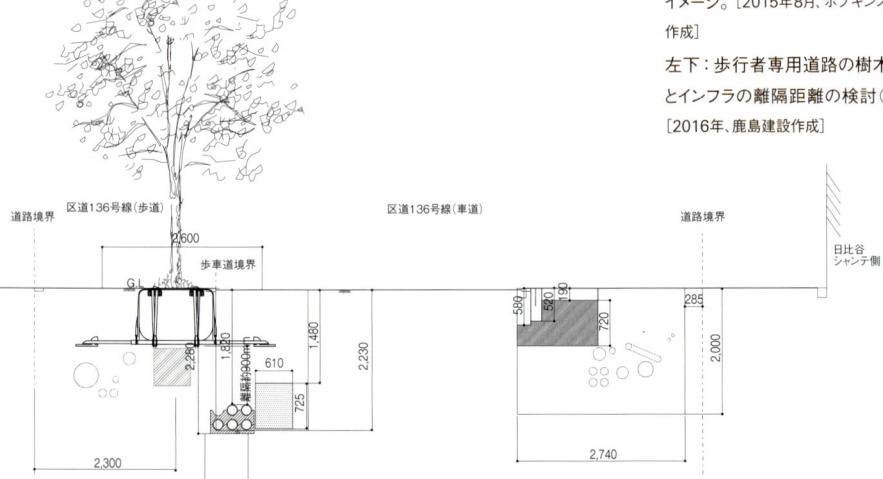

左上：日比谷仲通りのランドスケープの断面イメージ。[2015年8月、ホプキンス・アーキテクツ作成]

左下：歩行者専用道路の樹木と地下支柱とインフラの離隔距離の検討(縮尺1/100)。[2016年、鹿島建設作成]

Top Left: Cross-sectional image of the landscape of a pedestrian only road. [August 2015, created by Hopkins Architects]
Bottom Left: Consideration of the distance between trees and underground struts and infrastructure on a pedestrian only road (scale: 1/100). [2015, created by Kajima Corporation]

左下2点：日比谷仲通りの舗装モックアップ。 2 pictures on the bottom Left: Hibiya-Nakadori Street's pavement mock-up.

2点：マーカスバーネットスタジオが実際に畑を訪れ、樹木を選定。

2 pictures: Marcus Burnett studio visiting the field and selecting the trees.

東京ミットタウン日比谷と日比谷シャンテの間の日比谷仲通り。
Hibiya-Nakadori Street between Tokyo Midtown Hibiya and Hibiya Chanter.

日比谷仲通りを南西から見通す。
View of the Hibiya-Nakadori Street.

街を上品に照らし出すライティング

2015.1–
From work session 10 onwards =
Consideration of lighting design

Lighting, which elegantly illuminates the city

▎劇場の街をドラマチックに照らし出す照明計画
llumination plan that dramatically illuminates the theater city

ライティングデザインはDHAライティングというロンドンのライティングデザイン事務所にお願いした。DHAライティングは劇場の照明計画を手掛けていたバックグラウンドがあり、そのドラマティックさを建築の照明にも活かしている。マスターデザインの踊る女性のプリーツの柔らかさを表現できるよう、タワー部のラップ部分や頂部のクラウンの曲線の美しさを際立たせる照明や、日比谷通り側の石のファサードを照らす照明が提案された。[HA]オフィステナントや周囲のビルから眩しく感じないような照明計画とすることも重要だった。また、遠くからビルを眺めて適切な明るさとなっているかどうかも難しい検討だった。デザイナー提案を具現化するため、フォーライツに参画してもらい、シミュレーションや器具選定を行い現場で調整を繰り返し、実現に至った。[KD]

DHA Lighting, a lighting design office in London was requested to do the lighting design. DHA Lighting had the background of working on the illumination plan of the theater and have utilized that dramatism for architectural illumination. To express the softness of pleats of the master design's dancing lady, illumination that highlights the beauty of the curve of the crown at the top and the lap portion of the tower part and illumination that lights up the stone facade on the Hibiya-dori side, were proposed. [HA] It was important for the illumination plan that it does not appear too dazzling to office tenants or when seen from the surrounding buildings. Also, it was difficult to consider whether the building was suitably bright or not, watching it from afar. In order to realize the design proposal, FORLIGHTS were requested to participate, simulation and equipment selection were carried out and an implementation was arrived at. [KD]

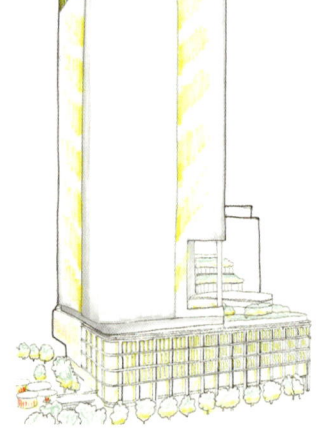

DHAライティングから提出された照明計画のイメージスケッチ。左が日比谷通り側低層部、右がタワー部の照明。光るのではなく、柔らかく照らされているイメージが提案された。[2015年10月、DHAライティング作成]

Image sketch of the illumination plan submitted by DHA lighting. On the left is the Hibiya-dori side low-rise section, tower part illumination on the right. A softly lit but not shining image, was proposed. [October 2015, created by DHA Lighting]

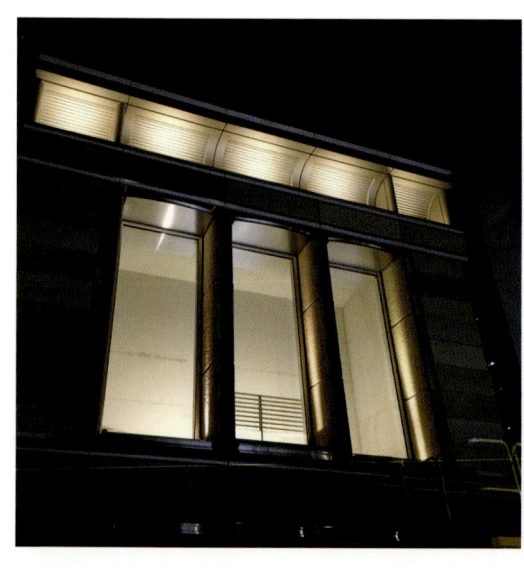

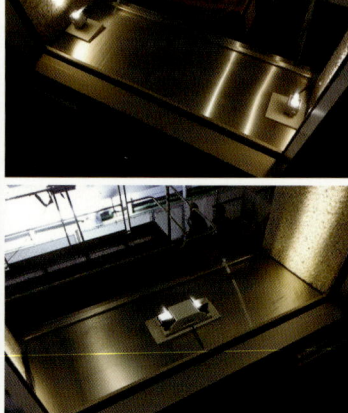

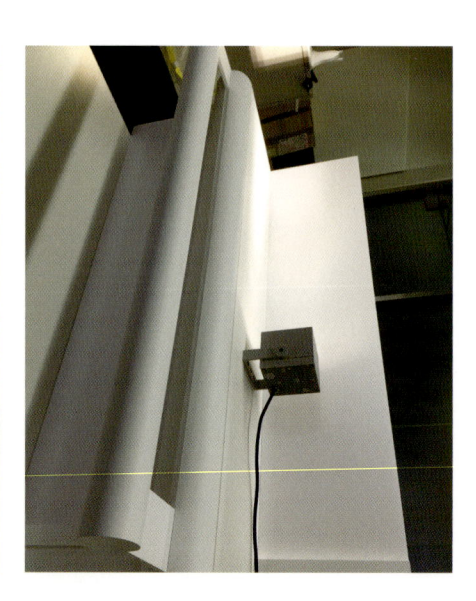

左3点：日比谷通り側低層部のライトアップテスト。

右：低層部カーテンウォールの原寸サイズの模型を製作し、照明のテストを行った。

3 pictures on the left: State of light-up test on low-rise Hibiya-dori side.
Right: Lighting test was carried out by making a full size model of the low-rise section curtain wall.

飯田橋方向から見る夕景。
Evening view from the Iidabashi direction.

アクティビティのきっかけを生むアート

2016.1
Participation of art designers

Art that will create a chance for activity

■ 和泉正敏氏による日比谷ステップ広場に ふさわしい石のアート
Befitting stone art at Hibiya Step Square by Mr. Masatoshi Izumi

左：香川県牟礼の和泉氏のアトリエでの打ち合わせ。右：工房にて石の配置を検討。

Left: Meeting at Mr. Izumi's Atelier in Mure, Kagawa prefecture. Right: Consideration of the placement of stone in the studio.

歴史を表す3つの石が 生み出す人との対話

和泉正敏［彫刻家］

3 stones revealing History, in dialogue with people visiting

Masatoshi Izumi ［Stone sculptor］

日比谷通りを挟んで西側に日比谷公園が位置する広大な地に、東京ミッドタウン日比谷は建設されました。建物内から皇居、丸の内ビル街が一望できる建築の基礎工事が行われている頃、ビル関係者一同が瀬戸内海の石を調べに香川県・牟礼に来てくれました。そこで完成時の想いを交わし、石置き場でもいろいろな意見が出てきました。

周辺には皇居の石積みや、日比谷公園の素晴らしい石も多いのですが、周りの環境に合った、東京ミッドタウン日比谷にふさわしい石の選定が始まりました。

候補として選ばれた石は、雨風に晒された永い年月を経過した肌が美しい自然の形状で、250年ほど前に割られた大きい2個の石肌にはその歴史が表れています。

日比谷ステップ広場脇の通路のために、3個の瀬戸内海の石と庵治石を組み合わせた「明」をつくりました。敷石と夜の照明、荷重、安全、搬入に至るまで、何度も東京と牟礼の地で意見交換を行いました。

石は人間の魂をも支え、太陽、月、時間の光といったそれぞれの美が石と人との関係を生み出します。

この日比谷の石「明」と、東京ミッドタウン日比谷を訪れる人との対話が楽しみです。

Tokyo Midtown Hibiya was built on the west side across Hibiya-dori, in the vast area where Hibiya Park is located. Around the time when the foundation work of the building, from where there is an unbroken view of the Imperial Palace and Marunouchi Building Street, was done, all the authorized people concerned with the building, visited Mure, Kagawa prefecture to examine stones from Seto Inland Sea. There, with thoughts arising regarding the completion, various opinions arose even at the stone yard.

Though there were the Imperial Palace's masonry and the many wonderful stones of Hibiya Park around, the selection of stones suiting the surrounding environment began in Tokyo Midtown Hibiya. The candidate stone selected, with a beautiful natural shape with a natural texture due to its exposure to wind and rains for a long time, on two large textured stones split about 250 years ago, depicts that history. For the pathway by the side of Hibiya Step Square, "*Mei: Sun and Moon*" was made combining 3 stones from Seto Inland Sea and Aji stones. Many opinion exchanges were carried out in Tokyo and Mure until the carrying in, safety, loading, paving of stones and night illumination were done.

Stones support the soul of human beings and each of these beauty - the sun, moon, light of the time - creates a relationship between stones and people.

A dialogue with people visiting this stone of Hibiya "*Mei: Sun and Moon*" and Tokyo Midtown Hibiya, is a pleasure.

上：日比谷ステップ広場に設けられた和泉氏によるアート「明」。左下：9階スカイロビー天井に設置されたSTUDIO SAWADA DESIGNによるシャンデリアアート。右下：9階スカイガーデンに設置されたNicolas Fedorenkoによる「Hopeful」。（アートディレクション：TOSHIO SHIMIZU ART OFFICE）

Top: Art "*Mei*: Sun and Moon" set up in Hibiya Step Square by Mr. Izumi. Bottom Left: Chandelier art installed on the 9th floor Sky Lobby ceiling by STUDIO SAWADA DESIGN. Bottom Right: "Hopeful" (Art direction: TOSHIO SHIMIZU ART OFFICE) installed in 9th floor Sky Garden by Nicolas Fedorenko.

左上：シャトルエレベータホールからかご室を見る。右上：かご室。8基あるかご室はすべて異なる意匠となっている。下：1階シャトルエレベータホール。

Top Left: View of the cabin from the Shuttle Elevator Hall. Top Right: Cabin. All the 8 cabins are of different design. Bottom: First floor Shuttle Elevator Hall.

伝統産業の和紙と最先端技術の融合がつくり出す豊かな空間

堀木エリ子 ［和紙デザイナー］

A Rich Space Created by the Fusion of Traditional Japanese Industry of Washi and the State-of-the-Art Technology

Eriko Horiki ［Washi designer］

「建築空間に生きる和紙造形の創造」をテーマに仕事に取り組み、30周年を迎えた頃に、「エレベータの中に和紙作品を」という、今回のご依頼をいただきました。通常の建築空間以上に多くの機能性が求められるエレベータの中で、新たな抄紙技術の開発と共に進めてきた、燃えない、汚れない、破れない、退色しない、精度を上げるという二次加工を、最大限に活かした表現にしたいと思いました。和紙合わせガラスの加工は、万一割れても破片が落下しない安全性があり、表面に無反射加工を施して和紙の質感を損なわない技術でできています。

和紙のデザインは、「Dancing Tower」という東京ミッドタウン日比谷のコンセプトを受けて、軽やかなステップの曲線の軌道を「透かし」という手法で、リボン状に漉き上げました。和紙素材を和的に表現するのではなく、オフィス空間への動線にふさわしい、和洋の域を超えた心地よさを目指しました。

また光を透過する効果のある和紙は、適度に映り込みのある素材や鏡と組み合わせて、小さな空間が万華鏡のように広がる効果を生み出しています。

導光板による現代の最先端技術の光源と、伝統的な手漉き和紙を融合させることで、用途や機能を広げ、伝統産業を未来へ、世界へと広げていくための新たな一歩に繋がりました。

At the time about thirty years passed since I have worked under the theme "Creation of washi (traditional Japanese paper) art & design which can be utilized in architectural spaces," I got this job offer, which is to "incorporate washi works in elevators." Elevators are required to have more functionalities than common architectural spaces. In such environment, I was hoping to create washi works making the most of secondary processing, which is to make washi works non-flammable, antifouling, untearable, and antifading, as well as making them more precise. I have worked on this secondary processing along with the development of new papermaking technology. The laminated glass combined with washi is safe because even in the event of being damaged, its debris won't fall. Further, it incorporates the technology for preventing the texture of washi from being deteriorated, by making the surface non-reflective. As for the design of washi, under the concept of "Dancing Tower" of Tokyo Midtown Hibiya, I used the method of "Sukashi" (watermarking) to draw curved tracks in ribbon shapes, expressing springy steps. Instead of using washi material as traditional Japanese expression, I tried to make it suitable for flow lines in the office space, for achieving comfort beyond the border of Japanese and western culture.

Since washi transmits light, when used with mirrors or other moderately reflective materials, they create an effect like a kaleidoscope, and a small space seems broadened.

When a light source using a light guide plate, which is modern state-of-the-art technology and traditional hand-made washi are fused, they expanded the applications and functions. They led us to a new step to develop a traditional industry to the future and the world.

■ オフィス来訪者の気持ちを高める和紙を用いたエレベータのかご室空間
Elevator cabin space with washi, lifting the spirits of office visitors

左：モックアップの検討。
中：紙漉きの様子。
右：受け入れ検査の様子。

Left: Consideration of mockup.
Middle: State of paper making.
Right: State of acceptance testing.

着工に向けて1番列車を走らせる
―実施設計1

Run train No.1 oriented towards starting the construction
– The execution design 1

■ 着工に向けたテクニカルな
デザインのブラッシュアップ

KD 全体の大きなスケジュールの中で着工を守るために、まず1番列車の実施設計をとりまとめました。作図の中では各種申請や認可もクリアし、着工を可能にするコンディションを整えることが、1番列車の実施設計でのミッションでした。

たとえば、DD図で示された形とディテールに対し、施工性・品質・コスト・法規と、プランの整合性・合理性の観点から、技術検討を行いました。また、安心安全な建物を実現するための構造計画やBCP対策など、精度を高めた検討も行いました。テクニカルな部分を建築デザインへブラッシュアップしていく検討を6～8カ月ほど継続していきました。

MF これまでのデザイン案に対して、事業性を確認する必要があります。さらに押さえておかなければいけない性能をきめ細かく確認しました。また、コスト面でのVE案の要求や運営管理の視点も明確にしてお伝えしました。たとえばオフィスでいうと、コア回りの貸室の形状をできるだけ整形にしたかったので、曲率を若干変えたり、設備や階段の配置などを工夫してもらいながら、全体としての印象は絶対変えないよう、どこまで許容できるかスタディを繰り返しました。

HA デザインに関わるVEや設計上の変更は、うまくワークセッションに乗せていただき、チームで一緒になって丁寧に検証を行いました。

■ 建物を支える構造計画
Structural plan to support the building

2011年3月11日に発生した東日本大震災後、将来起こり得る東海・東南海・南海地震をはじめとした巨大地震への対応が必要とされている。建築用制震ダンパーとして世界初となる振動エネルギー回生システムVERS（Vibration Energy Recovery System）を搭載した新世代制震オイルダンパー「HiDAX-R（Revolution）」を鹿島建設で開発し、今回初めて実適用した。

解析モデルに東日本大震災時に観測された地震動を入力し地震時および地震終了後の建物の揺れの違いを検証した。制震装置を鋼製ダンパーのみとしたケースと比較すると、揺れ幅が約半減、後揺れの時間が1/9に低減され、より安心な建物であることを確認した。[KD]

After the Great East Japan Earthquake on 11th March, 2011, it is necessary to take measures for huge earthquakes that may occur in future including the Tokai, Tonankai and Nankai Earthquakes. This tower is the first structure in the world to feature the high-performance oil damper "HiDAX-R (Revolution)" which is equipped with vibration energy recovery system, it's developed by Kajima Corporation. In order to verify the effect of the new oil dampers, we analyzed by seismic motion observed in the Great East Japan Earthquake. It is possible to reduce the tremor amplitude to about half and shorten the vibration convergence time to 1/9th after the end of the earthquake compared with the building which have only the steel damper for the damping devices. So not only the seismic performance of the building but also the secure performance can be greatly improved. [KD]

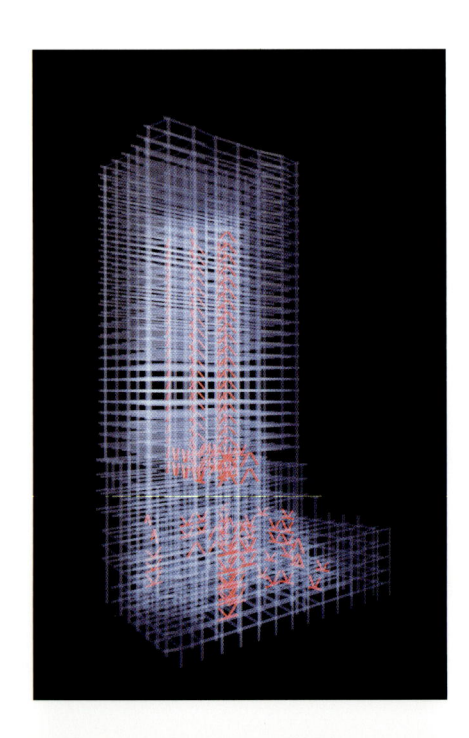

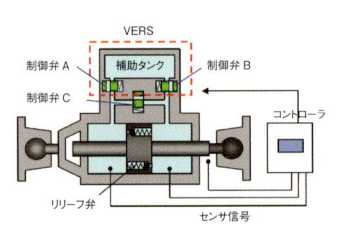

左：建物全体の構造CG。赤い部分が制震装置。右上2点：HiDAX-Rの外観（左）と内部機構の概念図（右）。右下：東日本大震災の東京・大手町での記録に対する解析。[いずれも、2015年7月、KAJIMA DESIGN作成]

Left: Structure of whole building CG. Red part is the damping device. Top Two on the right: Appearance of HiDAX-R (Left) and conceptual diagram of internal mechanism (Right). Bottom Right: Analysis of records of the Great East Japan Earthquake at Tokyo, Otemachi. [all images: July 2015, created by KAJIMA DESIGN]

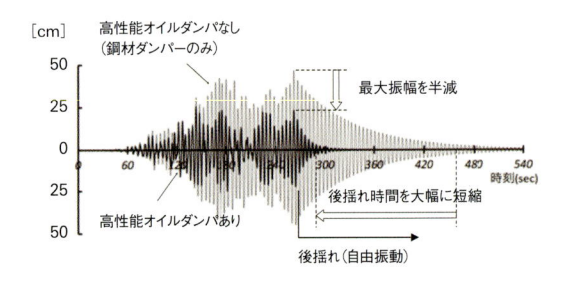

■ Technical design brush-up oriented towards starting the construction

KD   Since the start of construction date was fixed as the whole big schedule, the execution design of train No.1 was compiled. Since various applications and authorizations were required during the construction, it was a mission of the execution design of train No.1 to clear all those and prepare the conditions for starting the construction.

For example, corresponding to the exterior line and design detail shown in the Design Development Document (DD document), technology was considered from the perspective of workability, quality, cost, regulations, consistency and rationality of the plan. Also, structural plan and BCP countermeasures etc., to realize the construction of a safe and secure building, were considered with high accuracy. The study to brush up the technical parts to architectural design was also continued for around six to eight months.

MF   It is necessary to confirm the feasibility of the design proposal so far. Further, indispensable performance was determined and studied in detail. Also, in terms of cost, we also clarified the view points of the requirements and management control of the VE plan and conveyed the same. For example, in the office part, since we wanted to give good shaping to the rental rooms around the core, we changed the curvature slightly, while devising the placement of facilities and stairs, we repeatedly studied how much can be allowed, in such a way that the total impression remained the same.

HA   Design related VE and any design changes, were well included in the work sessions and verification was carried out carefully by the team.

低層階に大空間を必要とするTOHOシネマ
ズ 日比谷のシアターやアトリウムが計画され
ているため、上層部を支えている6本の柱を、
M6〜8階の3層をまたぐ三角形状のトランス
ファー架構により支持することで、高層からの
高い柱軸力を隣接する柱に伝達させ、下階
の吹き抜け空間を可能とした。[KD]

Because a large open space is required for some theaters of TOHO Cinemas Hibiya and the Atrium of commercial zone on the lower floors, six columns supporting the upper floors are replaced with the large triangular transfer frames to be transmitted the columnar force of the upper floor to the adjacent columns. [KD]

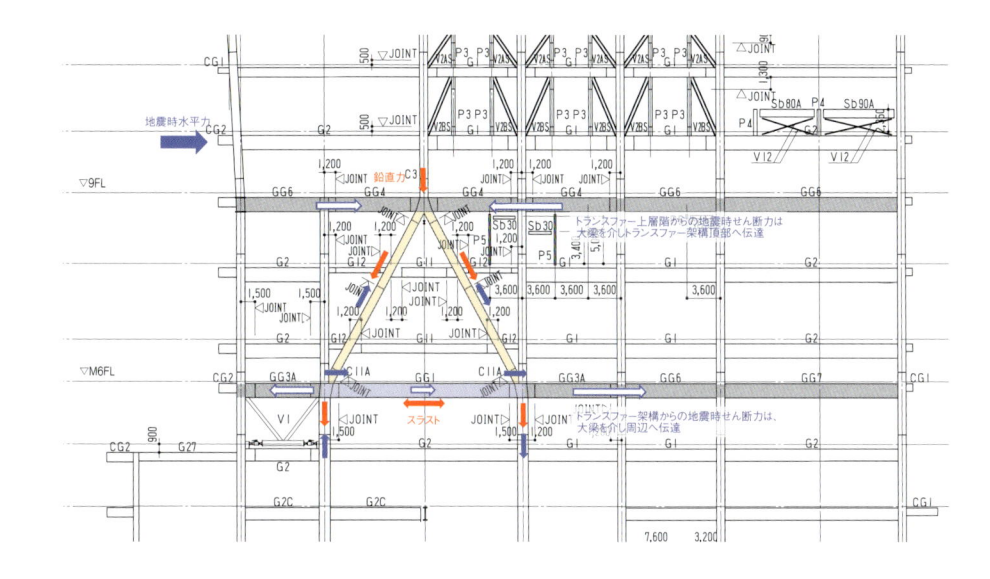

M6〜9階のトランスファー架構概念断面。
[2015年7月、KAJIMA DESIGN作成]

Transfer conceptual sectional diagram of structure from M6th to 9th floor . [July 2015, created by KAJIMA DESIGN]

左：パイルド・ラフト基礎の解析モデル。工
期短縮、基礎躯体合理化のため逆打工法
を採用し、逆打用杭基礎を本設利用し直接
基礎との併用基礎とした。[2015年7月、
KAJIMA DESIGN作成]

右：建物角部の約30mの長柱を見る。上
下に取り合う梁の剛性、層の水平剛性、初
期不整や地震時の水平変位を考慮した弾
性座屈解析による検証、断面設計を行うこと
で、7〜11階までの建物角部が一部切り欠
かれた建築計画を実現。

Left: Analysis model for piled raft foundation. The piled raft foundation is adopted to be rationalized the foundation of this building, it was possible to reduce the construction period by the inverted construction method.

Right: View of the long column. The middle part of the west side of the tower has been scooped except for the about 30m long column which supports at the corner of the high-rise building. In the design of this column, it is demonstrated that the cross section is safe through elastic buckling analysis considering with the condition of the peripheral members.

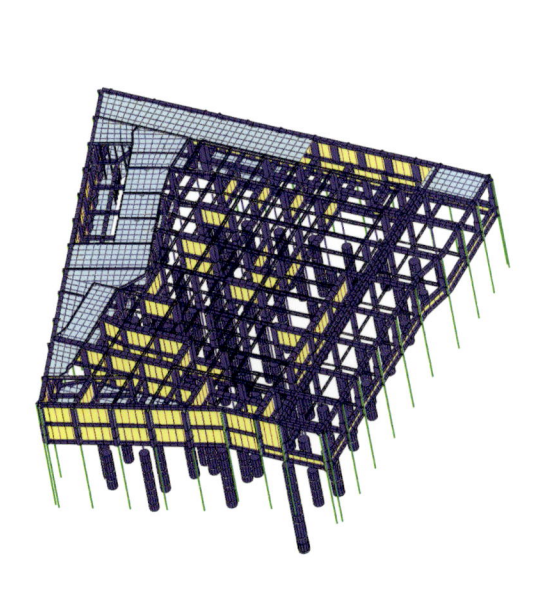

日比谷公園側からタワー部の切り欠き部分を支える長柱を見る。
View of the long column supporting the notch of the tower section from Hibiya Park side.

安心安全のためのBCP計画
BCP plan for safety and security

さまざまな人が集う拠点施設として、国内最高水準の安心安全の提供が重要となる。千代田区最大級となる帰宅困難者の一時滞在施設（約5,800m²）を整備し、災害用備品を保管する備蓄倉庫（約200m²）を確保。約3,000人の帰宅困難者を受け入れることができる。さらにデジタルサイネージ等を利用して、帰宅困難者に災害時の情報提供を行う。また、災害時の電力供給の自立性を高め

る取り組みとして、ガスコージェネレーションシステムを導入。ガス供給は耐震性能に優れた中圧導管で行い、さらにA重油、中圧導管双方に対応したデュアルフューエル型非常用発電機など、高効率で自立性の高いエネルギーシステムを採用。災害時には日比谷ステップ広場や地域冷暖房（DHC）施設にも電力供給を行う。［MF］

As a base facility where various people gather, it becomes important to provide the highest standard of safety and security in the country. Consolidate a temporary accommodation facility (about 5,800m²) for those who find it difficult to return home, which will become the largest ranking in Chiyoda-ku, secure an emergency storehouse (about 200m²) for safekeeping of disaster equipment. Approximately 3,000 people who find it difficult to return home can be accepted. Furthermore, using digital signage etc., provide information on disasters to those who find it difficult to return

home. Also, introduced a gas cogeneration system as an effort to increase the autonomy of electricity supply in the event of a disaster. Gas supply is carried out with medium pressure conduit excellent in seismic performance, furthermore, it adopts high efficiency self-sustaining energy system such as dual fuel type emergency generator corresponding to both A heavy oil and medium pressure pipe. In the event of a disaster, it will also supply power to neighboring Hibiya Step Square and District Heating and Cooling (DHC) facilities. [MF]

設備配置の構成図。［2014年5月、KAJIMA DESIGN作成］

Configuration diagram of facility arrangement. [May 2014, created by KAJIMA DESIGN]

[高圧変電設備]
・高層事務室用、低層事務室用、商業用を分散して配置
・二次側負荷近くに計画し、エネルギーロスが少なく、合理的

マネジメントオフィス

[コージェネレーション設備]
・高効率ガスエンジン発電機による電力と蒸気の効率的な利用による環境負荷の低減
・中圧導管による常用発電

[中央熱源（DHC施設）]
・地域冷暖房の主機械室

[非常用発電機設備]
・A重油と都市ガス（中圧）のデュアルフューエルタイプとし、ガス供給が継続している場合には長時間運転可能
・BCP時備蓄燃料にて保安電力の供給を行う

[特別高圧受変電設備]
・特別高圧受変電設備は浸水被害のない8階に設置

防災センター

[水槽類・中水設備・雨水排水再利用・井戸ろ過設備]
・水槽類・中水設備は水密区画内で水没時も利用可能な対応
・雨水、空調ドレン水、冷却塔ブロー水を再利用
・BCP対応時に防災井戸を利用

[A重油オイルタンク]
・非常用発電機連続運転72時間分（3日分）の備蓄

[蓄熱槽]
・建物内エネルギー需要の平準化で高効率運用
・BCP対応時に利用

[中央熱源（DHC施設）]
・地域冷暖房の供給を受ける
・浸水被害のない水密機械室に計画

特別高圧線
中圧ガス管
油配管
上水引込管

PHASE 3

■ デザインと品質・施工性を両立させる
Make design, quality and constructability compatible

高層部外装のプリーツの形状について、DD図では平面段差が400mmであったが、型材構成や基準階からの眺望などを合わせて検討し、最終的に255mmの段差へと変更を行った。また、外装の曲率とアルミカーテンウォール型材の整理を行い、5種類の型材をプラスマイナス1度の組み合わせバリエーションで、曲面を描く高層部の全体を構成することが可能となった。[KD]

Regarding the shape of the pleats on the high-rise exterior, the level difference in the DD documents was 400mm, but by examining the configuration of the metal profiles and the view from the typical floors, the difference was eventually changed to 255mm. In addition, coordinating the curvature of the exterior and aluminum curtain wall profiles allowed the entire curved high rise part to be constructed with five types of profiles variously combined at plus and minus one degree. [KD]

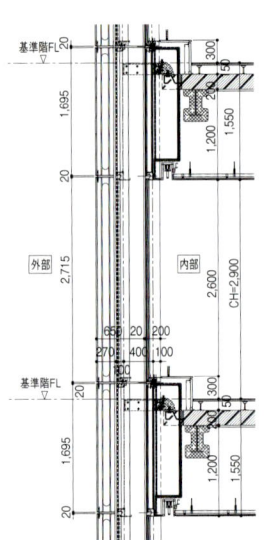

断面詳細　縮尺1/100
Sectional detail | scale: 1/100

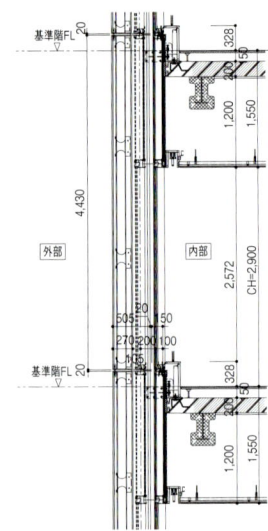

断面詳細　縮尺1/100
Sectional detail | scale: 1/100

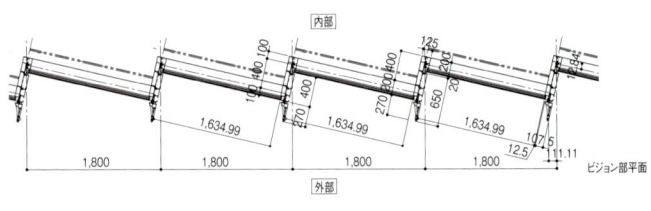

平面詳細　縮尺1/100
Detailed plan | scale: 1/100

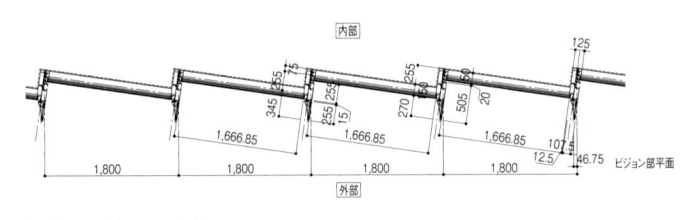

平面詳細　縮尺1/100
Detailed plan | scale: 1/100

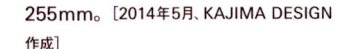

高層部アルミカーテンウォールの形状検討。左が平面段差400mm、右が平面段差255mm。[2014年5月、KAJIMA DESIGN作成]

Consider the shape of the high-rise area aluminum curtain wall. On the left, planar step 400mm, on the right, flat step 255mm. [May 2014, created by KAJIMA DESIGN]

高層部カーテンウォール。
High-rise curtain wall.

2014.12–
デザイナー定例スタート

2014.12–
Designer regular meeting start

デザインを実現する設計図面への落とし込み

Capture the drawing for design creation

■ DD図を基にデザイン議論で深化させる
Deepen in the design discussion based on Design Development Document

1番列車の実施設計が進む一方、たとえば低層部のファサードの検討などまだ議論しきれていない部分が残っていた。そこで、DD図をベースとしつつ、デザイナーであるホプキンス・アーキテクツと日建設計、KAJIMA DESIGNと鹿島建設の施工部門のメンバーで直接コミュニケーションを取り、CGや模型、モックアップなどを用いて検討を行った。[KD]

As the execution design 1 of train No.1 was going on, there were still parts remained that were not yet discussed, such as considering the facade on the low-rise. Therefore, not only the Design Development Document (DD document), but with the DD document as a base, discussions were carried out using CG, model, mockup etc., establishing direct communication with the designers Hopkins Architects and Nikken Sekkei, KAJIMA DESIGN and members of the construction division of Kajima Corporation. [KD]

デザイナー定例時の低層部ファサードの検討。左2点：模型写真。右：DD図の意図を施工者と共有するための、基準となる設計資料。[2014年11月、KAJIMA DESIGN作成]

Consideration of low-rise facade at the designer regular meeting. 2 pictures on the left: photo of the model. Right: Drawing for communicating clearly, the construction contents of the DD document to the constructor. [November 2014, created by KAJIMA DESIGN]

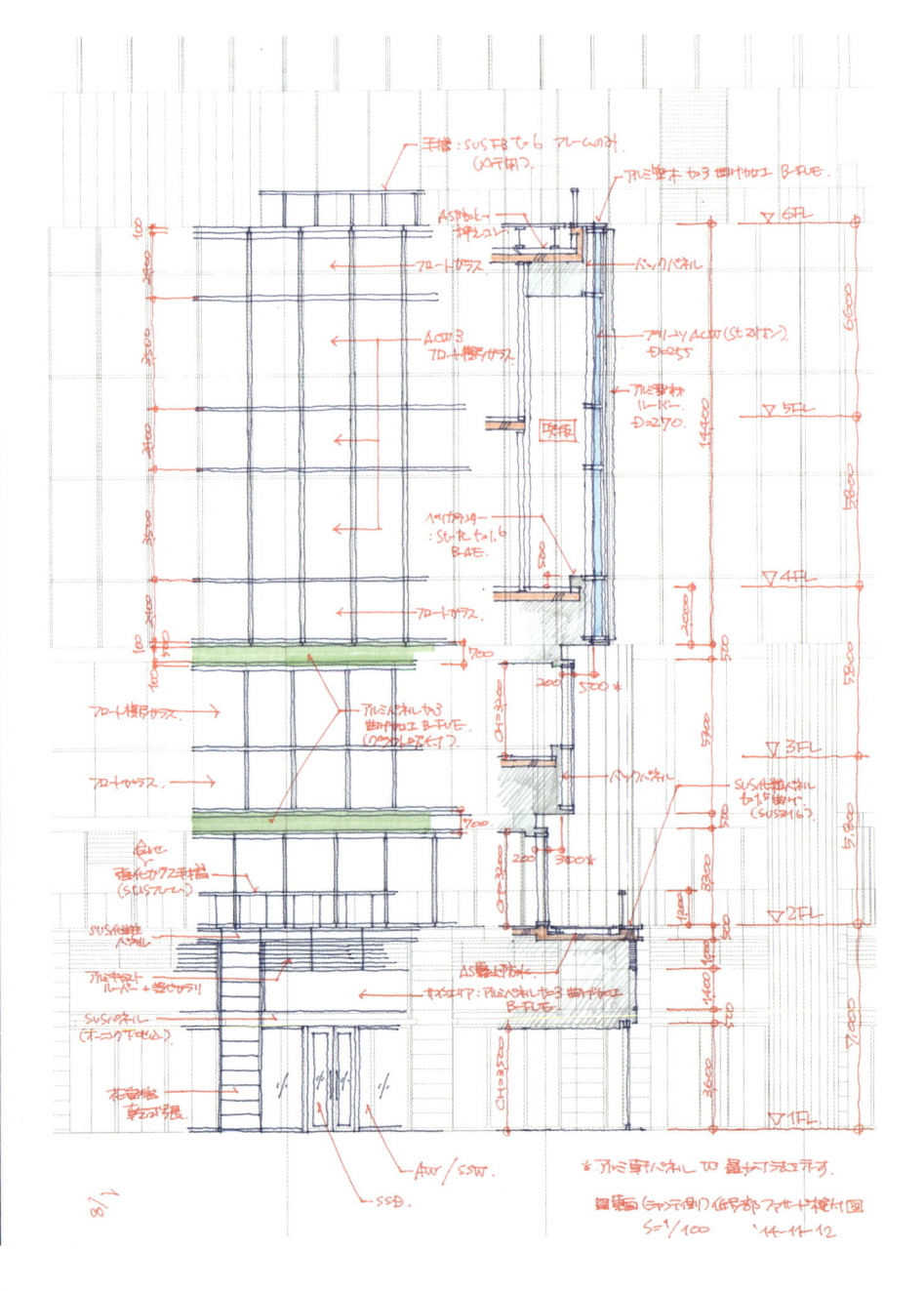

2点：デザイナー定例の様子。現場でモックアップを前にデザイナーと設計者、施工者が議論を行う。

2 pictures: State of designer regular. Designer, architect and constructor carry out discussion before mock-up on site.

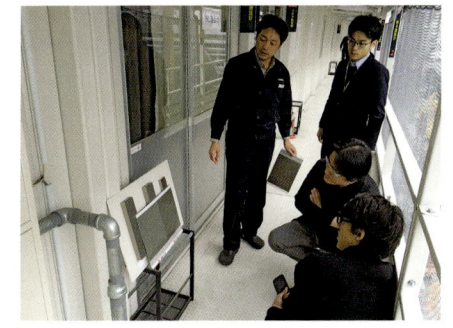

デザイナー定例時のパークビューガーデンの検討。
左：模型写真。右：DD図の意図を施工者と共有するための、基準となる設計資料。
［2014年12月、KAJIMA DESIGN作成］

Verification of Park View Garden at the designer regular meeting.
Left: photo of the model. Right: Drawing for communicating clearly, the construction contents of the DD document to the constructor.
[December 2014, created by KAJIMA DESIGN]

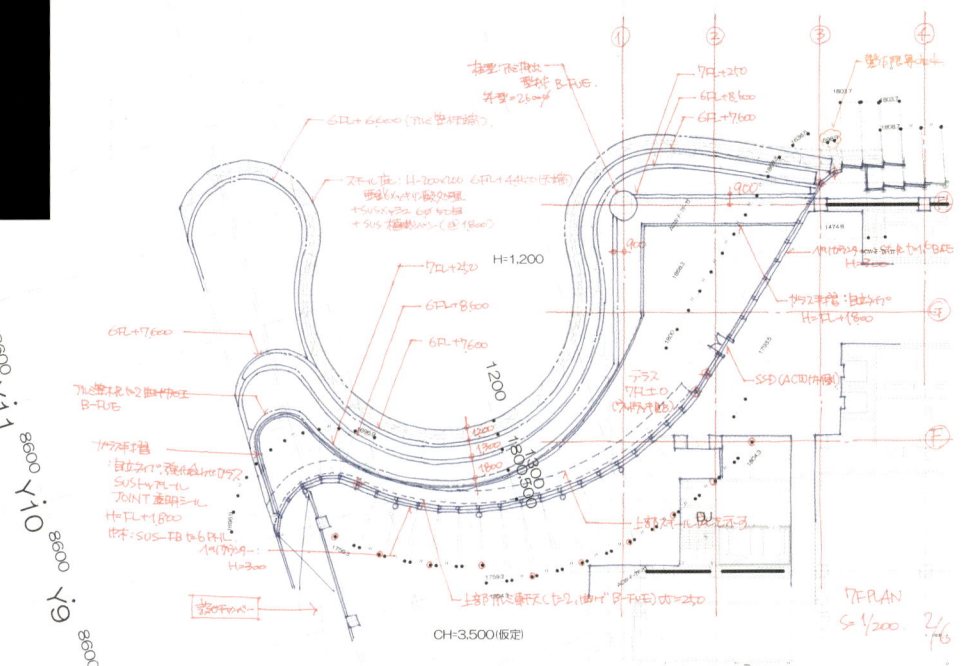

デザイナー定例時の商業エリアのエントランスの検討。
左：模型写真。右：設計デザインの意図を共有するためのディテールスケッチ。［2015年9月、KAJIMA DESIGN作成］

Verification of commercial zone entrance at the designer regular meeting.
Left: photo of the model. Right: Detail drawing for communicating the construction contents of the design.
[September 2015, created by KAJIMA DESIGN]

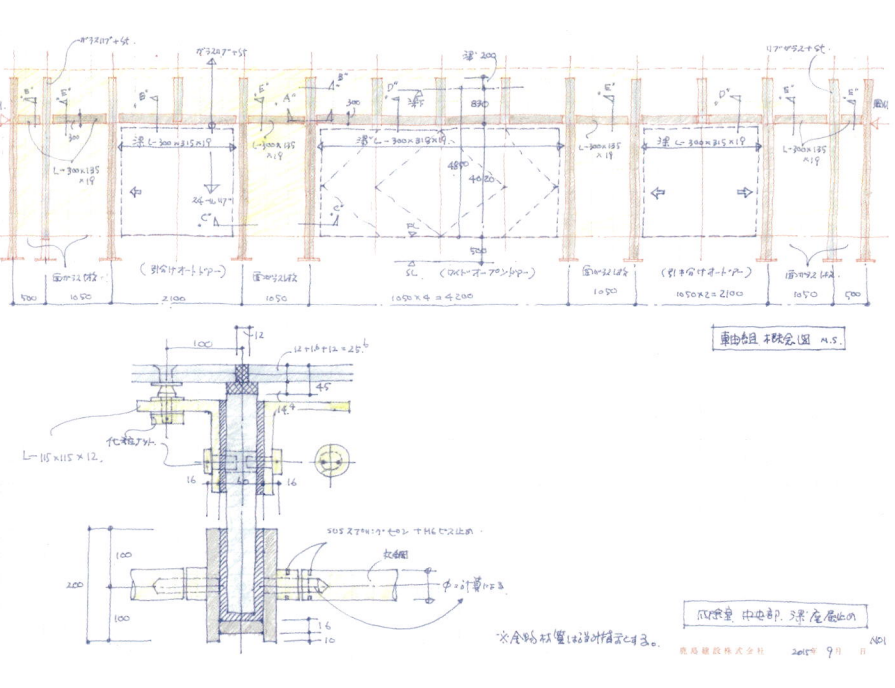

PHASE 3

総合検討を深めるための
2番列車を走らせる―実施設計2

Run train No.2 for comprehensive study
– The execution design 2

▌テナント像や使われ方をイメージしたオフィス基準階
Office standard floor with the visualization of tenant image and its usage

1番列車の実施設計における検討を深度化し、建物設計の品質をより高めるために、プラン整理をさらに進め、外装ディテールのブラッシュアップと合理化、コアアメニティの向上、動線の整理など、各種品質向上を進めた。また外装割り付けや詳細ディテール等、設計段階でのデザイン検討を繰り返し、デザインチームの合意を形成した。［KD］

オフィスを検討するにあたり、どういう企業にご入居いただけるかを議論した。1棟貸しではなく、キーテナントが2〜3社いるマルチテナントとなることをイメージしながらオフィス設計を進めていった。［MF］

By deepening the content of consideration in train No.1's of the execution design, in order to increase the quality of the exterior design, we promoted various quality improvements such as further advancing the plan adjustment, brushing up and rationalization of exterior details, improving core amenities, organizing flow lines etc. We repeated the design considerations at the design stage such as overall assignment and finer details and made a design team agreement. [KD]

In connection with office consideration, the location of tenant's target was discussed. Since everyone could not be loaned to a single company, it would become multi-tenants and we visualized that the key tenants could be placed in two to three companies. [MF]

オフィスの基準階プランの検討（縮尺1/800）。左が実施設計1、右が実施設計2。エレベータの台数と階段位置、機械室構成などを調整し、アメニティの向上を図った。［2014年11月、KAJIMA DESIGN作成］

Consideration of typical office floor plan (scale: 1/800). On the left, at the time of train No.1 of the execution design 1, on the right, at the time of train No.2 of the execution design 2. The number of elevators, the stair position, machine room composition etc. were adjusted and amenity improvisations were planned. [November 2014, created by KAJIMA DESIGN]

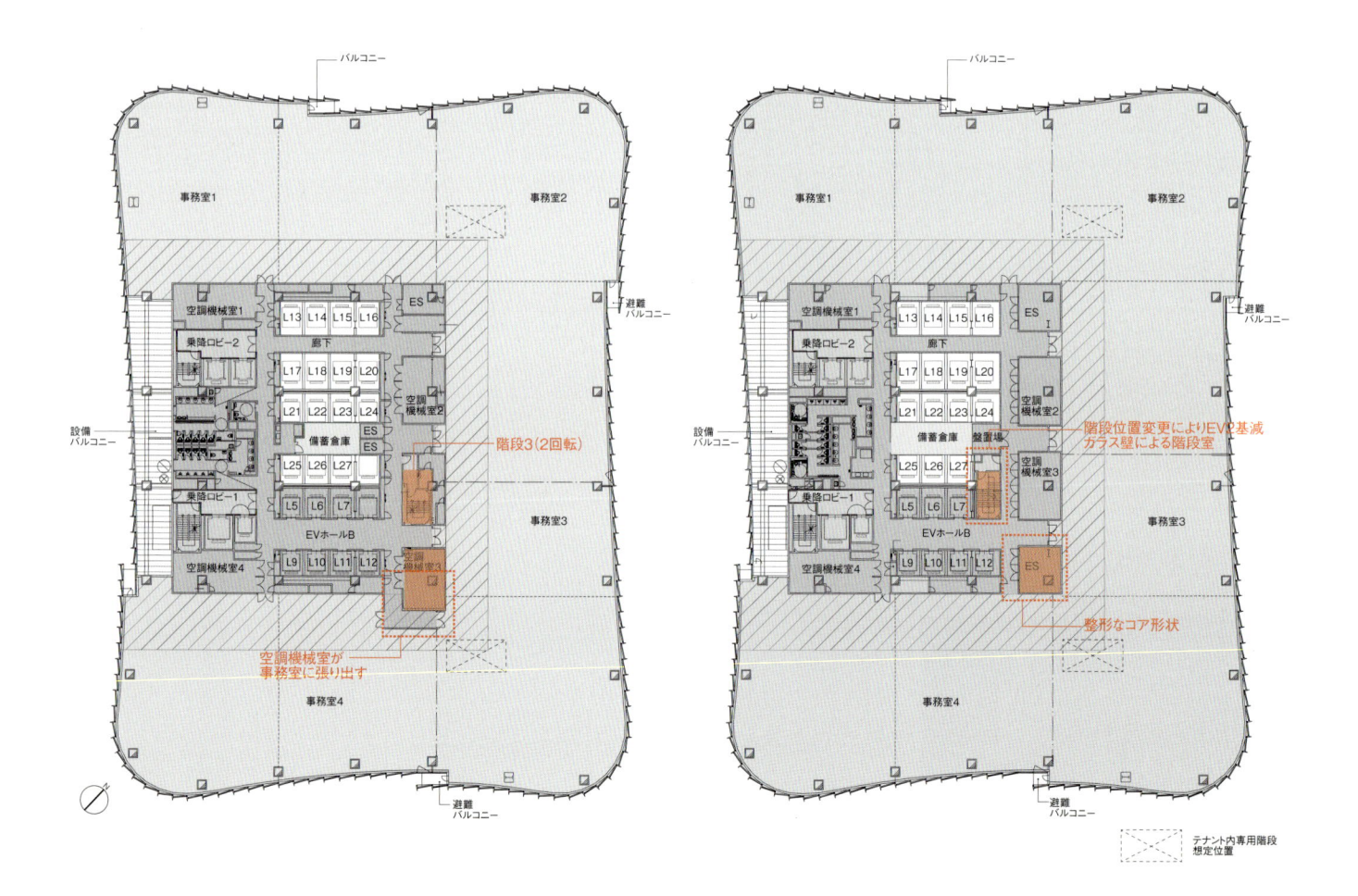

基準階オフィスのコーナー部を見る。
View of the typical office floor corner.

左上：32～33階に設けられたオフィスフロア テナントワーカー専用ラウンジスペース。左下： オフィス基準階男子トイレの手洗いスペース。

右上：オフィス基準階廊下から階段室が見 える。

右下：オフィス基準階の設備バルコニー。

Top Left: Lounge space exclusively for office floor tenant workers, set up on floors 32 and 33. Bottom Left: typical office floor washroom space for male

toilet. Top Right: Staircase hall can be seen from the typical office floor corridor. Bottom: Facility balcony of the typical office floor.

PHASE 3

■ 基準階のトイレのプランニング
Planning of toilets on a standard floor

トイレ部分の有効スペースを拡大することで、個数可変式プランの採用や採光窓の実現、マルチパーパスブースの設置やインターロッキング式だれでもトイレの設置など、Sクラスビルにふさわしい、ユニークで高品質なゆとりあるトイレプランを実現した。[KD]

By expanding the effective space of the toilet part, we were able to adopt a variable number plan with lighting window implementation, installation of a multipurpose booth, interlocking and an anyone-can-install toilet, thereby realizing a unique, high quality and clear toilet plan suitable for S class building. [KD]

左：オフィス基準階のトイレプラン検討（縮尺1/120）。男子トイレの大2室に男女間の間仕切りが移動可能な仕組みを採用し、女性比率の高いテナントニーズに対応できる。

［2015年4月、KAJIMA DESIGN作成］
右：トイレ手洗いスペースのデザインスケッチ。［2015年4月、イリア作成］

Left: Consideration of toilet plan of office standard (scale 1/120). By adopting a mechanism where the partitioning between the male and female can move into the two large rooms of a male toilet, we can respond to tenant needs with high female ratio. [April 2015, created by KAJIMA DESIGN]
Right: Design sketch of washroom space in the toilet. [April 2015, created by Ilya Corporation]

■ シャトルエレベータの滞留シミュレーション
Congestion simulation of shuttle elevator

シャトルエレベータの利用では、出社時や昼食時など利用が集中する可能性が高い時間帯に、当初目標に対して輸送能力の不足がないかどうか、想定される利用者が、シャトルエレベータの乗降時に利用するエレベータホールほかの近傍スペースにて乗降待ち等、問題なく一定時間滞留可能かをシミュレーションにより確認した。[KD]

For shuttle elevator usage, its operation during concentrated usage timings such as arrival time at work or lunch time etc., whether there is any shortage of transport capacity relative to the initial target, whether the assumed users can wait in a nearby space other than the elevator hall used when getting on or off the shuttle elevator and stay for a certain period without problems etc., were confirmed by simulation. [KD]

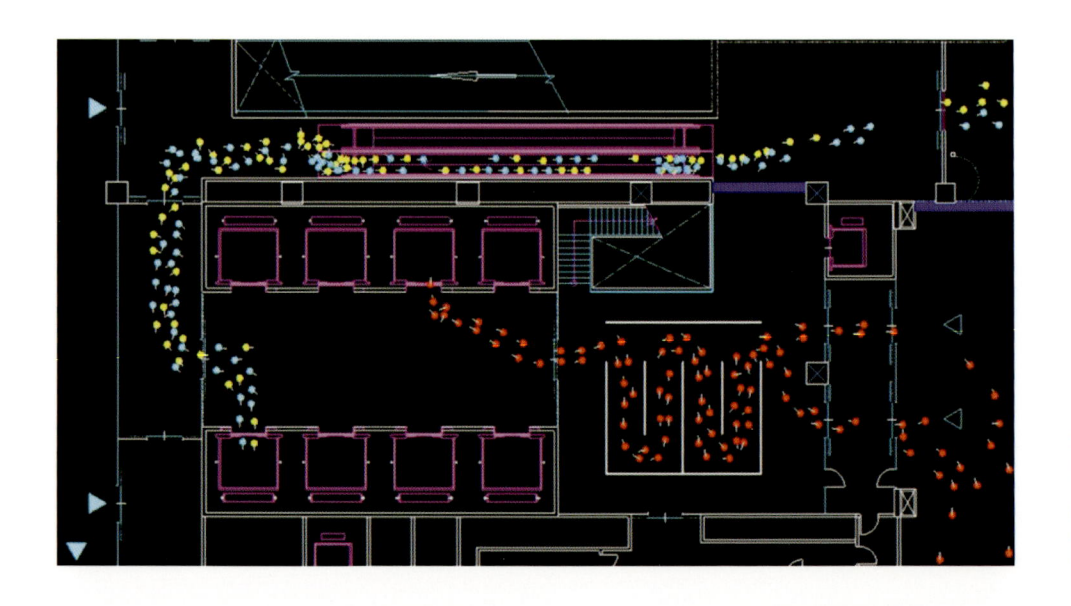

シャトルエレベータの滞留シミュレーション。［2014年7月、KAJIMA DESIGN作成］

Congestion simulation of shuttle elevator. [July 2014, created by KAJIMA DESIGN]

■ タワー部ファサードのラップ部分
Lap part of tower facade

基準階に4カ所あるラップ部分に設定されていた避難バルコニーが、法的要件や構造的要件、また安全性確保の面でDD図の意図を満たしていなかったため、2方向避難をラップ部分のバルコニーを介さずに成立させるコアプランを再検討し、ラップ部分の避難バルコニー機能を中止した。またラップ部分に設定されていたアルミカーテンウォールのユニット数を2ユニットから1ユニットへ削減し構成を合理化することで、基準階有効面積の拡大および意匠性の向上と合わせ、コスト削減や施工性・品質の向上も同時に実現した。[KD]

Since the evacuation balcony, set at 4 locations in the lap portions of a standard floor, did not satisfy the intention of the DD document from the view point of legal requirements, structural requirements and safety assurance in terms of design, the core plan to establish two-way evacuation without going through the lap portion's balcony was reconsidered and the lap section's evacuation balcony function was cancelled. The unit number of aluminum curtain wall was reduced from 2 units to 1 unit and its composition was rationalized. That fulfilled cost saving, improvement of constraints of construction and quality as well as expansion of standard floor effective area and improvement of design. [KD]

ラップ部分の形状検討。左がカーテンウォールを2ユニット分のラップ、右が1ユニット分のラップ。[2015年4月、鹿島建設作成]

Shape consideration of the lap portion. On the left, 2 units lap of curtain wall, on the right, 1 unit lap. [April 2015, created by Kajima Corporation]

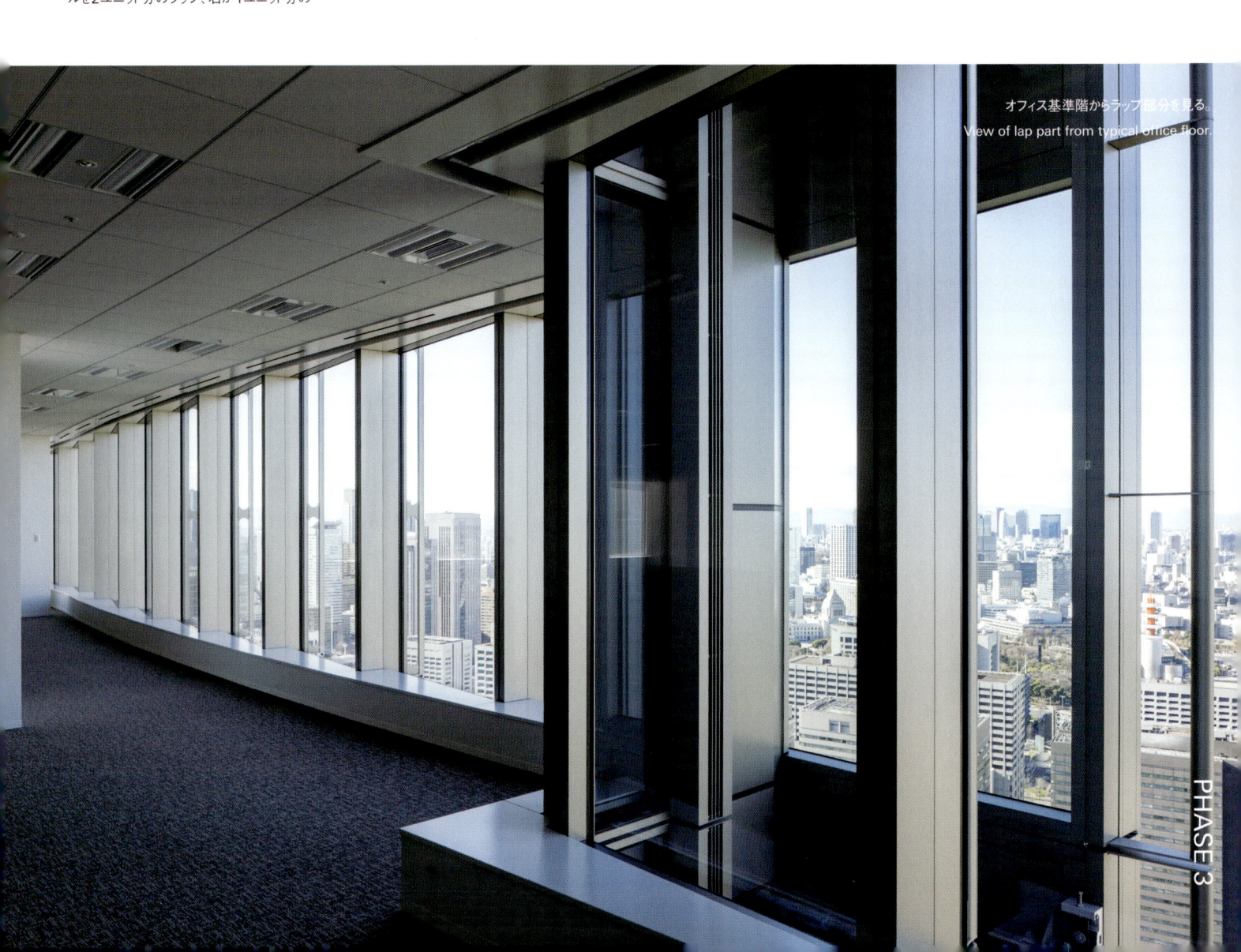

オフィス基準階からラップ部分を見る。
View of lap part from typical office floor.

PHASE3

モックアップで確認・検討し、合意形成を進める

2014.10–2015.3
Mockup production

Promote confirmation, consideration and consensus building by mock-up

▌モックアップをチーム全員で確認し、その場ですべて検討・解決する
Confirmation of mockup by the whole team, consideration and resolution of everything, on the same spot

三信ビルディングを踏襲すること、また、日生劇場と隣接して日比谷通りの顔をつくることを意識し、石でチャレンジしようと考えた。[HA]
日比谷通り側の低層部の石のモックアップを確認した。小口が非常に分厚く、ノミ切り仕上げで、この石のセレクトに込められた気概を改めて共有し、同時に本プロジェクトがどれだけ特別なものなのかということも再認識できたように思う。また外装だけでなくオフィス内部もモックアップを作成し、納まりや手順を確認した。[NS]

Conscious of making Hibiya-dori's face, also adjoining the Nissay theatre and following Sanshin Building, we thought of challenging by stone. [HA]
We confirmed the mock-up of the stone on the Hibiya-dori side low-rise exterior. Sharing again the spirit of this stone selection with an unusually thick small entrance and only cutting finish, we think we were able to recognize how special this project was, at the same time. Also, we created the mockup for not only the exterior but also the inside of the office and confirmed the settlement and procedures. [NS]

左2点：低層部外装の石のモックアップ。
右：高層部のガラスのモックアップ。

2 pictures on the left: Low-rise exterior stone mock-up.
Right: High-rise glass's mock-up.

下：低層部外装モックアップ。右上：高層部外装モックアップ。右下：高層部外装モックアップの内部。インテリアを再現することで、

意匠面だけでなく、納まりや施工手順なども合わせて確認する。

Bottom: Low-rise exterior mock-up. Top Right: High-rise exterior mock-up.
Bottom Right: Inside state of high-rise

exterior's mock-up. Confirm not only the design surface but also the settlement and construction procedure.

日比谷公園側から見る。高さを100尺（約31m）にすることで、右側の日生劇場と合わせた街区の一体感がデザインされている。

View from the Hibiya Park side. By setting the height to 100 shaku (about 31m), it is designed to feel the unity of the block together with the Nissay Theatre on the right side.

PHASE 4

技術と人に支えられ実現した街づくり

Town Development Realized by the Power of Technology and People

2015.1
建築確認取得
Acquired Building Confirmation

2015.5
区有施設
建築確認取得
Acquired Building Confirmation on facilities owned by the ward

2015.8
第1回計画変更
確認取得
Acquired Confirmation of the 1st Change of the Plan

2015.8
ワークセッション13
Work session 13

2015.8
第1回中間検査
The 1st intermediate inspection

2015.10
ワークセッション14
Work session 14

2015.11
第2回中間検査
The 2nd intermediate inspection

2016.5
ワークセッション15
Work session 15

2016.5
第2回計画変更
確認取得
Acquired Confirmation of the 2nd Change of the Plan

街づくり・都市計画｜Town Development and Urban Planning

建築設計｜Architectural Design

施工｜Construction

2015.1−6
構真柱工事
Pile foundation construction

2015.6−10
地下鉄骨工事
Underground steel-frame construction

2015.10.21
地上鉄骨建て方
開始（立柱式）
Steel-frame erection construction on the ground started (the ceremony of installing pillars)

2016.4
オイルタンク搬入開始
Installing the oil tanks started

2015.1.28（3.23）
新築着工（起工式）
Construction started (the groundbreaking ceremony)

2016.6−
外装工事開始
Exterior work started

2015年10月空撮。
Aerial view in October 2015.

2016年6月空撮。
Aerial view in June 2016.

PHASE 4では、実際にどのように施工されたのかを紹介する。
延床面積約193,000m²、工期36カ月、最盛期で1,800人の作業員が従事した工事は、
さまざまな技術に支えられ、少しずつ日比谷の街の風景を変えながら進んでいった。

We explain how this project was carried out in PHASE 4.
The construction which had 193,000m² of the architectural area, required a 36-month construction period and
1,800 workers had been carried out in the peak period while making the scenery in the city of Hibiya
around the construction site changed gradually.

2016.11
ワークセッション16
Work session 16

2017.7
第4回計画変更 確認取得
Acquired Confirmation of
the 4th Change of the Plan

2017.11
第5回計画変更 確認取得
Acquired Confirmation of
the 5th Change of the Plan

2017.3
第3回計画変更 確認取得
Acquired Confirmation of
the 3rd Change of the Plan

2018.1
完了検査
The final
inspection

2018.3.29
街びらき
Opening of the
Town

2016.7
地下掘削工事
完了（鎮物埋納式）
Excavation
construction
finished.
(*Shizumemono
mainou shiki*, a part
of the construction
ceremony)

2016.10
基礎躯体
完了
Construction
of basic
structure
finished

2016.12
外装取り付け完了
Exterior work
finished

2017.2
地下躯体完了
Construction of
underground
structure
finished

2017.6
受電 試運転開始
Test operation with
receiving power
started

2018.2.1
竣工
Completion

2016.8
内装工事
開始
Interior
work started

2016.11.7
鉄骨建て方完了
（上棟式）
Steel-frame erection
construction finished
(framework completion
ceremony)

2017年1月空撮。
Aerial view in January 2017.

2018年1月空撮。
Aerial view in January 2018.

36カ月にわたる工事のスタート

2015.1
Koji-anzen-kigan-sai
(Construction started)

Construction which takes 36 months started

▍着工 | Start of Construction

当時東洋最大級のオフィスビルとなった「日比谷三井ビルディング」（1960年竣工）の建て替えである当工事は、鹿島建設にとって歴史的に特別な思い入れがある。2015年1月に着工して36カ月の工期を無事故・無災害で竣工まで終わらせるべく、工事安全祈願祭を挙行し、安全に対しての決意を新たにした。［KC］

The rebuilding construction of "Hibiya Mitsui Building" which was constructed in 1960 as one of the largest office buildings in the East at that time has a special meaning for Kajima Corporation. We reaffirmed our determination for safety of the construction by having a *koji-anzen-kigan-sai* (a ceremony performed to pray for safety) to pray to finish the 36-month construction started in January 2015 without an accident or disaster. [KC]

日比谷通り側を主要な搬出入動線とした。基準階の鉄骨建て方は北側と南西側をヤードとして使用し、700tクラスのタワークレーン3台で行った。また、建屋内に3台の工事用エレベータを設置し、仕上げ材および外装材の揚重を行った。鉄骨やその他躯体関連部材（タワークレーンによる揚重）と外装材（工事用エレベータによる内部揚重）を分離することにより、地上階の躯体から外装工事の工程短縮を図った。[KC]

We decided that we would bring in and out building materials and other equipment at the side of Hibiya-dori. The steel-frame erection of the typical floor was performed with three 700t class tower cranes using the north and south-west sides as yards. And also, three elevators for construction were installed inside the building to lift finishing and exterior materials. We aimed to shorten the process of steel-frame and exterior construction by separating steel-frame materials lifting (with tower cranes) and exterior materials lifting (with elevators for construction). [KC]

左頁上2点：工事安全祈願祭。[2015年1月]
左頁下：日比谷公園側から工事がスタートした敷地を見る。[2015年10月]
右：地上仮設計画図　縮尺1/1,200

2 pictures on the top on the left page: Scenes of the *koji-anzen-kigan-sai*. [January 2015]
Bottom of the left page: The site viewed from the side of Hibiya Park at the time of starting the construction [October 2015]
Right: project drawing of temporary construction on the ground (scale: 1/1,200)

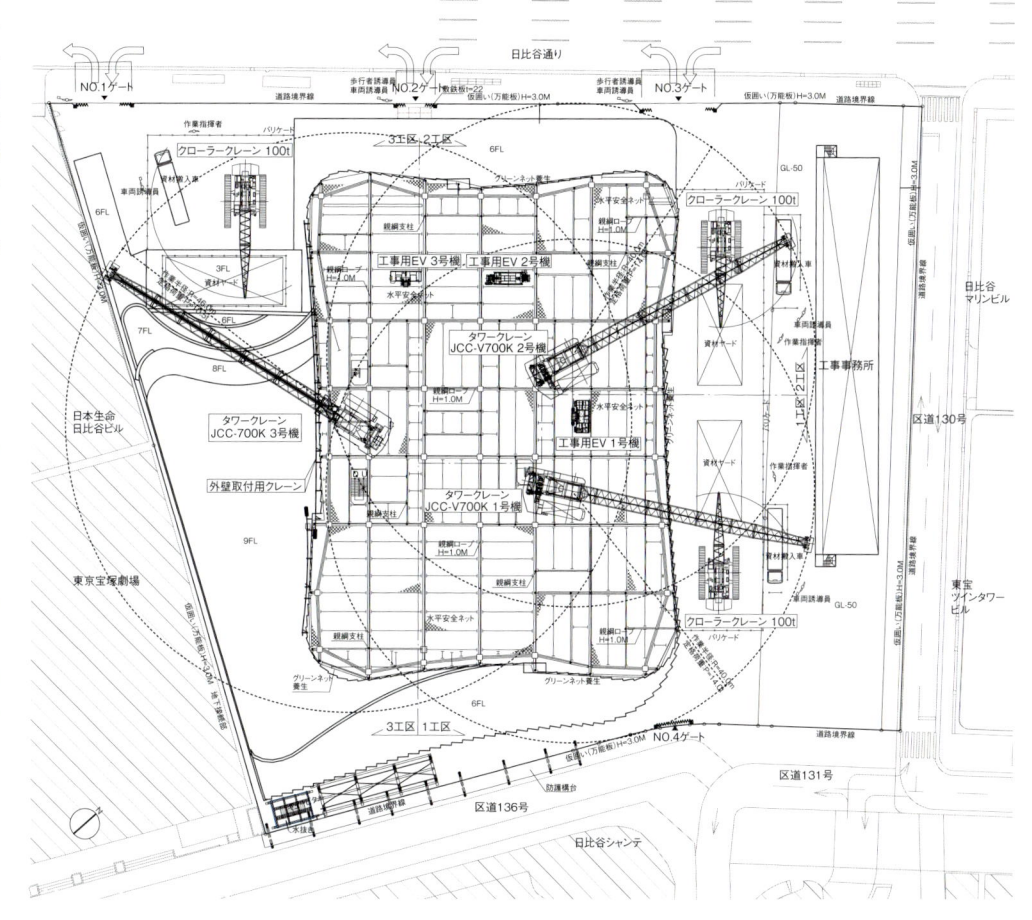

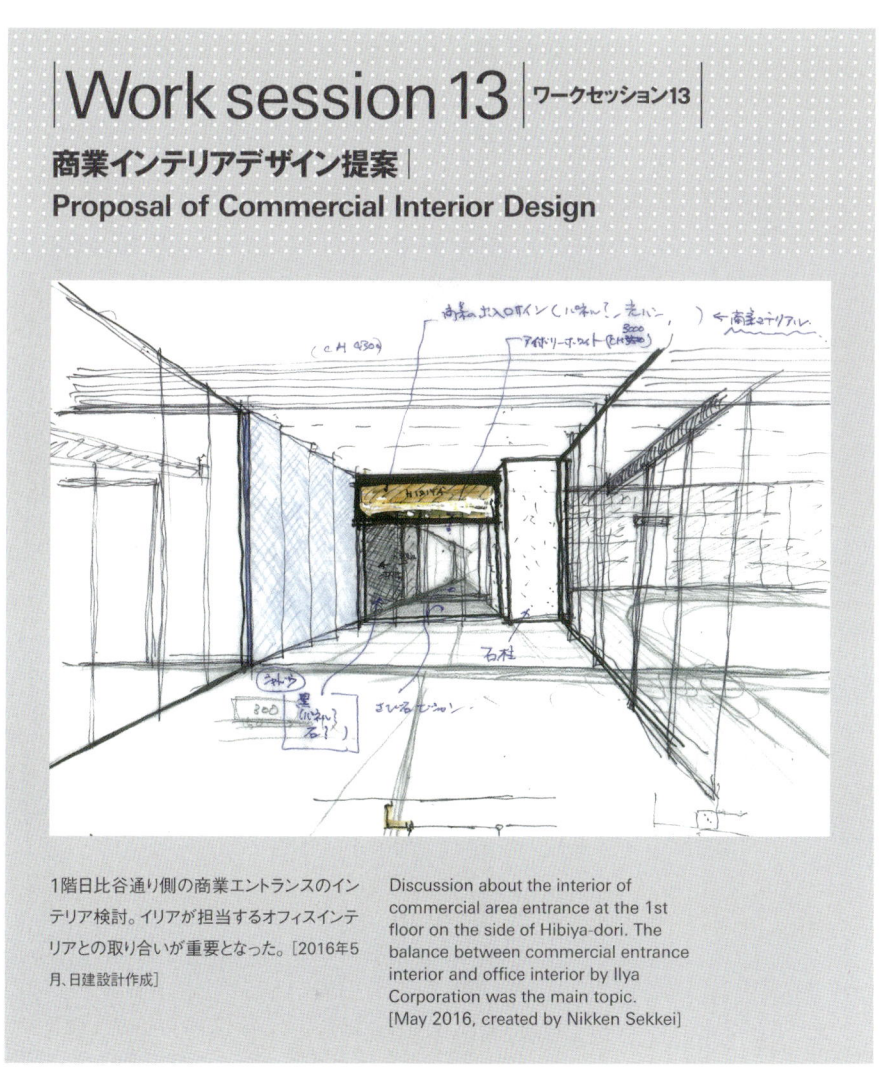

Work session 13 ｜ワークセッション13

商業インテリアデザイン提案｜
Proposal of Commercial Interior Design

1階日比谷通り側の商業エントランスのインテリア検討。イリアが担当するオフィスインテリアとの取り合いが重要となった。[2016年5月、日建設計作成]

Discussion about the interior of commercial area entrance at the 1st floor on the side of Hibiya-dori. The balance between commercial entrance interior and office interior by Ilya Corporation was the main topic. [May 2016, created by Nikken Sekkei]

PHASE 4

■ 地下掘削工事
Excavation construction

都心部での超軟弱地盤（GL-20m付近までがN値ゼロ）における大規模（約1ha）かつ大深度工事（約27m）であり、地下鉄東京メトロ千代田線、劇場や宿泊施設も近接していたため、基本計画段階から施工者が設計者と協議して慎重に進めた。既存躯体の外周部を残置させ山留壁として利用し、構真柱を打設し、1階、地下1階、地下2階を逆打ちすると共に、地下3階以深はグランドアンカーによる純打ち工法を併用することで解体・掘削工事の合理化を図った「ハイブリッド逆打ち工法」を初めて採用。周辺環境の維持や地下鉄への影響を抑制すると共に、工期全体も約5カ月短縮することが可能となった。[KC]

The constructor carried out the excavation construction upon consultation with the designer from the stage of basic plan because the construction has a large scale (approximately 1ha) and large depth (approximately 27m) in a downtown and at the soft ground (N value is 0 around GL-20m), and also, there were

The Tokyo Metro Chiyoda Line and theaters and accommodations in the vicinity of the site. We used "Hybrid inverted construction method" for the first time where the periphery of the current building frame was left as retaining walls, pile foundation was installed, inverted construction method was used for G, B1, B2 and ordinary

basement construction method with ground anchors was used for B3 or lower level aiming to increase efficiency of demolition and excavation process. We managed to minimize effects to the environment surrounding the site and the subway and also decrease five months work from the total construction period. [KC]

左：地下掘削工事。[2015年10月]

右上：地下掘削工事。三信ビルディングの松杭の撤去。[2015年12月]

右下：地下掘削工事。[2015年12月]

Left: Excavation construction [October 2015]/ Right top: Excavation construction. Removing pine piles of Sanshin Building [December 2015] /Right bottom: Excavation construction [December 2015]

PHASE 4

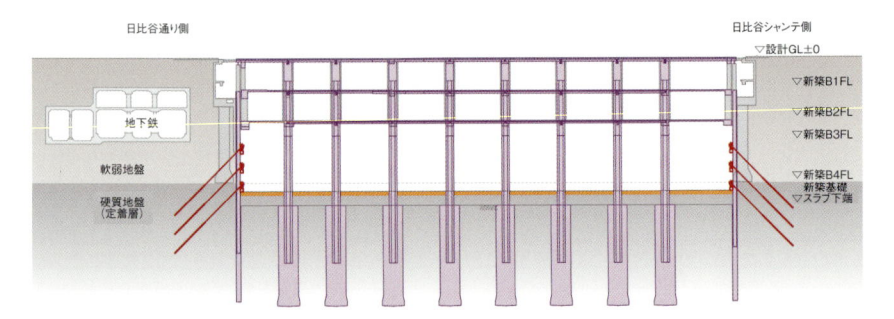

日比谷通り側　　　　　　　　　　　　　　　　　　　日比谷シャンテ側
　　　　　　　　　　　　　　　　　　　　　　　　　▽設計GL±0

地下鉄　　　　　　　　　　　　　　　　　　　　　　▽新築B1FL

　　　　　　　　　　　　　　　　　　　　　　　　　▽新築B2FL

軟弱地盤　　　　　　　　　　　　　　　　　　　　　▽新築B3FL

硬質地盤　　　　　　　　　　　　　　　　　　　　　▽新築B4FL
（定着層）　　　　　　　　　　　　　　　　　　　　新築基礎
　　　　　　　　　　　　　　　　　　　　　　　　　▽スラブ下端

上：地下掘削工事。[2016年7月]
左下：地下部分断面。
右下2点：鎮物埋納式の様子。地下の掘
削工事がすべて完了。[2016年7月]

Top: Excavation construction. [July 2016]
Bottom left: Sectional details of the underground
2 pictures at bottom right: Scenes of *Shizumemono mainou shiki*, a part of the construction ceremony. All excavation construction finished. [July 2016]

いよいよ建物が立ち上がる

2015.10
The ceremony of installing pillars
[Steel-frame erection
construction on the ground]

The building finally erected

立柱式［地上部鉄骨建て方］

▌地上鉄骨建て方スタート
Steel-frame erection construction on the ground started

2015年10月に1階先行床のコンクリート打設が完了し、10月21日に立柱式を執り行った。これより、16節（地上35階、屋上付帯鉄骨含む）約34,000tにおよぶ地上の鉄骨建て方工事に着手した（鉄骨総重量は約39,000t）。
［KC］

The floor concrete at the 1st floor was completed in October 2015, and we conducted a ceremony of installing pillars on October 21. After this, we started to work on steel-frame erection construction which had 16 joints (35 floors above ground, including steel-frame on the roof top) and approximately weighted 34,000t (the total weight is approximately 39,000t).
[KC]

日本生命日比谷ビル上部から敷地を見る。
［2015年10月］

The site viewed from the top of Nissay Hibiya Building. [October 2015]

Work session 14 | ワークセッション14

石のアート検討 | Discussion about the Stone Art

和泉正敏氏による石のアートの配置計画。
[2017年2月、和泉氏作成]

An arrangement plan of the stone art
by Masatoshi Izumi [February 2017,
created by Izumi]

上3点：立柱式の様子。地上の鉄骨建て方
工事がスタート。[2015年10月]
下2点：現場で行われた餅つき大会の様子。

3 pictures at the top: Scenes of the
ceremony of installing pillars. Steel-
frame erection construction on the
ground started. [October 2015]
2 pictures at the bottom: a rice cake
pounding event on the site.

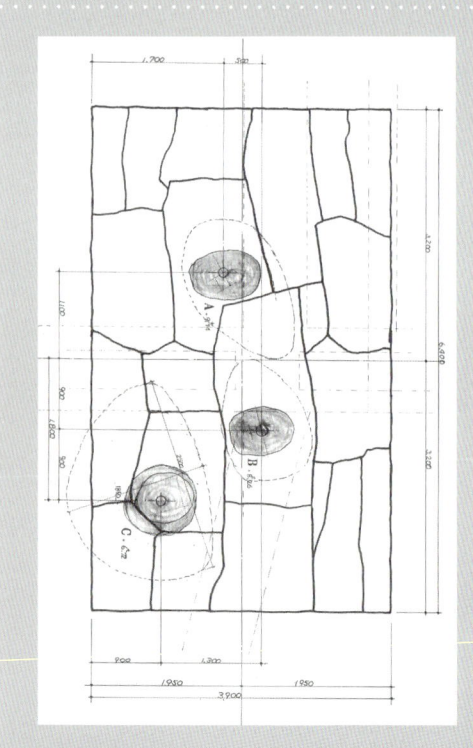

上：日比谷シャンテ別館側から敷地を見る。
［2015年12月］
下：北側から見る。700tクレーン3基を使用
しての工事。［2016年1月］

Top: The site viewed from Hibiya
Chanter Annex. [December 2015]
Bottom: The site viewed from the north
side. Construction with 700t 3 cranes.
[January 2016]

PHASE 4

建物の機能を止めない備え（BCP）

Preventative Measures against Disruption of the Building (BCP)

▌大型設備機器の搬入・埋設
Large Equipment was Brought in and Installed

躯体工事の進捗に合わせたピンポイントの工程の中で、建物西側外構部分にビル用60,000ℓ×4基、テナント用75,000ℓ×2基（計390,000ℓ）のオイルタンクを工程進捗ごとでの危険物係の消防検査を受検しながら据付、埋設工事を実施した。[KC]

At specific points of the construction process that meet the progress of the framework construction, four 60,000-liter oil tanks for the building and two 75,000-liter ones for the tenants (a total of 390,000 liters) were installed and buried outside on the west side of the building while undergoing the fire inspections by the hazardous materials section at each construction process. [KC]

左：敷地北西側の地下へのオイルタンク搬入。[2016年4月]
右3点：オイルタンク埋設工事。[2016年4月]

Left: An oil tank was brought in to underground at the north west side of the site. [April 2016]
3 pictures on right: Installing construction of oil tanks [April 2016]

PHASE 4

地下鉄との接続

Connecting a tunnel to the subway

▌地下推進工事
Tunnel Excavation Work

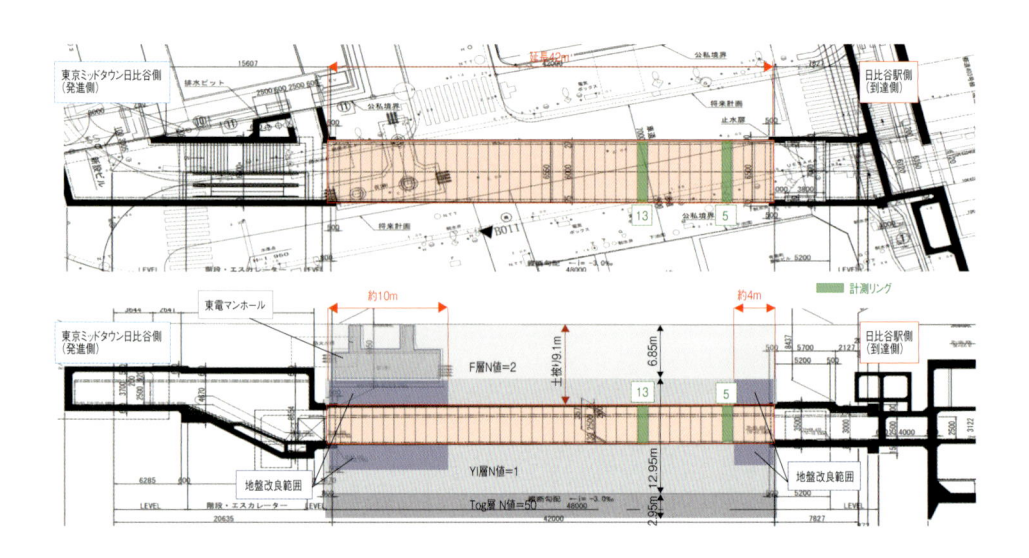

本工法は、掘削機の上部に装着した屋根（ルーフ）が、先行掘削することにより掘削中の地盤沈下などを防止し、周辺環境への影響を最小限に留めながらトンネルを構築することができる。地下鉄日比谷線との地下接続工事に適用し、無事に掘削を完了した。［KC］

This method enables to excavate a tunnel while preventing the land around a construction site from sinking and minimize affecting the surrounding environment with a roof attached on the top of the tunnel boring machine which precedes to excavate a tunnel. We used this method to connect a tunnel to Tokyo Metro Hibiya Line and completed the tunnel. [KC]

上：地下推進工事平面
中：地下推進工事断面

左下：掘削を行う3連のR-SWING機。
右中：R-SWING機の裏側を見る。この部分を推進機と接続させる。
右下：掘削後の状況。［2016年2月］

Top: A floor plan of the tunnel excavation work
Center: A cross section plan of the tunnel excavation work

Bottom left: Triplet R-SWING machine which excavates a tunnel.
Right center: The back side of R-SWING machine which is to be connected to a propulsion machine.
Bottom right: A scene after an excavation work [February 2016]

上：北側から見る。［2016年3月］
下：日比谷公園から見る。［2016年6月］

Top: View from the north side. [March 2016]
Bottom: View from Hibiya Park. [June 2016]

PHASE 4

Dancing Towerを印象付ける
外装取り付け

Finishing Exterior to Make the Dancing Tower Unique

本頁：南東側から見る。［2016年6月］

右頁上4点：高層部外装詳細　縮尺1/50

右頁下3点：高層部カーテンウォール取り付け工事。［2016年11月］

This page: View from the southeast side. [June 2016]
4 items on the top on the right page: detailed plan and section of upper part exterior (scale: 1/50)
3 pictures on the bottom of the right page: Scenes of installing curtain walls on the upper part of the building [November 2016]

■ カーテンウォール取り付け
Installing Curtain Walls

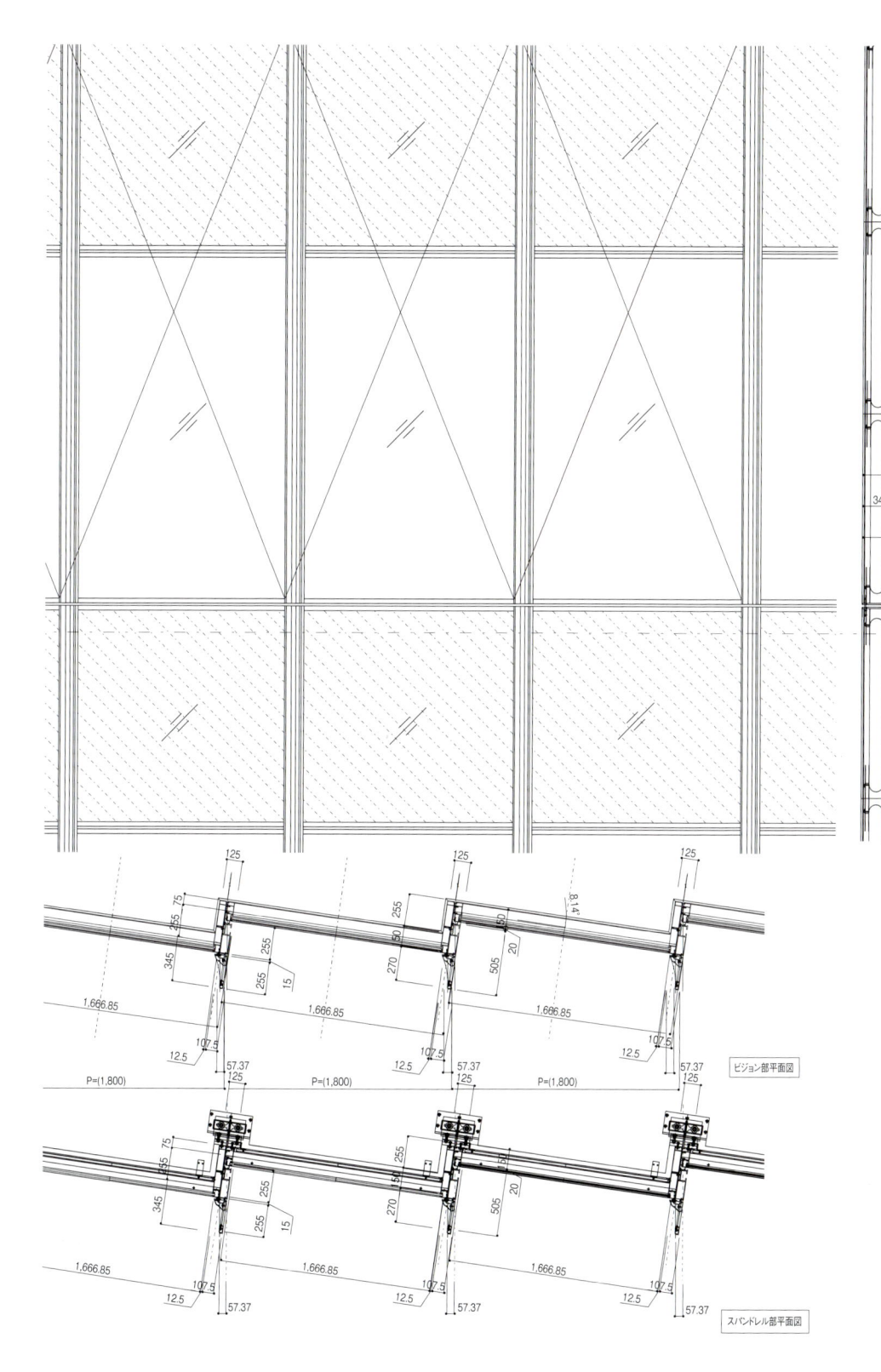

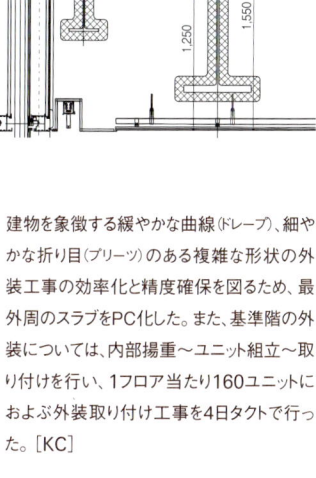

ビジョン部平面図

スパンドレル部平面図

建物を象徴する緩やかな曲線（ドレープ）、細やかな折り目（プリーツ）のある複雑な形状の外装工事の効率化と精度確保を図るため、最外周のスラブをPC化した。また、基準階の外装については、内部揚重〜ユニット組立〜取り付けを行い、1フロア当たり160ユニットにおよぶ外装取り付け工事を4日タクトで行った。[KC]

We used precast concrete slabs for the outermost peripheral part to improve efficiency and accuracy of exterior construction with gentle drapes and fine pleats which are symbol of this building. The typical floors' exterior was done by lifting material with elevator for construction work, assembling each unit, and then installing it. We finished this exterior installation task with 160 units per floor for four days. [KC]

PHASE 4

本頁上：大手町方向から見る。[2016年10月]
本頁下：南側から見る。[2016年9月]
右頁：有楽町方向から見る。[2016年10月]

The top on this page: View from the Otemachi side. [October 2016]
The bottom on this page: View from the south side. [September 2016]

Right page: View from the Yurakucho side. [October 2016]

街への存在感が立ち現れる

2016.11
Framework Completion
Ceremony

The existence of the building is emerging

■ 鉄骨建て方完了
Steel-frame Erection
Construction Finished

左頁・本頁 3点：上棟式。[2016年11月7日]
Left page, 3 pictures on this page:
Scenes from the framework completion
ceremony. [November 2016]

|Work session 16 | ワークセッション16

日比谷ステップ広場ファサード検討、タワー部照明確認
Discussion about of the Facade of Hibiya Step Square and lighting check for the tower

左2点：日比谷ステップ広場のファサード検
討の様子。
右：タワー部の照明効果検討CGパース。
[2016年9月、フォーライツ作成]。

2 pictures on the left: Scenes of
discussion about the facade of Hibiya
Step Square.
Right: CG Perspective for discussion
about lighting of the tower part.
[November 2016, created by FORLIGHTS]

2016.8–
内装工事スタート

たくさんの職人に支えられる工事現場

2016.8–
Interior work started

The construction site where many craftsmen
contributed to this project

左頁：現場で毎朝行われる体操。[2016年9月]
本頁上：屋上での鉄骨工事。[2016年11月]
本頁下：工事最盛期には1日2,000人もの
作業員が現場に従事していた。[2016年2月]

Left page: A morning routine exercise at the site. [September 2016]
Top on this page: Steel-frame construction on the roof. [November 2016]
Bottom on this page: At its peak of construction, there were 2,000 workers per day at the site. [February 2016]

PHASE 4

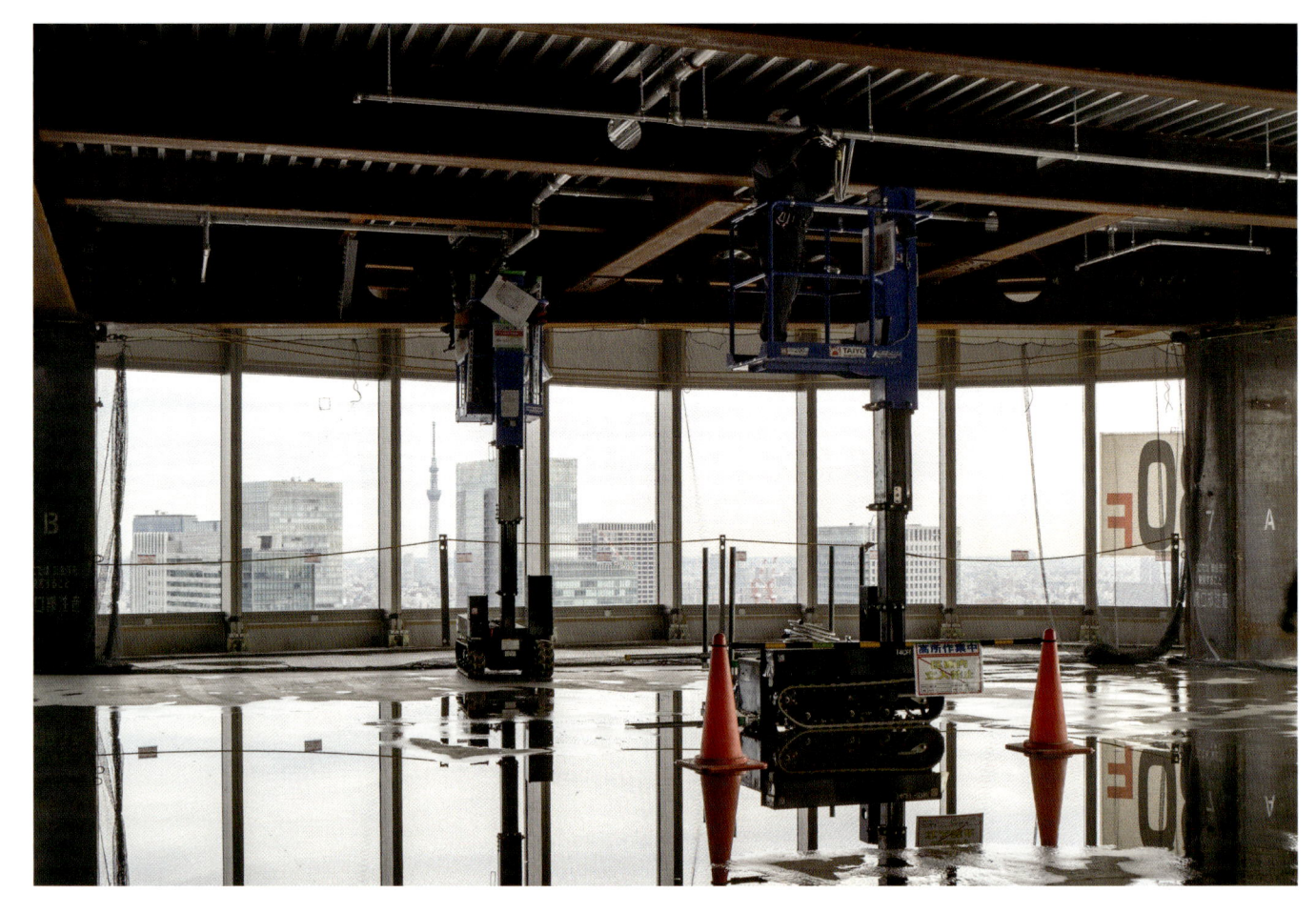

上：オフィス基準階の配管工事。［2016年11月］
左中：女性技術者も多く従事。
右中：3階の商業アトリウム工事。［2017年9月］

左下：現場での体操。［2016年12月］
右下：地下1階日比谷アーケード工事。［2017年8月］

Top: Piping work at the typical office floors. [November 2016]
Center left: Many female engineers were working at the site.
Center right: Construction of commercial zone Atrium on the third floor. [September 2017]

Bottom left: Exercise at the site. [December 2016]
Bottom right: Construction of an Hibiya Arcade on the basement 1st floor. [August 2017]

上：日比谷ステップ広場の工事。［2017年7月］
下：日比谷ステップ広場の外構工事。［2017年10月］

Top: Construction of Hibiya Step Square. [July 2017]
Bottom: Construction of the outdoor facilities of Hibiya Step Square. [October 2017]

PHASE 4

日比谷濠から見る。[2017年1月]

The site viewed from Hibiya moat.
[January 2017]

▌高品位な建物の竣工を支える監理業務
Management operation that supports the final completion of a sophisticated construction

本プロジェクトのような超大型複合建築物における監理業務は、より一層複雑かつ膨大となる。多岐にわたる各種工程検査や書類確認および製品検査等を通じて、工程の順守と高い施工品質の確保を実現する要となった。[KD]

The management operation for a large construction complex as in this project becomes more complicated and enormous. The broader process of inspections and document check work including product inspections served to observe each construction process and secure high construction quality. [KD]

右上：法定中間検査の様子。[2015年7月]
右下：中国での製品検査（外装石材）の様子。[2017年3月]

Top right: Legal interim inspections.
[July 2015]
Bottom right: Product inspection (exterior stone material) in China.
[March 2017]

■竣工式
Completion Ceremony

4点：竣工式の様子。[2018年1月30日]

4 pictures: Scenes of the completion ceremony. [30, January 2018]

たくさんの人の関わりで実現した難易度の高い工事

桐生雅文 ［鹿島建設 東京ミッドタウン日比谷現場所長］

A Difficult Construction Work Realized with the Involvement of Many People

Masafumi Kiryu ［Kajima Corporation］

当プロジェクトの周辺には、劇場、映画館、ホテルなどが隣接しており、昼夜を問わず振動・騒音には細心の配慮が必要であったため、事前に施工実験を行い、部位ごとに作業時間帯を決めて工事を進めた。また、当該地は非常に軟弱な地盤であるため、周辺建物や地下鉄への影響を考慮し、発注者・設計者と協議し、既存建物の外周部を残し、山留壁として利用することとし、その影響を最小限に留めた。

地上階では、構造の切り替え階でのトランスファー鉄骨や複雑な形状の外装カーテンウォールの製作施工管理など、非常に難易度の高い工事であった。最盛期1日2,000人の作業員が現場に従事したが、労働災害をなくすために、職長会を中心に風通しのよい現場づくりを目指した。また、「鹿島たんぽぽ運動」の代表現場として、女性技術者・技能者によるイベントや現場周囲の環境活動なども現場の雰囲気づくりに貢献した。

当工事は、「鹿島建築発祥の地」でのプロジェクトであり、当社にとって歴史的に特別な思い入れがある建物の建て替え計画であったが、当社の総合力を結集してつくり上げることができた。この「東京ミッドタウン日比谷」が、日比谷を活性化する核となり、多くの人に長きにわたり満足し愛され続ける建物となることを確信している。

Since stage theaters, movie theaters, hotels, and other facilities are located around the place of this project, we had to pay the most careful attention to vibration and noise control irrespective of day and night. Therefore, we conducted a preliminary construction experiment before the beginning of construction work, and carried out the construction section by section, specifying the working hour for each section. Also, since the ground of this site is quite soft, after discussion with the contractee and the designer, we decided to leave the outer peripheral part of the existing building to use it as a bracing wall, intending to minimize the influence of the construction to the buildings in the vicinity and the subways. The construction of the above-ground building was tough. What made it difficult included the transfer steel frame construction for the floor where the structure is switched, the manufacturing and construction control of the exterior curtain wall of complex shape, etc. As about 2,000 workers per day were engaged in the work at its peak, we tried to eliminate occupational injuries, and the meeting of chiefs took the initiative and make efforts to create an "open" work site. Additionally, as a representative site of "Kajima Tanpopo Activity," female engineers and skilled workers held an event at this site, and we carried out environmental activities in the areas around the work site of this project. Our attempts including such activities contributed to developing a favorable working environment.

This construction work was a plan to rebuild a building for which we have a special feeling in our history at the "place of origin for Kajima Corporation." We are sure that we have completed this project with gathering our collective strength. We believe that "Tokyo Midtown Hibiya" will be a core of revitalizing Hibiya. We also believe that people will continue to satisfy with this building and love it for a long time.

日比谷公園から見る
View from Hibiya Park

商業エリアアトリウム。開業1カ月を前に来街者が200万人を超え、
現在も月に100万人以上もの人が訪れている。

A scene from the commercial zone Atrium.
More than two million people have visited the commercial area
even before its one-month anniversary.
Now, more than a million people visits here each month.

6階パークビューガーデン越しに日比谷公園や皇居のお堀を見る。

Hibiya Park and the Imperial Palace moats viewed through
Park View Garden on the sixth floor.

賑わいの中心となる日比谷ステップ広場でさまざまなイベントを開催すると共に、
周辺施設とも連携している。

Various events are held in Hibiya Step Square, which is the center of the
bustling town, and collaborate with facilities in the vicinity of the area.

日比谷シネマフェスティバル2018での映画上映の様子。
日比谷ステップ広場の階段部分が観客席となっている。

A movie display scene during HIBIYA CINEMA FESTIVAL 2018.
The steps in Hibiya Step Square were used as seats for the audience.

日比谷シネマフェスティバル2018で
日比谷ステップ広場に設置された巨大スクリーンを見る。
Hibiya Step Square with a giant-screen at the HIBIYA CINEMA FESTIVAL 2018.

ふつうじゃない 2020 展の様子。
A scene from Futsuujyanai 2020 Exhibition.

日比谷フェスティバルの様子。
A scene form HIBIYA FESTIVAL.

日比谷フェスティバルの様子。
A scene form HIBIYA FESTIVAL.

TOKYO MIDTOW

新しい文化を取り込む 日比谷エリアの特性と可能性

岸井隆幸［日本大学理工学部 特任教授］

日比谷エリアの特性

日比谷エリアの象徴は何といっても日比谷公園である。この公園は1889（明治22）年の市区改正設計で位置付けられ、1903（明治36）年わが国最初の「近代的洋風」公園として開園された。その後、1905（明治38）年に音楽堂（現小音楽堂）、1908（明治41）年に図書館、1923（大正12）年に野外音楽堂、1929（昭和4）年に日比谷公会堂が整備され今日に至っている。

ただ、実はこの日比谷公園が東京都都市計画中央公園の一部であることはあまり知られていない。中央公園とは、日比谷公園・皇居外苑・皇居東御苑・北の丸公園・九段坂公園・千鳥ヶ淵戦没者墓苑・千鳥ヶ淵公園という皇居を取り巻く一群の公園緑地の総称である。現在は東京都・環境省・宮内庁・千代田区などが区分して管理しているため、われわれには一体としての存在が十分に感じられない。このことは実にもったいないとしか言いようがない。皇居周辺の航空写真を見てもらうと、その一群の緑の豊かさと貴重な水の存在を再確認することができる。大都市東京の中心にこの巨大なボイド空間が存在するのである。そして、そのボイド空間の中でさまざまな活動を受け止めているのが日比谷公園である。

また、歴史的に見ると日比谷エリアはさまざまな新文化を紹介する地域であった。明治期には鹿鳴館（1883［明治16］年）や帝国ホテル（1890［明治23］年）が建設され、国際的な接遇空間として活用された。1898（明治31）年に東京市役所が設置され、1910（明治43）年には山手線有楽町駅が開業した。この有楽町駅周辺には東京日日新聞（現毎日新聞）、報知新聞、読売新聞、朝日新聞が進出、新聞文化の中心地となった。一方、1908（明治41）年に「有楽座」が日本最初の洋風劇場として誕生、1911（明治44）年に「帝国劇場」、1933（昭和8）年に「日劇」、1934（昭和9）年に「東京宝塚劇場」、「日比谷映画劇場」などが加わり、この地域は一大アミューズメントセンターに変貌していく。日活、東宝、新東宝など日本映画産業大手6社の本社も有楽町に集中、戦後も1957（昭和32）年に「芸術座」、1963（昭和38）年に「日生劇場」、1966（昭和41）年に新しい「帝国劇場」が整備された。そして近年、地域の再開発が進み、1984（昭和59）年に「有楽町マリオン」、1987（昭和62）年に「日比谷シャンテ」、2007（平成19）年に「有楽町イトシア」、そして昨年「東京ミッドタウン日比谷」がオープンした。

日比谷エリアは常に新しい文化を受け入れて紹介する街であった。

・・・・・

なお、この日比谷エリアの交通利便性は目を見張るものがある。JR山手線の有楽町駅と新橋駅に近接しているし、地下鉄も東京メトロ日比谷・千代田線の日比谷駅、有楽町線の有楽町駅、丸の内線の銀座駅、都営三田線の内幸町駅・日比谷駅など多数の駅が利用できる。東京駅、新橋駅、神田駅に比べるとこの地区の地下鉄ネットワークの充実度が卓越していることがよく分かる。鉄道を通じて東京のさまざまな地域と結ばれているのがこの地区の特徴であり、結果として夜遅くまでこの地区で楽しんでいても公共交通を利用して家路につくことが可能である。

日比谷エリアの可能性

・・・・・

先日、東京都が日比谷公園のグランドデザインを発表したが、そこでは「街と公園を結ぶ」ことが強く意識されている。公園が街の一部として機能することはもちろん、公園がより積極的に街の中へと出ていく、あるいは公園の中に街の機能の一部を取り込んで公園自身が変わっていくという姿勢が示されている。東京ミッドタウン日比谷をはじめとする各種エンターテインメント施設と公園との融合が街に新たな賑わいをもたらすことは間違いがない。グランドデザイン実現に向けて、関係者の思い切った施策展開を期待したい。

また、公園として都市計画中央公園内の他の地区との連携強化についても期待したい。それぞれを縦割りに管理するのではなく、面として一体的に運営する仕組みができ上がれば、東京の魅力は一段と高まりを見せる。堀の水質維持や地域の広域防災についても大きな成果に結び付くであろう。そして中央公園周辺の民間開発にも大きな影響をおよぼすことは間違いがない。世界にも類がないような都心の巨大公園緑地に接する地域の価値はきわめて高いのである。

また、日比谷エリアの北側には大丸有地区（大手町・丸の内・有楽町地区）が広がり、ここでも着実に都市の再生が進められている。また、南側は新橋駅周辺に繋がっているが、その先には環状2号線沿いの都市開発が動いている。それぞれの地域にエリアマネジメント団体があり、東京ミッドタウン日比谷エリアにも新たな組織が設立された。こうした一連の動きを広域的視点で捉えることも必要である。日本橋から日本橋川に沿って大丸有地区へ、そして丸の内仲通りを抜けて日比谷地区へ、そこから環状2号線へと繋がって虎ノ門・六本木地区へ。エリアマネジメント組織の連携が実現すれば、東京の中心部に歩いて楽しい空間の強固なネットワークが浮かび上がってくる。歩いて楽しめる街「東京」に広がりが生まれる。

・・・・・

日比谷公園の周辺に「洋風」と称された新しい文化を取り込み人びとに発信する地域が生まれた、それがここ「日比谷エリア」であった。現在もその歴史は続いている。日比谷エリアにはまだこれから再開発を目指す地区がいくつも存在している。また、日本橋の議論を契機として首都高速道路のあり方も議論されるようになった。国土交通省交通政策審議会で議論されたTXの臨海部への延伸もこの地域の近くを通ることになり、これらに合わせて東京都庁跡地の開発も動き出すであろう。

まだまだ日比谷は変わる。

周辺部のさらなる再開発、中央公園としての設え、有楽町エリアの再生、JRを越えて繋がる街の連続性など大きな可能性を秘めている。

日比谷エリアが内包している「東京を変える大きな力」に期待したい。

岸井隆幸｜きしい・たかゆき
1953年兵庫県生まれ／1975年東京大学工学部都市工学科卒業／1977年同大学大学院都市工学専攻修士課程修了／1977〜92年建設省／1992年日本大学理工学部土木工学科専任講師／1995〜98年同大学助教授／1998年〜同大学理工学部土木工学科教授／2017〜18年日比谷公園グランドデザイン検討会副座長／2017年〜計量計画研究所 代表理事／2018年〜日本大学理工学部 特任教授

皇居周辺の俯瞰。
A bird's eye view of the Imperial Palace.

Characteristics and Possibilities of Hibiya Area, Embracing New Cultures

Takayuki Kishii [Professor of Nihon University]

Characteristics of Hibiya Area

• • • • •

Hibiya Park is, above all others, the symbol of Hibiya area. This park was defined as a park in the city development design planned in 1889 and opened to the public as the first "modern Western-style" park in Japan in 1903. After that, the music hall (currently called as small music hall) in 1905, the library in 1908, the Open-Air Concert Hall in 1923, and the Hibiya Public Hall were constructed in 1929. and the park became what it is now.

In fact, it is not well known that Hibiya Park is a part of the Central Park defined under Tokyo's urban planning. "Central Park" is a generic name for a group of parks and green spaces surrounding the Imperial Palace, including Hibiya Park, Kokyogaien National Gardens, the East Gardens of the Imperial Palace, Kitanomaru Garden, Kudanzaka Park, Chidorigafuchi National Cemetery, and Chidorigafuchi Park. Since these parks and green spaces are separately administered by the Tokyo Metropolitan Government, the Ministry of the Environment, the Imperial Household Agency, or the Chiyoda Ward government, the public does not fully feel the presence of them as one park. Such a lack of unity is truly regrettable. If you see an aerial photo of the area around the Imperial Palace, you will rediscover the abundance of green and the presence of precious water there. Such a huge void area is present in the Tokyo metropolis. Hibiya Park accepts various activities in this void area. Historically, Hibiya area has been introduced various new cultures. In the Meiji era, Rokumeikan (in 1883) and the Imperial Hotel (in 1890) were built and used as international hospitality spaces. In 1898, the Tokyo City Office was established, and in 1910, Yurakucho Station on Yamanote Line opened. Since several newspaper companies including Tokyo Nichi Nichi Shimbun (currently Mainichi Shimbun), Hochi Shimbun, Yomiuri Shimbun, and Asahi Shimbun moved to places near Yurakucho Station, the area became a center of the newspaper culture. Meanwhile, in 1908, "Yurakuza" opened as the first Western-style theater in Japan, followed by "Imperial Theatre" in 1911, "Nichigeki Theater" in 1933 , "Tokyo Takarazuka Theater" and "Hibiya Movie Theater" in 1934, etc. In this trend, the area transformed into a major amusement center. The six major Japanese movie companies including enterprises such as Nikkatsu, Toho, and Shin-Toho also placed their head offices in Yurakucho. Even after the World War II, "Geijutsuza" (in 1957), "Nissay

Theatre" (in 1963), and the new "Imperial Theatre" (in 1966) were built. In recent years, the area has been redeveloped and "Yurakucho Mullion" (in 1984), "Hibiya Chanter" (in 1987), "Yurakucho ITOCiA" (in 2007) opened, and then "Tokyo Midtown Hibiya" opened last year. Hibiya area has always been a town that accepts and introduces new cultures.

• • • • •

Another point to note about Hibiya area is traffic convenience. The area is close to Yurakucho Station and Shimbashi Station on JR Yamanote Line, and many subway stations including Hibiya Station on Tokyo Metro Hibiya Line and Chiyoda Line, Yurakucho Station on Yurakucho Line, Ginza Station on Marunouchi Line, and Uchisaiwaicho Station and Hibiya Station on Toei Mita Line. Compared to Tokyo Station, Shimbashi Station, and Kanda Station, the subway network around Hibiya area is outstanding. One characteristic of this area is that it is connected with various regions in Tokyo via railways. Consequently, people can get to their home by public transportation even if they enjoy the nightlife in this area until late.

Possibilities of Hibiya Area

• • • • •

In the Grand Design of Hibiya Park that the Tokyo Metropolitan Government announced recently, consideration for the concept of "connecting the town and parks" is strongly reflected. In that design, the attitude is indicated that the parks should not only assume a role as a part of a town but also proactively advance into the town, or incorporate a part of functions of the town into them to transform themselves. The fusion of parks and various entertainment facilities including Tokyo Midtown Hibiya will surely bring new prosperity to the town. For the realization of the Grand Design, drastic developments of the measures by the concerned parties are looked forward to.

In terms of a park, enhancement of collaboration with other areas in the Central Park defined under Tokyo's urban planning is also being expected. If the sections of the Central Park could be managed integrally instead of being administered compartmentally, Tokyo would become more attractive. We believe that such an approach will significantly contribute to maintaining the water quality of the moat, as well as to the wide-area disaster prevention. We also believe that it will have a major impact on the development of the area around the Central Park by private sectors. The value of the areas that lie adjacent to a massive land of parks and green spaces in the center of the metropolis, which is very

rare worldwide, is extremely high.

On the north side of Hibiya area, Daimaruyu area (i.e., the Otemachi, Marunouchi, and Yurakucho areas) extends, and the city regeneration initiatives steadily take place there as well. The south side of Hibiya area is in contact with the area around the Shimbashi Station, and beyond that, the city development is being promoted in the areas along the Loop Road No.2. Each area is managed by different area management organization, and a new organization was established for Tokyo Midtown Hibiya area. It is also necessary to view each movement from a wide area perspective which is from Nihonbashi, along the Nihonbashi River to Daimaruyu area, and to Hibiya area via the Nakadori street, from there connected to the Loop Road No.2, and then to Toranomon and Roppongi areas. If the alliance of the area management organizations is realized, a strong network is created and a fun space to walk along emerges in the middle of Tokyo. A city, "Tokyo", that people enjoy walking broadens.

• • • • •

Around Hibiya Park, an area was born which accepts new cultures called the "Western-style" and transmits it to the public. That is "Hibiya area." The history of such characteristics continues until now. In Hibiya area, there are still many areas that are intended to be redeveloped from now on. Also, discussion about Nihonbashi brought about the discussion on how the Metropolitan Expressway should be. Extension of TX to the waterfront area, which was discussed at the Council of Transport Policy of the Ministry of Land, Infrastructure, Transport and Tourism, will be near this area. Along with these movements, the development of the old site of the Tokyo Metropolitan Government Building will possibly be started.

Hibiya will continue to change.

Hibiya possesses great potential, including further redevelopments of the surrounding areas, arrangement as the Central Park, regeneration of Yurakucho area, and the continuity of towns being connected beyond JR.

We would like to expect "strong power to change Tokyo" that Hibiya area possesses.

Takayuki Kishii
1953 Born in Hyogo / 1975 B.A. in Department of Urban Engineering, the University of Tokyo / 1977 Completed the Master course, Graduate School of Engineering, the University of Tokyo / 1977-92 Ministry of Construction / 1992- Assistant Professor of the College of Science and Technology, Nihon University / 1995-98 Associate Professor / 1998- Professor of the College of Science and Technology, Nihon University / 2017-18 Planning Committee on Hibiya Park Grand Design Vice -chairperson / 2017- President, The Institute of Behavioral Sciences

所在地
東京都千代田区有楽町1-1-2

主要用途
事務所／店舗／文化交流施設／
産業支援施設／映画館／駐車場／
地域冷暖房施設（DHC）

事業主
三井不動産

▌設計

マスターデザインアーキテクト
ホプキンス・アーキテクツ
［デザイン最高顧問］
サー・マイケル・ホプキンス
［統括・担当］
サイモン・フレイザー
星野裕明
［デザインチーム］
宮本雅人／アンドリュー・アーディル／
モハメド・アシャー／ジョナサン・デイビス／
ジョアンナ・ユウ／星野希／
和田圭太／宮下依子

ガーデンデザイナー
マーカスバーネットスタジオ
［担当］パトリック・クラーク

照明デザイナー
DHAライティング
［担当］ジョナサン・ハワード

都市計画・基本設計・デザイン監修
日建設計
［統括］
川島克也
［都市計画担当］
大松敦／橋尾和博／木村由布子／
能田悟／宮本裕太／高田絵美／
浦田裕彦／湊太郎／北村亜砂／
倉石雄太／中野良子／桜間志野／
牧村和紀／長塚秀次／村井美由紀／
登山暁夫／朝田志郎／内原英理子／
川窪千壽／中村晋子／三浦裕美
［建築担当］
朝田志郎／小嶋隆／右高博之／
松崎愛彦／谷内啓太郎／森岡俊介／
友口理央／青木勇／古市博明／
石上智章／新田山直紀／佐藤洋子／
平田可弥穂
［構造担当］
小板橋裕一／柳原雅直／榊原啓太
［設備担当］
岸克巳／小林護／岡田悠介／
谷口洋平／長谷川巌／中島勝美／
伊藤浩士／石川富夫／中西理幸

実施設計・監理
KAJIMA DESIGN
［統括］
田名網雅人
［建築担当］
深井繁人／皆川典久／栗田孝久／
高森和志／角郁男／久保田聡／
真鍋寛／仙石正博／桝井亜沙美／
小林靖志／嶌岡耕平／丹羽雄一／
竜田英行／中谷泉／長塚直美子／
朝田亮／足立優太／鈴木総一郎／
瀧田暁
［構造担当］
原健二／加藤敬史／田中裕之
［設備担当］
渡部裕一／滝村徹／佐々木豊／
大坂泰／八木崇／高橋賢伍／
杉崎聡／中村佐和子／太田和好／
鈴木順一／鈴木智彰／大眉純明／
内田哲晴
［開発担当］
佐藤克久／松村崇／丹野聡明／
寺田香織／柿元淳子／古川健吾／
田野井雄吾／藤岡諒
［監理担当］
根崎秀彦／重田清志／大森文夫／
岡崎浩司／山口哲也／高岡智彦／
橋本洋／山口博由／大井英之

外構実施設計協力
ランドスケープデザイン
［担当］小池孝幸／岩崎哲治

外構・外観照明実施設計協力
フォーライツ
［担当］稲葉裕

商業環境デザイン
乃村工藝社
［担当］
奥山裕／數坂幸生／松本祐輔／
大井悠平／西本陽

オフィス共用部環境デザイン
イリア
［統括］
中込育子
［担当］
沖野俊則／姫井新／水上敬／
渡邊宏子／宮坂亮子／下村牧子／
田川賢三／進藤篤

サインデザイン
井原理安デザイン事務所
［担当］井原由朋

石アート
和泉正敏

和紙デザイン
堀木エリ子

スカイガーデンアート
TOSHIO SHIMIZU ART OFFICE

▌施工

鹿島建設
［建築担当］
桐生雅文／廣田裕介／近藤智則／
東谷卓哉／山川祐司／横田光司／岡田聡
［設備担当］
根本昌文
［土木担当］
上木泰裕／工藤耕一

▌規模

敷地面積
10,702.32m²（日比谷三井タワー）
1,990.01m²（日比谷ステップ広場関連施設）

建築面積
8,652.41m²（日比谷三井タワー）
930.69m²（日比谷ステップ広場関連施設）

延床面積
189,244.95m²（日比谷三井タワー）
3,602.43m²（日比谷ステップ広場関連施設）

日比谷三井タワー
地下1階：8,946.31m²
1階：7,094.72m²
2階：6,817.62m²
基準階：4,411.54m²
塔屋：260.85m²
建蔽率：80.84%（許容：100%）
容積率：1,449.97%（許容：1450%）
階数：地下4階／地上35階／塔屋1階

日比谷ステップ広場関連施設
地下1階：1,356.16m²
1階：462.38m²
2階：37.97m²
建蔽率：46.76%（許容：100%）
容積率：154.09%（許容：900%）
階数：地下2階／地上2階

連絡通路
延長：70m（42m：R-SWING工法）

▌寸法

日比谷三井タワー
最高高：191,460mm
軒高：183,860mm
階高：基準階事務室＝4,450mm
天井高：基準階事務室＝2,900mm
主なスパン：10,800×9,000mm

日比谷ステップ広場関連施設
最高高：11,890mm
軒高：11,195mm
階高：地下2階店舗階＝4,300mm
天井高：地下2階店舗階＝3,000mm
主なスパン：10,800×6,800mm

連絡通路
セグメント外径：

幅7,250mm×高さ7,275mm
セグメント内径：
幅6,550mm×高さ6,575mm

▌敷地条件

地域地区
商業地域／防火地域／都市再生特別地区／
駐車場整備地区／土地区画整理事業地区／
地区整備計画区域／有楽町日比谷地区／
地区計画／国家戦略特別区域

道路幅員
東11m,22m／西44m／北12m

駐車台数
400台

▌構造

日比谷三井タワー
主体構造／鉄骨造／鉄筋コンクリート造／
鉄骨鉄筋コンクリート造／
杭・基礎／パイルド・ラフト基礎

日比谷ステップ広場関連施設
主体構造／鉄筋コンクリート造／
杭・基礎／杭基礎

連絡通路
六面鋼殻合成セグメント造

▌設備

日比谷三井タワー
［環境配慮技術］
BEMS／LED照明（調光）／
中水利用（厨房排水・雨水）／
太陽光発電設備／
コージェネレーションシステム（排熱利用）／
明るさセンサー照明制御／
人感センサー照明制御／
外装ACW縦フィン＋自動制御ブラインドに
よる日射制御
●PAL=0.80／BEI=0.65
［空調設備］
空調方式：
商業＝外調機＋ファンコイルユニット方式
オフィス＝エアハンドリングユニット＋単一ダクト
VAV方式
熱源：地域冷暖房／排熱利用冷凍機
［衛生設備］
給水：
低層＝受水槽＋加圧給水方式
高層＝高架水槽方式
給湯：電気貯湯式局所給湯方式
排水：
建屋内＝汚水・雑排水分流方式
屋外＝雨水分流方式
［電気設備］
受電方式：
特別高圧22,000V／本線・予備線／
予備電源線（3回線）
契約電力：3,500kW
設備容量：
特別高圧変圧器／

12,000kVA×2台
予備電源：
デュアルヒューエルガスタービン発電機／
4,000kVA×2台
［防災設備］
消火：
スプリンクラー設備（湿式,放水型）／
屋内消火栓設備／窒素ガス消火設備／
閉鎖型噴霧消火設備／
連結送水管設備消防用水
排煙：機械排煙
昇降機：乗用×49台／非常用×3台
日比谷ステップ広場関連施設
［環境配慮技術］
BEMS／LED照明（調光）
●PAL=0.56／BEI=0.94

［空調設備］
空調方式：
外調機＋ファンコイルユニット方式
熱源：
東京ミッドタウン日比谷より供給（冷水・温水）
［衛生設備］
給水：受水槽＋加圧給水方式
給湯：局所給湯方式
排水：
建屋内＝汚水・雑排水分流方式
屋外＝雨水分流方式
［電気設備］
受電方式：
東京ミッドタウン日比谷より供給（高圧2回線）
契約電力：東京ミッドタウン日比谷に含む
設備容量：高圧変圧器／1,500kVA
予備電源：東京ミッドタウン日比谷より供給
［防災設備］
消火：
スプリンクラー設備（湿式）／屋内消火栓設備／
閉鎖型噴霧消火設備／連結送水管設備／
消防用水
排煙：機械排煙／自然排煙
昇降機：乗用×3台

┃ 工程

設計期間：2012年5月〜2014年12月
施工期間：2015年1月〜2018年2月

┃ 外部仕上げ

日比谷三井タワー
［屋根］
アスファルト防水／コンクリート押え
［外壁］
（柱型・梁型）花崗岩乾式張り
（トロピカルゴールド t=100mm ノミ切り仕上げ）
［開口部］
アルミカーテンウォール＋
高透過Low-Eガラス
［外構］
自然石舗装／植栽整備／一部水景
日比谷ステップ広場関連施設
［屋根］

アスファルト防水／コンクリート押え／
自然石仕上げ
［外壁］
花崗岩乾式張り
（トロピカルゴールド t=30mm 荒びしゃん仕上げ）
［開口部］
アルミカーテンウォール＋SSD
［外構］
自然石舗装／植栽整備／一部水景

┃ 内部仕上げ

日比谷三井タワー
［基準階オフィス］
床：タイルカーペット
壁：EP塗装
天井：DR（システム天井 600グリッド）

［9・10階スカイロビー］
床：大判タイル
（Fiandre: Marmi Maximum MERCURY）
壁：大判タイル
（Fiandre: Marmi Maximum TRAVERTINO）
天井：GB-R＋EP
（一部化粧ライン：アルミ＋SUS FB）
日比谷ステップ広場関連施設
［地下広場］
床：磁器質タイル（マラッツィ ジャパン：
モノリス／ヴェンゲ／ブッチャルダート）
壁：花崗岩乾式張り
（トロピカルゴールド t=30mm 荒びしゃん仕上げ）
天井：GB-R＋EP
連絡通路
床：磁器質タイル
壁：大理石乾式張り／ガラススクリーン
天井：アルミ不燃複合板 t=4mm

東京ミッドタウン日比谷
新たな街づくりの手法

—

2019年3月29日
初版第1刷発行
定価：本体4,000円＋税

—

監修：三井不動産株式会社　日比谷街づくり推進部

—

発行者：吉田信之
発行所：株式会社新建築社
〒100-6017
東京都千代田区霞が関三丁目2番5号
霞が関ビルディング17階
tel. 03-6205-4380
fax. 03-6205-4386
https://shinkenchiku.online

—

翻訳：トライベクトル株式会社
フォーマットデザイン：刈谷悠三＋角田奈央／neucitora
印刷所：凸版印刷株式会社

—

TOKYO MIDTOWN HIBIYA
New Technique of Town Planning

—

First Edition: 29 March 2019

—

Editorial supervisor: Mitsui Fudosan Co., Ltd.

—

Publisher: Nobuyuki Yoshida
Shinkenchiku-sha Co., Ltd.
Kasumigaseki Building 17F, 3-2-5
Kasumigaseki, Chiyoda-ku Tokyo
100-6017, Japan
tel. +81-3-6205-4380
fax. +81-3-6205-4386
https://shinkenchiku.online

—

English Translation: Trivector Co., Ltd.
Format Design:
Yuzo Kariya + Nao Kakuta/ neucitora
Printed by TOPPAN PRINTING CO., LTD.

—